EATING
DISORDERS

WILEY SERIES IN PSYCHOTHERAPY AND COUNSELLING

SERIES EDITORS
Franz Epting, *Dept of Psychology, University of Florida, USA*
Bonnie Strickland, *Dept of Psychology, University of Massachusetts, USA*
John Allen, *Dept of Community Studies, University of Brighton, UK*

EATING DISORDERS

Personal Construct Therapy and Change

Eric Button

*Eating Disorders Service and
Department of Clinical Psychology
Psychiatric Department, Leicester General Hospital,
UK*

JOHN WILEY & SONS
Chichester · New York · Brisbane · Toronto · Singapore

Other Wiley Editorial Offices

John Wiley & Sons, Inc., 605 Third Avenue,
New York, NY 10158-0012, USA

Jacaranda Wiley Ltd, G.P.O. Box 859, Brisbane,
Queensland 4001, Australia

John Wiley & Sons (Canada) Ltd, 22 Worcester Road,
Rexdale, Ontario M9W 1L1, Canada

John Wiley & Sons (SEA) Pte Ltd, 37 Jalan Pemimpin #05-04,
Block B, Union Industrial Building, Singapore 2057

British Library Cataloguing in Publication Data

A catalogue record for this book is available from the British Library

ISBN 0-471-94094-1 (paper)

Typeset in 10/12 Times from author's disks by Inforum, Rowlands Castle, Hants
Printed and bound in Great Britain by Biddles Ltd, Guildford, Surrey

To my parents

Contents

Series preface

The Wiley Series in Psychotherapy and Counselling is designed to fulfil many different needs in advancing knowledge and practice in the helping professions. What unifies the books in this series is the importance attached to presenting clear authoritative accounts of theory, research and experience in ways which will inform practice and understanding.

One of the frequent criticisms of the literature on personal construct therapy is that it is difficult to comprehend and apply. Eric Button's book, however, is refreshingly clear and written in a manner that leads naturally into concrete and specific clinical applications. The reader with no knowledge of personal construct theory will find that this book presents a complete review of theoretical issues. The book also provides a rich source of illustrative case material. Those familiar with personal construct approaches will find the applied sections of this book especially useful.

Many clinicians will find that this book will inspire them to develop new ways of thinking about the problem of clients with eating disorders and to apply personal construct approaches in an innovative and exciting fashion.

It is with great enthusiasm that this volume is welcomed to the series.

John Allen
Series Editor

Preface

About 20 years ago, while training as a clinical psychologist, I discovered an approach to understanding people that made sense to me in a way that most psychology had failed to do. Having been disappointed by the psychology I had encountered at university, I was struggling to understand the mental health problems that I was supposed to be helping people with. I first came across George Kelly's *The Psychology of Personal Constructs* (1955) through the excellent book *Inquiring Man* written by Don Bannister and Fay Fransella in 1971. For the first time since I had begun studying psychology, I found some ideas that offered some understanding of a person as a *whole* and in a very personal sense. In my subsequent career and personal life, I have found personal construct psychology to be invaluable in providing a framework for understanding the person.

The essence of the personal construct approach is quite a simple one, concerned with trying to understand a person in terms of his or her view of the world. Each person is seen to have a unique and potentially changing view of the world, which helps make sense out of things and chart a direction through life. No one view of the world is regarded as right or wrong, but without that view of the world we are lost, even psychologically dead. Taking the trouble to try to understand a person's view of the world, may give us some sense of what that person is aiming at, however bizarre, undesirable or unhealthy their behaviour may seem.

I first began to apply personal construct psychology to eating disorders when, in 1978, I went to work with Fay Fransella at the Royal Free Hospital in London. My personal construct research there on anorexia nervosa was to prove to be but the first chapter in my personal involvement in personal construct psychology. It was also to mark the beginning of a long exploration into the world of eating disorders. Although I have written a number of articles on my research and clinical work with eating disorders, it was not until I was approached by Glenys Parry (formerly one of the editors of the Wiley Series in Psychotherapy and Counselling) that I seriously entertained the idea of bringing my ideas together in book form. I was delighted to eventually bring this idea to fruition by participating in the Wiley Series in Psychotherapy and Counselling.

Eating disorders are often regarded as perplexing, and clients with eating disorders are typically viewed as difficult to work with therapeutically. I would like to share with you my efforts to make sense of and help people with these disorders. I will outline a theoretical perspective, a line of research and approach to helping and understanding. The structure of this book has been influenced by my anticipation of readers' backgrounds. On the one hand, some readers will be interested in and experienced in working with clients with eating disorders, but the personal construct approach may be new to them. On the other hand, readers may have a background in personal construct psychology, but may be intrigued as to how it might be applied to clients with eating disorders.

Part I, therefore, begins with an overview of eating disorders, which should be of particular value to readers with a primarily personal construct background. The main thrust of my position on eating disorders, however, is outlined in Part II. The concepts and techniques of personal construct psychology are described with particular reference to the context of people with eating disorders. I also advance my theoretical view of eating disorders and consider research carried out from a personal construct perspective. My personal interpretation of a personal construct approach to therapeutic relationships with eating disorders is sketched out and then further elaborated by a series of case studies in Part III. This is a central part of the book, primarily directed at professionals and others engaged in trying to understand and help people with eating disorders. In the fourth and final part, a number of specific issues that arise out of this work are considered within the fields of eating disorders and personal construct psychology. I also try to point towards some future directions in the field.

My hopes for the book are twofold. First, I hope that I will contribute towards a more personal approach to understanding people whose lives become taken over by food issues. Although medical and social perspectives help to explain many of the processes involved in both the initiation and maintenance of eating disorders, I also see a very personal path being taken by these people. Personal construct psychology seems to me to offer a valuable way of illuminating that path. Secondly, by sharing with you my particular explorations of the worlds within and beyond eating disorders, I hope that some sense is made of just what is involved in trying to move on. I am deeply grateful to the clients who have been prepared to share very personal aspects of their lives in this way. The personal construct perspective helps me to make sense of where my client may be going, but I offer no quick fix. There *is* life beyond an eating disorder, but it can be hard and painful to leave behind.

Eric Button

Acknowledgements

I wish to express my thanks to JAI Press Inc. for permission to reproduce the case study Jenny, including Figures 8.1 and 8.2. (In Button, E.J. (1992). Eating disorders and personal constructs. In R.A. Neimeyer and G.J. Neimeyer (Eds.) *Advances in Personal Construct Psychology* (vol. 2) (pp. 185–213). Greenwich, CT: JAI Press.) I also express my thanks to Croom Helm for permission to include Figure 7.1. (In Button, E.J. (1985c). Women with weight on their minds. In N. Beail (Ed.) *Repertory Grid Technique and Personal Constructs: Clinical and Educational Applications* (pp. 61–74). London: Croom Helm.)

I would like to thank my family for putting up with me over many evenings and weekends spent on this project. The support of my colleagues in the Eating Disorders Service and the Department of Clinical Psychology at Leicester General Hospital has also been much appreciated. My final thank you is to Fay Fransella, who gave me the opportunity to set off on the path that eventually led to this book.

Part I
INTRODUCTION TO EATING DISORDERS

1   The nature of eating disorders

Eating can be disordered in a number of different ways. Many illnesses lead to a reduction in eating and some can lead to overeating. Conversely, it is commonly argued nowadays that what we eat can make us ill, and this is no more evident than in the area of prevention of heart disease. As well as physical health, eating can also be affected by psychological factors, such as depression or anxiety. Children, in particular, are prone to use food as a weapon to try to control their parents. Thus, while disturbance in eating behaviour occurs diversely, the term 'eating disorders' has come to have a relatively narrowly defined meaning, particularly within the area of mental health. Rather than referring to all disordered eating behaviour, the term has come to be applied primarily to a spectrum of disorders associated with the avoidance of fatness and the pursuit of thinness.

It is no secret that contemporary Western society places considerable value upon the slimmer body, especially as far as women are concerned. Conversely, the more well-rounded among us tend to be stigmatised from quite an early age. Trends suggest that this phenomenon may be increasingly permeating non-Western cultures – hardly surprising given the global marketplace for products such as diet versions of popular soft drinks. Nor should it be assumed that it is only females who are subject to such societal trends. Although still in the minority, males do succumb to eating disorders, albeit possibly in slightly different ways and for different motivations (Andersen, 1990).

It is with this rather narrower definition of eating disorders that this book will be concerned. Specifically, the main focus will be on the disorders known as anorexia nervosa and bulimia nervosa, as well as their subclinical variants. People who fall into this broad category of eating disorders may differ from each other in numerous ways, but they share one common feature: their lives are dominated by concerns about their perceived need to control their weight and, by implication, their eating. Although very many of us go on diets at some time, for most people this will be a temporary period of abstemiousness that will come to an end without going too far. The person with an eating disorder, however, tends to be engaged in a relentless pursuit, which becomes all-consuming and takes over life. Neither does the person necessarily stop at a sensible level. It is as if the pursuit of the goal becomes more important than the goal itself. The emphasis on the qualitative difference between eating disorder and dieting does not mean that there is a sharp dividing line between the two – far from it. In agreement with a number of other writers (e.g. Nylander, 1971), it seems to me that there is a continuum of eating disorders, but clearly there is a time and place for drawing lines, even if those lines may appear arbitrary. We will return to the idea of a spectrum later, but let us now turn to those segments of the spectrum where lines have been fairly clearly drawn, namely to the disorders anorexia nervosa and bulimia nervosa.

Anorexia nervosa

It is now a little over a century since Gull (1874) and Lasègue (1873) identified the disorder now known as anorexia nervosa. Their strikingly similar descriptions drew the attention of the medical world to this still baffling disorder, but it is likely that the earliest systematic description was offered by Morton (1694) under the different title of 'a nervous consumption'. Gull's term has so far stood the test of time, in spite of the fact that the loss of appetite implied by the word 'anorexia' is not usually present until very late in the starvation process. Thus the term is something of a misnomer; in fact, many sufferers report a voracious appetite, which they are constantly battling against. In spite of its inaccuracy, the term anorexia nervosa persists, probably because no-one can come up with a satisfactory alternative that would concisely convey the essence of the disorder.

So what exactly is anorexia nervosa? There have been many conflicting attempts to define the disorder over the years, but the current convention has centred around the Diagnostic and Statistical Manual of the American Psychiatric Association (American Psychiatric Association, 1987) – the so-called DSM111R criteria. These are as follows:

A.   Refusal to maintain body weight over a minimal weight for age and height, for example, weight loss leading to maintenance of body weight 15% below that expected, or failure to make expected weight gain during period of growth, leading to body weight 15% below that expected.

B. Intense fear of gaining weight or becoming fat, even though underweight.
C. Disturbance in the way in which one's body weight, size, or shape is experienced, for example, the person claims to 'feel fat' even when emaciated, believes that one area of the body is 'too fat' even when obviously underweight.
D. In females, absence of at least three consecutive menstrual cycles when otherwise expected to occur (primary or secondary amenorrhoea). A woman is considered to have amenorrhoea if her periods occur only following hormone (e.g. oestrogen) administration.

Although these criteria are widely applied in the research literature, none is without problems. A minimum normal weight is hard to define, the intensity of fear of fatness is difficult to measure, body image is not always disturbed and the menstrual criterion poses problems with women who take the contraceptive pill. Although there is very little doubt in extreme cases, those on the edge of the disorder are not clear-cut. Of course, for the person in difficulty, the precise label may not be important and it is unlikely that someone would be turned away from help simply because they did not meet the current diagnostic convention. The example below is of someone for whom there was no doubt whatsoever about the use of the term anorexia nervosa.

Case example: Wendy

Wendy first presented for specialist help when she was aged 21, but her decline into anorexia nervosa had originated about a year previously. She had had an unsettled childhood; her parents split up when she was quite young, and there was much toing and froing between parents. Perhaps not surprisingly, she had shown evidence of being anxious, insecure and very dependent from an early age. Possibly partly as an escape, she left home when 16 and married a year later. The stabilising effect of her marriage was soon broken when her husband had an affair. This did not last for long, but she became very concerned that she needed to be slimmer to hold on to him and she went on a diet. Initially she was about 10 st. (140 lb) and aimed for 9 st. (126 lb), which she reached in about six weeks. But she was not satisfied with 9 st. and continued revising her aim downwards until she had reached 7 st. (98 lb) by the time of her assessment, which was very thin, given that she was 5'8".

It seemed that no weight could satisfy her and indeed this spiral continued in the coming months, with accompanying ever-increasing anxiety about weight gain. She had achieved this weight loss by a very low intake and had also turned to vomiting most days after her main meal. In spite of the fact that she was wasting away, she herself felt fat and seemed oblivious to the danger of her state. But she was not happy with her plight and had become low in mood, weepy, irritable and occasionally had felt life was not worth living. She felt she had changed from her former 'bubbly' self and it was clear that achieving thinness had done nothing for her self-confidence, which remained very low. In spite of her ambivalence, however, she realised she could not get out of the mess she was in and agreed to be referred for help.

The example of Wendy illustrates many of the typical features of anorexia nervosa. These are as follows:

● it is a disorder that mainly affects females
● it typically originates during the teenage years
● it involves a combination of psychological and physical symptoms
● the precise aetiology is unknown
● sufferers tend to deny they are ill and resist treatment
● in a significant proportion of cases the disorder can be fatal.

Psychological characteristics

Although there is a close link between psychological and physical characteristics, it is convenient to subdivide the symptoms of anorexia nervosa into those that appear to be more psychological in origin and those that have a clearer biological basis. The main psychological features emanate from the central pathology of a 'morbid fear of fatness' (Russell, 1970). Associated with this fear of fatness there is a corresponding drive for thinness, which far exceeds that which most people would regard as healthy slimness. Typically this will be accompanied by intense concern with body weight as a crucial marker of whether the person is achieving his or her aims.

Although it seems that people who are actually overweight have an increased vulnerability to anorexia nervosa, in many cases the anorectic path is taken by those who would not objectively be classified as obese. They may well feel fat, perhaps because they have experienced a pubertal growth spurt, which will naturally lead to increased fat deposition. To at least some extent the media would seem to play a part in this process. Girls, in particular, soon tune in to the prevailing image of slimness as a desirable state and there is compelling evidence that the ideal shape is significantly leaner than that which is typical of actual young women today.

The initial path towards anorexia nervosa may be unnoticed or seen as a normal diet, but achievement of the initial target weight will not satisfy and an ever-increasing downward spiral ensues. The person becomes engaged in a constant struggle to defend the latest weight from any increase and possibly to seek even further weight loss. It is not hard to see that if one becomes excessively fearful about any weight increase, however small, that the likely outcome is continuing weight loss. Weighing may occur many times a day or in some cases may be avoided altogether because it creates so much anxiety.

One of the obvious consequences of this single-minded pursuit is that food intake will need to be drastically curtailed. Typically, this will involve selective cutting out of foods commonly perceived as fattening, such as potatoes, bread, cake, sweet things and fatty food. In some cases it may involve eating nothing, but usually there will be a repertoire of 'acceptable' food, for example, cottage cheese, lettuce, yoghurt, etc. Some sufferers develop bizarre eating patterns and rituals, for example, eating butter on its own or raw meat. There are many other ways of facilitating weight loss, of course, including vigorous exercise, self-induced vomiting and laxatives. Although in most cases there will be extreme dietary restraint, for some this may not be absolute and they may have periods of 'binge-eating'. Rather than risk weight gain, however, they will counter it by self-induced vomiting or by taking laxatives, sometimes in huge quantities. This sub-group of anorectics are usually referred to as the bulimic subtype, as opposed to the restrictor subtype who do not binge-eat.

Preoccupation with food and weight issues is undoubtedly the most specific psychological characteristic of anorexia nervosa. But it has also been suggested that anorectics share other psychological tendencies that are relevant to the disorder. For example, Bruch (1962) has hypothesised an inability to identify and respond accurately to internal cues, such as are associated with emotions, hunger and satiety. She has also suggested that there is a primary deficit of an 'overwhelming sense of ineffectiveness' which becomes translated into an attempt to achieve control through self-starvation. Crisp (e.g. 1967) has contended that the central psychopathology is the desire to avoid the psychobiological consequences of maturity. Authors such as Bruch and Crisp are thus suggesting that underlying the main symptoms of anorexia nervosa there are more fundamental psychological deficits that make the individual unable to cope effectively with the demands of adult life. One of the problems with such theorising is that many of these psychological characteristics could be secondary to the disorder, rather than being an underlying cause. Strober (1981) attempted to overcome this by comparing recent onset anorectic adolescents with matched groups of depressed and antisocial adolescent females. He found that the anorectic adolescents' personality was characterised by greater conformity, neurotic anxieties, control of emotionality and stimulus avoidance. While such studies are not conclusive, they do suggest that the resolution of anorexia nervosa requires attention to the broader psychological context beyond food and weight.

Physical characteristics

When people go without much food, it is hardly surprising that their body suffers. This is most visibly apparent by a state of emaciation reminiscent of images from Belsen, or as Gull (1874) put it, 'a skeleton clad in skin'. In addition to looking ill, many body systems may become impaired. Without detailing the medical technicalities, the physical symptoms are wide-ranging and include deterioration of the skin, teeth and bones, hypothermia, chemical imbalance and dehydration. Such changes can lead to dangerous complications, such as acute gastric dilatation or cardiac abnormalities, which could prove fatal.

Endocrine disturbance is most manifest by the cessation of menstruation, crucial to the diagnosis in females. Amenorrhoea tends to occur at an early stage in the disorder and often persists long after weight is restored to normal. It is associated with reduced oestrogen and other hormones and in male sufferers there is an analogous reduction in testosterone, with associated reduced sexual drive. Both emotional disturbance and poor nutrition seem to play a part in causing the endocrine dysfunction.

In addition to these physical consequences of starvation, a number of psychological symptoms seem to derive from this state of deprivation. Depression and irritability are quite common and the sufferer may be extremely restless and agitated, in no small part because they are hungry. The extreme preoccupation with food seems also to be a result of starving, just as was shown to be the case among prisoner of war victims of the holocaust.

Keys et al (1950) conducted an experimental study in which 36 young men were voluntarily semi-starved over a period of about six months. All subjects became preoccupied with food and eating, some dreamed about eating and others developed bizarre eating habits. All reported increased lethargy, poor concentration, loss of sexual interest, irritability, moodiness and insomnia. Several admitted to breaking the diet and bingeing outside the experimental situation. After a prolonged period of rehabilitation, all subjects eventually recovered, but this rather extreme experiment demonstrates that many of the symptoms of anorexia nervosa are attributable to the effects of starvation. Most of these symptoms are reversible on restoration of weight, but some people are less fortunate and may be left permanently impaired. Death, through either suicide or the effects of emaciation, is also a significant risk. Although some long-term studies have shown mortality of at least 15% (e.g. Theander, 1985), Hsu's (1990) review of intermediate follow-up studies points to the possibility that effective treatment can reduce mortality to below 5%.

Bulimia nervosa

In marked contrast to anorexia nervosa, the sufferer of bulimia nervosa would be unlikely to stand out in a crowd. Although bulimia nervosa can accompany anorexia nervosa, most bulimics are at least average in weight and some are unquestionably obese. As well as generally not looking un-well, they may give no clues to others that there is anything wrong. Feelings of guilt and disgust at their behaviour lead them to be secretive and possibly this may explain why the disorder was not formally identified until the 1970s. Although there had been earlier references to similar concepts, the term bulimia nervosa was first coined by Russell in 1979. Out of his research into anorexia nervosa, Russell identified what he termed 'an ominous variant of anorexia nervosa'. Although there is no doubt that the disorder can be closely associated with anorexia nervosa, it is also the case that bulimia nervosa often occurs without any evidence of anorexia nervosa. Russell's diagnostic criteria consisted of: powerful and intractable urges to overeat; the avoidance of the fattening effects of food by inducing vomiting and/or abusing purgatives; a 'morbid' fear of becoming fat.

Since Russell's seminal work, there has been a fair amount of controversy, both over what to call the disorder and how to define it. Terms such as 'bulimarexia' (Boskind-Lodahl and White, 1978) and 'dietary chaos syndrome' (Palmer, 1979) were proposed at around the same time as Russell's bulimia nervosa. For a while the term bulimia was popular in North America, but this was dropped by the American Psychiatric Association in 1987 in favour of the term bulimia nervosa. Their DSM111R diagnostic criteria have since achieved the status of an international convention and they comprise:

A. Recurrent episodes of binge-eating (rapid consumption of a large amount of food in a discrete period of time).
B. A feeling of lack of control over eating behaviour during eating binges.
C. The person regularly engages in either self-induced vomiting, use of laxatives or diuretics, strict dieting or fasting, or vigorous exercise in order to prevent weight gain.
D. A minimum average of two binge-eating episodes a week for at least three months.
E. Persistent over-concern with body shape and weight.

Once again, these criteria are not without problems, with most difficulty being associated with the definition of binge-eating, a term subject to rather loose usage. Their adoption, however, has at least ensured that a degree of homogeneity has emerged from more recent studies of the disorder.

Case example: Vicky

Vicky was almost 21 and in her first year of university when she was first referred for help. She described her problem as being unable to control her eating. She used to feel that eating was the one thing she could control, but now she could not control anything and she felt very depressed about it all. There was no real pattern to her eating. At times she would eat very little apart from some cereal at breakfast, at other times she would 'binge', eating anything she could get her hands on. For example, on one occasion she began by having a reasonable lunch of tuna and pasta, with green beans and some chocolate pudding for dessert, but she was unable to stop and proceeded to eat four slices of toast with peanut butter; two slices of bread with peanut butter; a packet of crisps; two Danish pastries; two chocolate bars and six cream biscuits. At the time, she reported feeling depressed, fat, out of control, hating herself and wanting to hurt herself. She was angry because she felt she had ruined everything; she felt guilty and she despised herself. She temporarily relieved herself by inducing vomiting, but later on in the day repeated a similar cycle and ended the day feeling she wanted to die. The same kind of pattern followed on the next day until she once again went into her dieting mode.

All this had begun about three years previously, when after Christmas she decided to go on a diet. At that time she weighed about 8 st. 4 lb (116 lb), which for someone of her height (5'6") was well within normal limits, but she said she felt fat and that she looked it. She proceeded to eat very little and took to vomiting and excessive exercising, which resulted in her losing weight, but she said this did not last and before long she had developed into a cyclical pattern of binge-eating and dieting. As a result her weight had fluctuated quite a lot. At her lowest, she was down to about 7 st. 9 lb (107 lb), but still felt fat. At the present time she weighed 9.5 st. (133 lb) and felt fat, heavy and clumsy, although by most standards this again was within normal limits for someone of her height.

Vicky's background was of having quite a happy childhood and family life, in which she says there was no special emphasis on food or appearance. But she had not been particularly happy in her latter school years, when she remembers feeling inferior to other girls, who were less shy and more wealthy than she was. Although she had made quite a lot of friends since coming to university, she was inclined to be shy and conscious of what people thought of her. She was also wary in relationships with the opposite sex, being fearful of being rejected for being fat. Although Vicky had had two previous unsuccessful attempts at treatment, she was keen for help, saying she wanted to be able to eat like everyone else and not be so worried about weight and appearance.

The case example of Vicky illustrates many of the typical features of bulimia nervosa. Life becomes dominated by the threat of eating too much and the fear of consequent excessive weight gain. The bulimic is on guard against weight gain and may aspire to strict dieting, but he or she is not persistently effective and breaks out into episodes of uncontrolled eating. Such behaviour is followed by shame/disgust, which may last for hours or days and is typically followed by greater restraint or self-induced vomiting, large doses of laxatives, excessive exercise or diuretics. As a result of this behaviour, weight is often rather volatile, with swings in weight of a stone (14 lb) or more not uncommon. This volatility in weight and eating be-haviour is often accompanied by a corresponding instability of mood. This may reach depressive proportions and there has been much interest in the relationship between bulimia nervosa and depression (e.g. Cooper and

Fairburn, 1986). Whatever the cause, the result is a kind of circle in which low mood leads to overeating, which leads to a worsening of mood, and so on. In some cases this pattern can go on for weeks at a time, to be ended by yet another period of food restriction – or being 'good' as it has often been described.

Attention has also been drawn to the fact that some bulimics turn to multiple substances – which would include food, but also alcohol, drugs or sex – in an impulsive attempt to deal with feelings of distress (see, for example, Lacey, 1985). There does indeed seem to be a subgroup of bulimics who present in such a way and Lacey refers to them as the 'personality disorder' group. Their volatility is in sharp contrast to the image of the highly controlled, restricting anorectic and it does generally seem to be the case that there are broad contrasts at the level of personality and emotional control between anorexia nervosa and bulimia nervosa. Anorectics tend to be emotionally controlled, introvert and conforming, whereas bulimics are more inclined to be impulsive, extravert and prone to excesses of behaviour. It should be reiterated, however, that such contrasts are stereotypes and there are many exceptions to this rule, including those many anorectics who also binge-eat.

In addition to the above psychological characteristics of bulimia nervosa, in similar vein to anorexia nervosa there are a number of possible physical complications of bulimia nervosa. The most serious of these is low levels of potassium, which is caused by excessive vomiting or excessive use of laxatives. This can cause cardiac arhythmias, which could prove fatal. Another common consequence of the vomiting is erosion of dental enamel and consequent decay. More generally, the skin and hair tend to deteriorate and a whole host of physical complications may arise. Although the disorder is generally not seen to be as life-threatening as anorexia nervosa, Patton (1988) found a 940% increased mortality among a group of 96 normal-weight bulimics. Two of these died in traffic accidents and one following a severe weight loss. This kind of finding needs confirmation from other studies, but it does underline how serious the disorder is. Moreover, the quality of life for the sufferer may be severely impaired and every bit as miserable an existence as can apply to anorexia nervosa.

Partial syndromes and the spectrum of eating disorders

It is very easy to form the impression from reading textbooks that psychological disorders fall into nice neat packages that are easily identifiable and separate from anything else. Any clinician will know that this is far from the case and there are many shades of grey. There is very little doubt that this principle applies in the field of eating disorders. It was possibly

Nylander (1971) who first drew attention to the concept of a continuum of eating disorders in his research focusing on dieting and feeling fat in teenagers. Back in 1981 Button and Whitehouse conducted a study of females in a college population, in which we identified a substantial number of young women who had many of the symptoms of anorexia nervosa, without fulfilling strict criteria. These girls were termed 'subclinical anorexia nervosa'. Szmukler (1983), however, has suggested that the term 'partial syndrome' may be more appropriate than subclinical, which tends to imply present but undetected disorder. Furthermore, it is clear that such partialness of disorder applies as much to bulimia nervosa as to anorexia nervosa.

It seems highly appropriate to conceive of a spectrum of degrees of eating disorder ranging from 'normal' eating through persistent dieters and partial syndromes to frank bulimia nervosa and anorexia nervosa. While there may be great differences in severity of such disorders, there might be much in common across this spectrum. The understanding of clinically defined eating disorders can be enhanced only by studying the whole spectrum. Indeed, it seems that people can move to and fro along this spectrum. Partial syndrome may thus turn out to be a prelude to the development of a more severe form of eating disorder. The main problem with the concept of partial syndromes is that there are no clearly defined criteria for marking the lower limits for the disorder. There is thus a danger of it being applied as a catch-all category that could stretch from mild anorexia nervosa through to normal dieting. There is clearly a case for some firming up of criteria here, but we should avoid being too rigid about where we draw lines.

Obesity

People who are overweight often have psychological problems, but it seems unlikely that they do so any more than anyone else (see, for example, Wadden and Stunkard, 1985). Nor is it possible to say that people who are overweight, in general, eat abnormally. As a group, however, there is very little doubt that they suffer from stigmatisation associated with a negative stereotype common in contemporary Western society (see, for example, Ciliska, 1990). It is not fashionable nowadays to be large and it seems that females are particularly subject to negative social pressures associated with this image. Thus, people tend to think badly of the overweight and this stereotype is evident from a very early age. It is no wonder, therefore, that many overweight people succumb to such pressures and internalise this negative image and feel very bad about themselves. In consequence, their eating behaviour may become secretive for fear of being accused of being greedy. Paradoxically, they may turn to binge-eating because of such pressures, thus partially confirming the stereotype.

Obesity is not generally classified as an eating disorder and there will not be a special section devoted to obesity in this book. But there is little doubt that the obese as a group are more vulnerable than more slender people to develop the kind of eating disorders to which this book refers. This will be reflected in the choice of case examples, several of whom will have been overweight at some time in their life and in one case (Sally, see Chapter 13) it was the predominant issue.

Epidemiology

What is the scale of the problem? Who gets eating disorders? These are the kinds of questions that tend to be embraced by those who have studied the epidemiology of eating disorders. It has frequently been asserted that eating disorders are on the increase. This is very difficult to predict accurately, partly because there is a tendency for theories to be self-fulfilling. Just as with aggressive pit-bull terriers, we notice the cases that come to attention and ignore all the exceptions. It may well be that we are more aware of eating disorders these days and this creates a misleading impression. It appears from the research literature that, irrespective of whether there ever was an increase in such disorders, this does not seem to be a sustained growth. Studies (e.g. Williams and King, 1987; Cooper, Charnock and Taylor, 1987) suggest a fair amount of stability in the prevalence of the main disorders. Thus, while more cases get noticed and referred for help, the underlying prevalence of the disorders may be fairly stable at present.

So what are the current figures? It would seem that, in the early 1990s, among females in the most vulnerable age group (say 16–35) the following approximate figures prevail:

- about 0.5% suffer from anorexia nervosa
- about 1-2% suffer from bulimia nervosa
- About 3% suffer from a partial syndrome eating disorder.

Thus, of the order of 5% of young women will at one time be experiencing marked problems associated with eating/weight. The ratio of females to males with eating disorders would appear to be of the order of 15–20:1, that is, about 0.3% of young men will be in similar difficulty.

Although eating disorders have primarily been identified within Western cultures, a number of studies have now appeared from various other parts of the world. These confirm that eating disorders do occur in non-Caucasian and non-Western cultures. They also tend to show the same clinical features and outcome, as well as predominantly affecting females. Several studies have suggested that the influence of Western cultural ideals is relevant to the development of the drive for thinness among people from Third World countries (e.g. Furnham and Alibhai, 1983; Nasser, 1986; Pumareiga, 1986).

Within any particular culture, it seems that other factors may place some individuals at higher risk. It is a common view, for example, that eating disorders are more prevalent among higher socioeconomic groups. The evidence on this is, however, not entirely consistent and it may well be that such groups are simply more likely to present for treatment at specialised centres. There is consistent evidence, however, that certain pursuits and occupations place people at a high risk. For example, Garner and Garfinkel (1980a) found about 7% of dance and modelling students to have anorexia nervosa. Similar figures were reported among ballet students by Szmukler, Eisler, Gillis and Hayward (1985). Jockeys, wrestlers and runners are also examples of groups who may be placed at risk by the need to control weight. Broadly speaking, it seems that an environment that emphasises slimness leads to an increase in both dieting and eating disorders.

Aetiology

The general consensus of opinion nowadays is that eating disorders are multifactorially determined. This was the view taken by Garfinkel and Garner (1982) in their well-known book on anorexia nervosa and their 'multidimensional perspective' seems to be also the generally accepted line in relation to bulimia nervosa. Broadly speaking, three classes of variables seem to be possibly implicated: social, biological and psychological.

The main evidence for the role of social factors comes from epidemiological data. The overwhelming preponderance of eating disorders in females is an immediate pointer in this direction. Is there something about being a woman these days that renders them more vulnerable? The general answer to this has been to point to the enormous popularity of dieting or slimming in young women in Western society. Most women are concerned about their weight and most will diet at some point. Polivy and Herman (1987) argue that among young women, dieting is more prevalent than non-dieting and as such is thus normative behaviour. As well as dieting being much more common in females, body dissatisfaction is higher and much more likely to be linked to self-esteem. From a historical point of view, there is also evidence that the cultural ideal of slimness for women has increased in recent times. In a famous study, Garner, Garfinkel, Schwartz and Thompson (1980) examined data from perhaps a dubious source, namely *Playboy* centrefolds and Miss America contestants between 1959 and 1978. Over this 20-year period, the average weight for height of the females in these contexts had decreased by 10%. Moreover, during this period, the number of articles pertaining to dieting in popular magazines had increased some sixfold. Similar findings have also come from non-American countries. For example Rossner (1984) reviewed statistics from the Miss Sweden contest and noted a drop in weight from 68 kg to 53 kg. Although such phenomena have traditionally not been associated with underdeveloped countries, several studies have pointed to the possible influence of 'Western' standards. For example, Furnham and Alibhai (1983) studied Kenyan women immigrants to Britain and found that those who had been in Britain for at least four years were more similar to their British counterparts than to those living in Kenya. The immigrants favoured a slimmer female figure, whereas traditional Kenyan women preferred larger figures. Similar findings have also been obtained in several other studies, all pointing to an all-pervasive cultural push towards slimness in women that potentially has no boundaries. Thus, in searching for aetiological factors, the high prevalence of dieting and preference for slimmer forms seems to underpin eating disorders. Quite simply, it seems reasonable to suppose that the more people diet, the more they will succumb to eating disorders.

Social factors alone cannot explain eating disorders. In spite of widespread social influences, it is only very much a minority of women who get into big trouble with eating. Biological factors may well play a role, it seems. A number of genetic studies have found a higher concordance rate amongst relatives with eating disorders. For example, in reviewing the evidence from a number of studies, Hsu (1990) estimated that the first degree relatives of people with eating disorders are perhaps about four to five times more likely than the general public to develop an eating disorder. themselves. Among twin studies, the figures are quite striking. For example, Holland et al (1984) found 56% and 7% concordance for anorexia nervosa among monozygotic and dizygotic twins respectively.

In addition to the evidence of increased concordance for eating disorders, there is also evidence of increased risk of other psychiatric disorders amongst relatives, with particular emphasis on affective disorder. Although there is always the problem of trying to disentangle the possibly complex interaction between genetic and environmental influences, the evidence does point to a fair degree of familial risk, although the mechanisms have not been elucidated. As well as potentially predisposing some individuals to an increased risk of developing eating disorders, biological factors seem to also play a role in perpetuating the disorder. For example, there is considerable evidence to support the presence of a disturbance in hypothalamic function in anorexia nervosa (see, for example, Wakeling, 1985). The weight of evidence, however, points to this as mainly being a result of malnutrition and possibly also emotional factors, rather than reflecting any primary abnormality. Similarly, there is substantial evidence that hunger and satiety mechanisms in bulimia nervosa have become disturbed, possibly mediated by hypothalamic/neurotransmitter dysfunction. Thus, it seems to be the case that biological factors may play a part both in the initiation and maintenance of eating disorders. But the bulk of the literature on eating disorders tends to point towards psychological factors as playing the most significant role.

The psychological literature on eating disorders points in several directions. On the one hand, personality factors have been invoked. As we have seen above, both clinical descriptions and empirical studies tend to point towards certain kinds of personality characteristics as predominating in eating disorders. Broadly speaking, in the case of the anorectic, phenomena such as emotional over-control, conceptual rigidity and lack of development of self have been described. Clinical descriptions typically portrayed the anorectic as being inclined towards over-compliance and perfectionism, but with a lack of ability to function effectively in the interpersonal world. Bulimics, in contrast, tend to show greater impulsivity and affective instability. Such impressions have been broadly borne out by empirical research using standardised measures, such as Strober's study (1981) referred to above.

Such personality characteristics have also formed the basis of a number of theoretical positions on the aetiology of eating disorders. Most notably, Bruch (1973) has construed anorexia nervosa as emerging as an individual's desperate attempt to gain competence and a feeling of control, set against a background of conceptual rigidity, a sense of ineffectiveness and a disturbance in interoceptive awareness. Evidence for such a viewpoint comes, for example, from Garner, Olmsted, Polivy and Garfinkel (1984) who found that anorectic women, compared with weight-preoccupied women, have a greater sense of ineffectiveness and interpersonal distrust, as well as a greater lack of interoceptive awareness. The phenomenon of conceptual rigidity, while frequently commented on in anorexia nervosa, has not been investigated too much in empirical studies, but it will be a central feature of the personal construct approach, as we shall see below. Similarly, although the cognitive approach has been very influential in the treatment of bulimia nervosa, the evidence of cognitive deficits in bulimia nervosa is rather limited.

Many of the theoretical positions on eating disorders postulate that the above kinds of strategies, particularly common in anorexia nervosa, may reflect a response to deficits in the relationship between the patient and family. For example, Palazzoli (1978) construes the anorectic to have equated the body with the introjection of a bad controlling mother, who has been internalised and identified with. Self-starvation is thus seen as an attempt to break away from this identification and to strive for a sense of separate identity. This is similar to the position of Bruch (1973), who argues that the deficits shown by the anorectic occur because of parents superimposing their own wishes and ignoring the child's needs and wants. The role of a dysfunctional family in anorexia nervosa is most associated with Minuchin, Rosman and Baker (1978). They argue that there are four features of such families, namely 'enmeshment', 'overprotection', 'rigidity' and 'lack of conflict resolution'. The evidence, reviewed by Hsu (1990) tends to point towards disturbed family interactions being more common in eating-disorder families, and that such disturbance tends to be more overtly expressed in the families of bulimics rather than those of restrictive anorectics. There do seem to be some differences between the family patterns of restrictive and bulimic anorectics, with the latter group tending to be more similar to normal weight bulimics. To what extent such patterns of interaction cause the disorder or are consequential remains to be seen.

In addition to personality characteristics, possibly associated with disturbed family interactions, the other psychological ingredient of eating disorders is thought to be a developmental one. The timing of the typical onset of eating disorders around early adulthood tends to point in this direction and indeed this is the major theme of Crisp (1967, 1980) in his theorising on anorexia nervosa. His view is that anorexia nervosa represents a kind of phobic avoidance of sexual maturation, which serves to protect the individual from the turmoils that can accompany adolescence. It is well known that adolescence is often marked by a degree of psychological distress. There is also considerable evidence that low self-esteem is closely associated with body dissatisfaction in this age group, particularly among females. Thus, the female adolescent or young adult who has low self-esteem may be highly prone to turn to weight control, through equating slimness with greater social success. The latter is born out by consistent evidence that fatter people are viewed more negatively, even among young children. Thus, in the short term at least, there is likely to be some social validation for the quest for slimness and weight control. A recent study (Button, 1990a) has shown that 11–12-year-old girls with particularly low self-esteem are about four times more likely to show concern with fatness than those with high self-esteem. These girls will be followed up when 15–16, which will test out the author's view that low self-esteem is a major vulnerability factor for the development of eating disorders.

In summary, although the precise aetiology of eating disorders is unknown, there is some support for the view that eating disorders are more likely to develop in females with psychological vulnerabilities affecting cognition, emotion, sense of self and interpersonal relationships. Such vulnerabilities may relate to both biological and familial experience and are likely to be put to considerable challenge during the emergence towards adulthood. The concept of vulnerability, however, may be a rather negative way of looking at eating disorders. Rutter (1979), for example, in relation to psychopathology in general, has argued for the role of *protective factors*, such as high self-esteem. Perhaps it may prove fruitful to look more towards characteristics and qualities that promote effective functioning and help protect individuals from succumbing to these disorders. As we shall see, this is very much in the spirit of a personal construct approach.

2   Treatment of eating disorders

The concern of the medical community to treat illness has led to no shortage of treatment procedures being offered for people presenting with eating disorders. Although most of the literature in this field has emerged from centres with a significant medical input, psychological forms of treatment form the backbone of the thrust to help people with these stubborn and distressing conditions. A wide array of types of treatment have been applied, particularly in the case of anorexia nervosa. Many decades of work using a wide variety of different approaches in all corners of the world has seemingly failed to produce convincing evidence that any treatment of anorexia nervosa is specifically beneficial. With bulimia nervosa, however, although the story is still unfolding, things look somewhat more promising and there tends to be far more consensus as to how to proceed in offering help.

The task of comprehensively surveying this field is not relevant to this book. But an overview of the main treatment approaches and the results of outcome studies will help to set the scene for the personal construct approach. Some readers may have a primarily psychotherapeutic background and, although interested in working with people with eating disorders, may not be too aware of the state of the art. This overview is presented with particular emphasis on themes that are relevant to a personal construct perspective.

The treatment of anorexia nervosa

Whatever treatment approach offered to the anorectic, the issue of the client's need for control and motivation for change will be at the forefront. This is an issue that is considered within the context of personal construct psychotherapy below, but it applies whatever approach is being taken. If the client's position is not sensitively handled, then that person will have been done a serious injustice and the chance of a successful outcome will have been decreased. For the medical profession, there are particular issues surrounding the area of medical responsibility and their orientation towards seeking to preserve life that create their own pressures. This text is written from a psychological perspective and will primarily focus on the kind of consideration relevant to a psychological therapist, whatever that person's professional background.

Physical treatment

A number of physical treatments have been applied to anorexia nervosa. These include the use of chlorpromazine and insulin, as advocated by Dally and Sargant (1960). The most drastic form of treatment is tube feeding, on a forced basis – a treatment which is generally regarded by experts as unwise and very much a last resort. Antidepressant medication has often been used, perhaps particularly in view of the accompanying depression often associated with anorexia nervosa. Many of these treatments have not formally been evaluated, but what evidence that exists suggests that some psychotropic medications can have a marginal effect by speeding up the rate of weight gain, when used in conjunction with other treatments. But this seems of little point, given that a fast rate of weight gain may be distressing and counter-productive in the long term. Although there may well be cases in which psychotropic medication may have a part to play in an overall treatment programme, there seems to be no basis for seeing it as having a major contribution in the treatment of anorexia nervosa.

Weight restoration

There is wide consensus that one of the first aims of treatment should be to help the anorectic to return to a 'healthy weight'. The main reason for this is that many of the symptoms of the disorder are secondary to a state of starvation. Until this is rectified, the client will probably remain preoccupied with food and suffer the many physical and psychological consequences of being malnourished. In spite of the fact that most clients will be at least anxious about the prospect of weight gain, there is also evidence that weight gain can lead to a reduction of such anxieties (Garfinkel and Garner, 1982; Morgan and Russell, 1975). This is perhaps not surprising, as we know that exposure is possibly the main component of successful treatment of phobic behaviour. Although there is a phobic element to anorectic behaviour (Crisp, 1967), I should not, however, wish to argue that anorexia nervosa is simply a phobia.

Traditionally, weight restoration has tended to be carried out on a client as a hospital in-patient. Centres vary in terms of the amount of weight gain that is aimed for, some aiming for a close approximation to a 'normal weight' and others seeking to merely achieve sufficient weight gain to reverse the worst effects of starvation and allow psychotherapy to take over. In-patient treatment may be in a psychiatric or medical context, although psychiatrists tend to warn against the danger of heavy-handed treatment by some physicians. Although in-patient treatment was dominant in the literature for many years, out-patient treatment became common during the 1980s. For example, in the Eating Disorders Service at Leicester, about four-fifths of anorectics are treated as out-patients. Recently there have also been reports of treatment on a day-patient basis (Piran and Kaplan, 1990). Although it seems that, in principle, weight restoration can occur in any of these contexts, in-patient treatment is more likely to be chosen if weight loss is extreme and/or continuing to slide, where there are physical complications and/or severe depression/risk of suicide. Day-patient treatment may be regarded as an intermediate choice for those people who do not respond well at out-patient level, but where the level of severity and/or other considerations make in-patient treatment less acceptable.

Irrespective of where treatment occurs, the underlying principles tend to be the same:

- establishing a therapeutic atmosphere in which there is trust and understanding
- presenting weight restoration as a phase in treatment within an overall psychotherapeutic climate
- aiming for a gradual rate of weight gain of the order of no more than 2–3 lb per week
- helping to contain the client's anxieties about eating and weight gain
- firmly confronting signs of behaviour, such as vomiting, purging or throwing food out of the window.

The overall thrust of such treatment is thus to bring about substantial weight gain within a firm, but understanding therapeutic climate. Although the main route to weight gain is clearly a matter of eating more, the process may be augmented by the use of reduced activity (bed rest in hospital) and an element of 'behavioural treatment' in which rewards and withdrawal of 'privileges' are made contingent upon weight gain and/or improved eating behaviour.

Where the above process occurs on an in-patient basis, it is usually the case that nursing staff play a prominent part in the supervision of meals and someone may sit with the anorectic. This may also be a feature of day-patient treatment, but at out-patient level the client is clearly in charge. Thus a much more collaborative relationship is possible. Eating may be focused upon mainly through the medium of an eating diary, with guidelines being suggested by the therapist. It is thus very easy for the client to 'cheat', but this can be monitored by the evidence of the scales. Once again, this will be confronted, but in a non-hostile way. In the case of in-patient treatment, the focus on weight gain is much more obvious. Indeed, it has been shown repeatedly that in the vast majority of cases, the client can be returned to within about 10–15% of 'normal weight' in this context. In out-patient treatment, the path towards weight gain may be less channelised and is more likely to overlap with the other psychological aspects of treatment. Within a day context, however, Piran and Kaplan (1990) have made weight gain an explicit target and, as shown below, the signs are that good results can potentially be achieved at this level.

Psychotherapy

Many forms of psychotherapy have been applied to anorexia nervosa, ranging from the behavioural to the psychodynamic. Usually, this would be individual psychotherapy, as anorectics are not generally thought to be very suitable for group treatment (see, for example, Hall, 1985). The most common form of behaviour modification has tended to use reinforcement principles in order to try to achieve weight gain. Typically, clients are weighed regularly and if a certain level of weight gain is achieved, the client is rewarded. Commonly used reinforcers include increased physical and social activity, which may be withheld until the required weight gain is achieved. Although crude behavioural principles tend to apply to in-patient treatment in general, there is no firm evidence that more precise and individualised schedules of reinforcement create better results (see, for example, Touyz, Beumont and Glaun, 1984). Another study failed to show any superiority of behaviour modification over 'milieu therapy' (Eckert et al, 1979). Overall, it seems that the specificity of behaviour modification has not had much impact on the long-term treatment of anorexia nervosa and also that it presents an overly naive approach to this complex problem.

Most experts in the field would argue that some form of psychotherapy is appropriate in the long-term management of anorexia nervosa. Often, the view is taken that psychotherapy should be delayed until a substantial amount of weight gain is achieved. In a number of approaches to psycho-therapy, however, there is a wish to de-emphasise the focus on weight gain. For example, Orbach (1985) makes an agreement with her clients that if they agree not to fall below their weight measured at the beginning of treatment, then she will not interfere with their food intake. In practice, in many centres psychotherapy often goes hand in hand with weight restoration, or at least dovetails with it.

Psychotherapy of anorexia nervosa perhaps really began to take off through the writings of Hilde Bruch (e.g. 1962, 1973). Earlier psychoanalytical approaches had sought to interpret anorectic behaviour in terms of such concepts as rejection of oral impregnation. But Bruch's experience of anorectics was that the more traditional psychoanalytic approach, which emphasised interpretation by the therapist, was inappropriate. Bruch instead saw the therapeutic task in terms of overcoming the anorectic's overwhelming sense of ineffectiveness. She aimed to help her clients to get in touch with their inner feelings and needs and to confront their need for approval and perfection. In essence, she was trying to help the anorectic to achieve identity without recourse to eating control. This kind of theme runs through many other forms of psychotherapy with anorexia nervosa, albeit with different language and theoretical conceptions. Goodsitt (1985), for example, also rejects interpretive psychotherapy and builds on the kind of ideas expressed by Bruch within the language of what he calls 'self psychology', an approach heavily influenced by Kohut (1971). He conceptualises the task of the therapist as providing an opportunity for growth and healing of the self. He aims to fill in the missing self structure by acting as a 'transitional object', as parent, guide, teacher and coach.

Although Orbach (e.g. 1985) is well known for her feminist conceptualisation of anorexia nervosa, her approach to treatment seems to be very similar to that of Bruch and Goodsitt. She refers to the 'making of the individual' as the 'raison d'être of the therapeutic work'. The emphasis is on discovery of who the client is and wishes to be. Weight and eating is put to one side until the client has a sufficiently developed sense of self to allow him or her to feel safe with letting go of control. She describes a process of moving from being highly defended, through a period of feeling chaos and lack of integration towards relationship and self-actualisation. It seems to be agreed that this type of in-depth psychotherapy is a long-term process. Orbach, for example, typically sees people for between 30 and 48 months.

In many people's eyes, the closest relative of a personal construct approach is cognitive therapy (sometimes expressed as cognitive-behavioural therapy), which in the case of anorexia nervosa is most closely associated with Garner and Bemis (1982). Their focus is on the significance of 'distorted thinking patterns', using techniques of treatment derived from Beck's (1976) cognitive model of depression. Thus a central aim of treatment is to identify the client's 'belief system', including attitudes about weight, assumptions of self-worth and so on. Although the authors stress the need to accept the client's belief system, they suggest lines of enquiry that may 'begin to introduce doubt . . . .'. Moreover, they repeatedly refer to

'reasoning errors', 'faulty beliefs' and substituting more 'realistic' interpretations, particularly in relation to attitudes about shape, size and self-
esteem. Thus, while displaying respect for the client's point of view, the
approach is fundamentally underpinned by an assumption of rationality, an
approach that is in quite sharp contrast with a personal construct approach.

Although some family work may form part of the overall treatment plan
in many centres, the use of family therapy as a primary mode of treatment
is most closely associated with Minuchin, Rosman and Baker (1978) and
Palazzoli (1978). In formal family therapy, the locus of the problem is seen
to be dysfunctional patterns of family interaction, which it is assumed
maintain and reinforce the syndrome of anorexia nervosa. Minuchin, Rosman and Baker (1978), for example, argue that there are five such patterns:
'enmeshment', 'overprotectiveness', 'rigidity', 'lack of conflict resolution'
and involvement of the sick child in unresolved parental conflict. The task
of family therapy is to change the behaviour of all members of the family,
not just the client. A wide variety of techniques and strategies may be
employed within this framework, the most well known of which is the so-
called 'family lunch'. In such sessions, the therapist/s join with the whole
family in a meal and make suggestions for how the client can eat more
autonomously, with collaborative parental direction, but without being
over-intrusive. In its original formulation (Minuchin, Rosman and Baker,
1978) great claims were made for its efficacy. Research by Russell,
Szmukler, Dare and Eisler (1987), however, suggests that while more beneficial for younger clients of recent onset, it is by no means a panacea.

The outcome of treatment for anorexia nervosa

Garner (1992) comments that although over 60 follow-up studies have
been conducted, there is a paucity of controlled research. Thus, although it
is now possible to make some general conclusions about how anorectics
progress over a period of some years, it is not really appropriate to link this
in any specific way with the nature or amount of treatment received. Hsu
(1980, 1990) has reviewed these studies and pointed out that methodological flaws are commonplace in these follow-up studies. In his recent review,
he selected five that met more strict methodological criteria, including a
follow-up of at least four years. In these five studies, 50–60% were at
'normal weight', 47–58% were regularly menstruating, but between 11–
20% were still markedly underweight. Although weight improvement was
common, about two-thirds were still intensely preoccupied with weight and
dieting. At the same time, there was evidence of impaired 'mental status',
such as depressive or anxiety symptoms, in quite a substantial proportion
of cases. Using Morgan and Russell's (1975) measure of overall outcome,

44% were classified as good outcome, 28% intermediate and 26% poor, the latter including 2% who died. This mortality rate is much lower than many earlier studies, which could perhaps be regarded as an indication that competent treatment is increasingly making an impact. But we should perhaps take note of Theander's (1985) 33-year follow-up. Whereas 18% had a poor outcome and 8% had died after five years follow-up, by 33 years the figures were 6% and 18% respectively. Within the above five studies reviewed by Hsu (1990), five factors predicted poor outcome: longer duration of illness, lower minimum weight, previous treatment, premorbid personality and social difficulties and disturbed family relationships.

Although it is not possible to infer any therapeutic effect from the above studies, Crisp et al (1991) have recently published a controlled study. Ninety clients were randomly allocated to one of three types of treatment (or back to the community): intensive in-patient treatment followed by 12 sessions of out-patient therapy; 12 out-patient individual and family psychotherapy sessions; 10 out-patient group psychotherapy sessions (for clients and parents separately). All treatment was accompanied by dietary counselling aimed at gradual weight restoration. At one year there were no significant differences between the three active treatments. Garner (1992) cites this study as evidence to challenge the old assumption that in-patient treatment was the treatment of choice. Moreover, there was 40% non-compliance for in-patient treatment compared with 10–15% for out-patient.

Treatment of bulimia nervosa

Since this disorder was first identified in the late 1970s, quite considerable progress has been made at the therapeutic level and there is a fair amount of consensus as to how to help reverse the vicious cycles associated with binge-eating and purging. It is generally recognised that with or without active treatment, an educational component is necessary and may in some cases be sufficient, particularly for those who are least symptomatic (Olmsted et al, 1991). Although 'educational' treatments vary in content and intensity, they tend to be based on the kind of arguments advanced first by Garner et al (1985). The essence of such treatment is the provision of information, particularly concerning the role of social and biological factors. This tends to place a fair amount of emphasis on the dietary side of eating disorders and will focus on the principles of good nutrition, biological factors controlling weight and the effects of vomiting and purging. A particularly important element is explaining the evidence for the relationship between starvation and binge-eating and of the likelihood of continued bingeing if one persists in striving for an unrealistically low weight. Garner et al (1985) suggest that clients should aim for a weight that is around 90% of highest weight prior to the eating disorder. Although most clients find the arguments plausible, the hardest part can be the acceptance of allowing one's weight to settle at a level higher than the perceived cultural ideal. If the client can be persuaded to at least give it a go, however, they are sometimes pleasantly surprised to find that as binge-eating reduces, their weight doesn't necessarily go up and may in fact go down.

If the client accepts the principles of an educational approach then they will be encouraged to eat regularly (three or four meals per day) and to gradually introduce 'forbidden foods', such as those high in carbohydrate. This, in itself, may for some clients be successful in reducing or eliminating binge-eating, quite simply because the biological urges have been counteracted. But it is generally the case that treatment will extend beyond this level. The most common form of treatment is cognitive-behavioural, originally formulated by Fairburn (1981). Such treatment typically includes an educational/dietary component, particularly in the early stages, but gradually the focus will have moved on to cognitive factors. This will be facilitated by the use of an eating diary, which should help to identify some of the 'antecedents' to binge-eating. As well as biological triggers, such as hunger, it will be possible to identify 'dysfunctional thoughts', such as 'I'm greedy because I ate a piece of chocolate' or 'Nobody would want to go out with me'. The principles of intervention are the same as used in Beck's treatment of depression (Beck, Rush Shaw and Emery, 1979) and involve four elements: identification of dysfunctional thoughts; examination of these thoughts; identification of underlying dysfunctional beliefs and values; and the examination of these beliefs and values. Thus, each thought that may surround a binge is challenged and alternatives sought. Generally, such treatment will occur over a period of several months, gradually tapering off in frequency and has been conducted both on an individual or group basis. At present, there seems to be no clear evidence in favour of individual versus group treatment.

Although educational/cognitive-behavioural treatment has tended to dominate the prevailing therapeutic ethos, two other forms of treatment have also been quite extensively applied. Pharmacotherapy, particularly the use of antidepressants, has been extensively applied. A variety of drugs have been used and Hsu (1990) in reviewing a number of studies concludes that such drugs result in a significant reduction in binge/purging in 60–70% of clients. There tends to be a consensus, however, that such drugs alone are not sufficient. In one study, Agras et al (1992) found that cognitive-behavioural treatment plus Desipramine was superior to both treatments used singly, provided the medication was continued for at least 24 weeks.

Other forms of psychological treatment have been applied with bulimia nervosa and these include those with a more analytical/insight approach. For example, Lacey (1985) argues for a combination of behavioural and insight-oriented therapy. The term 'interpersonal psychotherapy' has also been frequently applied. For example, Fairburn et al (1991) report on a comparison of 'interpersonal psychotherapy' with cognitive-behavioural and behavioural only treatment. The interpersonal psychotherapy was originally devised for depressed out-patients by Klerman, Weissman, Rounsaville and Chevron (1984). This form of treatment is based on psychodynamic techniques, but the primary focus is on current circumstances and relationships. Fairburn et al (1991) were trying to identify to what extent the specifics of cognitive treatment were important to its success, over and above any non-specific effects. Results indicated that all three treatments resulted in a reduction in binge-eating and general psychopathology, but that cognitive-behavioural treatment proved superior in modifying extreme dieting, vomiting and attitudes towards shape and size.

The outcome of treatment for bulimia nervosa

Although there have been no long-term follow-up studies of bulimia nervosa comparable to those for anorexia nervosa, there have been a number of short-term outcome studies, and Hsu (1990) summarises 13 of these. Although these studies vary in terms of treatment received and criteria of outcome, there is a reasonable amount of consistency. Using a criterion of less than two binges per week (the DSM111R criterion – American Psychiatric Association, 1987), at least two-thirds of clients were no longer diagnosable as bulimia nervosa after one year, having reduced binge-eating dramatically. Moreover, body weight change was minimal and there was no evidence of increased fasting. Improved eating behaviour was also generally accompanied by an improvement in overall psychopathology, with reduced depression and social anxiety. Little is known about mortality, although one study by Patton (1988) reports on three deaths out of 96 normal-weight bulimics, a finding that if replicated would point to a very high increase in mortality.

Overall, it would seem that there is a good chance of recovery or at least a much reduced frequency of binge-eating in bulimia nervosa, apparently pointing to a rather more favourable outcome than in anorexia nervosa. But authors such as Fairburn (1991) and Lacey (1985) have pointed to the heterogeneity of the disorder and the need for differing treatments depending on factors over and above the bulimic behaviour. One of these is the 'personality disorder' subgroup (Lacey, 1985), who tend to be impulsive and prone to accompanying drug and alcohol abuse. Although the term 'personality disorder' is a bit of a fuzzy concept, it seems that such clients may be among those most likely to have a poor outcome (Herzog, Hartmann, Sandholz and Stammer, 1991).

Summary

This short review of the treatment and outcome for anorexia nervosa and bulimia nervosa has revealed that people suffering from these disorders can and do often improve in terms of their presenting symptomatology. But there seems to be a wide range of possible outcomes, particularly in the case of anorexia nervosa. There is no convincing evidence that any form of treatment is especially effective for anorexia nervosa. The weight of clinical evidence, however, tends to point to the need for a rather long process, in which the establishment of a safe therapeutic relationship is critical to the client being able to emerge from the obsession with weight control and become a person in his or her own right. Although medical intervention typically becomes a more acute issue with extreme weight loss, recent research seems to cast doubt on the necessity for lengthy in-patient treatment.

In the case of bulimia nervosa, the consensus seems to be that relatively simple educational/cognitive-behavioural treatment can achieve good results in many cases, at least in terms of reduced binge-eating and related behaviours. The same seems to be true of certain forms of drug treatment. The indications are, however, that for some clients there are more complex underlying psychological issues, which do not necessarily respond too well to such treatment. In the early 1990s, insight-oriented treatment with an emphasis on interpersonal relationships seems to be most commonly applied in tackling these broader issues.

One of the striking things recorded in this literature is the way in which treatments are often applied to people with eating disorders as if they have to be cured of an illness, with relatively little regard for the personal nature of the issues that may surround the eating disorder. Cognitive therapy is a classic example of this, with its emphasis on reducing dysfunctional thoughts. This is also reflected by the assessment of treatment outcome, which typically focuses on eating behaviour and various general indices of well-being, and it is rare to find an assessment of what trying to let go of the eating behaviour means for the client. I would contend, however, that whatever treatment a client receives, the outcome will depend more on the meaning of personal change than to the particular technical bag of tricks brought by the therapist. As shown in the following chapters, the meaning of life with or without an eating disorder is very much the concern of the personal construct approach.

Part II

A PERSONAL CONSTRUCT APPROACH TO EATING DISORDERS

3 The psychology of personal constructs

In 1955, an American psychologist, George Kelly, published his magnum opus, *The Psychology of Personal Constructs*. This two-volume work presented a major contribution to twentieth century psychology that has enormous implications for our understanding of people in general and people in distress in particular. Kelly was a practising clinical psychologist as well as an academic and his ideas are both theoretically penetrating and clinically relevant. In fact, one whole volume, entitled *Clinical Diagnosis and Psychotherapy*, was devoted to the clinical context. Although his theory has wide applicability, amply demonstrated by its extensive application in diverse fields such as education and business, its focus is very much on the client in distress. Indeed, there has been a number of books written specifically on clinical applications (e.g. Epting, 1984; Button, 1985a; Neimeyer and Neimeyer, 1987; Winter, 1992).

First, we will look at Kelly's original ideas. In the 1950s in the USA, two traditions were dominant. Within psychology, behaviourism was still the predominant model. People were viewed by and large as responding to stimuli, a passive victim of reinforcement and conditioning. The therapy that was to emerge from this, namely behaviour therapy, took the view that treatment and change was a matter of producing new behaviour by tampering with a person's learning experiences. At a clinical level, however, the psychoanalytic tradition, to which Kelly had been exposed, was still very influential. In many ways this, too, presented a rather passive model of the person; in this case, however, the focus of that passivity was more from inside. People were seen to be driven by biological forces, notably sex and aggression, which the person had to struggle to deal with. Therapy was and still tends to be primarily about helping the client to achieve 'insight' into the defenses being used to reconcile the conflicts arising from the competing demands of inner and outer forces. Thus in both cases, the individual is viewed as a kind of victim who has to be rescued by the expert. *The Psychology of Personal Constructs* (Kelly, 1955) may be viewed in part as a reaction to these rather stifling views of the person.

The essence of Kelly's approach is indeed an optimistic one, which enshrines a sense of freedom and possibilities. This is encapsulated in his underlying philosophical assumptions.

First basic assumption

> We (Kelly) assume that all our present interpretations of the universe are subject to revision or replacement. (Kelly, 1955, p. 15)

This basic position implies that there are many and various ways of viewing the universe. By universe, Kelly implied that all aspects of a person's world, ranging from bowel movements through to thoughts about the meaning of life, may be the focus of our attention. We can view or interpret these things in a whole host of ways. Some ways may turn out to be better than others, but no interpretation is intrinsically right or wrong. However set and predictable things may seem, there is always another way of looking at it. No-one has to be the victim of his or her biography. In the context of eating disorders, there is a sense in which people can become trapped within the worlds of their creation, as brilliantly portrayed by Hilde Bruch (1978) in her metaphor of *The Golden Cage* for the plight of the anorexia nervosa sufferer. A common theme that runs through the lives of people afflicted with an eating disorder is indeed that they have become blinkered by one interpretation of the world. Broadly speaking, this focuses on the importance of weight. For example, faced with an invitation to go out to a party, this is interpreted less as an opportunity for fun, meeting someone, letting one's hair down, getting drunk, exploring ideas, making love, etc, than as a matter of weight/eating: 'I'm too fat' . . . 'I'd have to eat'. This limited frame of reference narrows the options in ways that may well serve a function for that person, but at the same time blinds the person to the possibility of other dimensions to experience. Before going any further, it should be stressed that this phenomenon applies as much to us, the therapist/clinician, as to our client. We too can become trapped by a kind of tunnel vision. For example, we can look at a client just in terms of emaciation, just in terms of vomiting or the fact that the person is a bulimic. Creative interaction with a client requires that we too can see other possibilities. Yes, the client may be a dangerously thin anorectic, but he or she could also be or become an artist, a person full of painful emotions, a tower of strength, or someone on the brink of something new. We can all become trapped or freed by our constructions.

Therapeutic implication

There is hope that things can change. It may not be easy and it may take time, but there are other perspectives on life besides the current one. Reconstruction can open up new and more fruitful avenues to the client's life.

Second basic assumption

A person's processes are psychologically channelised by the ways in which he anticipates events. (Kelly, 1955, p. 46)

The key word in this statement is *anticipation*. The emphasis is on looking ahead. Kelly was concerned with the ever-flowing stream of events that is life. In contrast to some schools of psychology and approaches to mankind that stress the reactive nature of people, we are seen as actively engaged in thinking, doing and feeling on the basis of what we anticipate or expect. For example, when clients meets us for the first time, they are not there just answering or refusing to answer our questions. They probably have an agenda too. On the basis of previous experience, they will be anticipating, correctly or incorrectly, what is going to happen, what you are like, what you are planning to do, etc. Indeed, their behaviour will probably reflect this. Their silence, crying, sharing and so on will be influenced by how they anticipate you will react and their degree of comfort with the situation.

In stressing anticipation, Kelly was not implying that this was the only way of looking at people, more that this might be a fruitful perspective on people. So what are the implications of taking this stance? A central implication is that we would pay more attention to the future as anticipated by a person, in contrast perhaps to focusing on the past. This does not imply that the past is unimportant, but that ultimately our perception of the past leads us to have a particular way of anticipating the future. For example, if a female client has been badly abused by a number of men in the past, she may well come to anticipate that other men will also be potential abusers. As a result of such construction, she may well behave in a way that seeks to confirm that construction. For example, she may keep her distance from men and avoid any possibility of getting too close. The important point here is that such construing will guide the way she approaches her life and will be a major consideration in any attempt to understand and work with her. Kelly's reference to 'psychological processes' implies that all aspects of a person will be influenced by such constructions. Thus, her thinking, feelings and behaviour will all be directed by the anticipation that men are abusers. It should be stressed here that the rightness of this construction is not at issue. There may well be a fair amount of social consensus for the construction, but the main concern from a personal construct perspective is that the construct will impose certain limitations as to what is possible for that person.

People with eating disorders are, in most respects, no different from people in general. Thus, they will be anticipating in areas such as relationships with other people, work, leisure and health. But we might speculate that they also have particularly important anticipations with regard to weight, food and eating. This might involve anticipating that life above 8 st. (112 lb) would be intolerable, that eating a piece of chocolate will make them fat or that if they gave up weight control, they would risk becoming an unacceptable person. These anticipations may be derived from the media or from direct experience of themselves and others. For example, a sexual relationship may have ended in an unwanted way. This could lead the person to have concluded that this was because he or she was too fat. It is not difficult to see how this might lead to an expectation that this would recur in other sexual relationships, unless weight was controlled strictly. Other aspects of the relationship, which may have been relevant, may be ignored, possibly because they held less meaning for the person. The weight explanation may seem like a much easier option.

As we shall see later, anticipation also applies to the therapeutic situation. Clients who are seeking help will be trying to anticipate what is coming. What are they letting themselves in for? What would their therapist be like? Will they risk losing what they value most in their life? Each client will have different agenda, as revealed by their anticipatory processes. They will be unlikely to engage and persist with treatment unless they feel reasonably able to anticipate what is involved, as well as feeling comfortable with what they do anticipate. Much of the initial work of therapy needs to be focused on what kinds of anticipations they are operating with.

Corollaries of personal construct theory

Kelly had a rather logical approach to his theorising and elaborated his basic assumptions by presenting a series of 11 further propositions about the person, which he labelled as 'corollaries'.

Construction corollary

> A person anticipates events by construing their replications. (Kelly, 1955, p. 50)

We are able to anticipate if we have succeeded in inferring some sort of pattern and order in our experience. Repeated observation of sets of traffic lights enable us to eventually know the sequence and what to do at particular points in the cycle. In the context of early feeding behaviour, mother and baby are both engaged in construing the other, until a point is reached where both can anticipate each other and act accordingly. In both of these contexts, the person's ability to anticipate emerges out of a detection of recurring patterns or themes. Much as listening to a piece of music, on first hearing it will be all new. It is only with repeated hearing, that we come to recognise the themes and are able to sing along, hum or whatever as evidence of our developing anticipation. Although Kelly uses the term 'replication', this does not mean that the events are identical, but that we detect sufficient similarity to recognise that they have something important in common. For example, no two Indian meals are exactly the same, but anyone who has had some experience of this cuisine will have no difficulty detecting the distinctive aroma that indicates that curry is on the menu and not roast beef.

Individuality corollary

> Persons differ from each other in their construction of events. (Kelly, 1955, p. 55)

An important point to stress about the process of construction is that it is a matter of personal interpretation, rather than a simple detection of reality. For example, it might be a therapist's experience that fat people are at least as likely to develop intimate relationships as their slimmer counterparts. The therapist's 'reality', however, might be quite different from the client's, who may be quite convinced that being fat rules out sexual relationships. The personal construct approach implies that neither of these constructions is intrinsically right; they are examples of alternative constructions potentially available. There are many others: for example, that people who construe people primarily by size tend to end up with superficial relationships.

The significance of 'events' has been highlighted in recent times by the study of 'life events' and their relevance to mental health (e.g. Paykel, 1978). The assumption was that an accumulation of many adverse events (e.g. bereavement, job loss, house move) can lead a person to be more susceptible to breakdown. Perhaps not surprisingly, more sophisticated research (e.g. Andrews, 1981) has shown that individual differences account for a much higher proportion of variance than the events per se. This is entirely consistent with a personal construct perspective, which points out that the significance of an event will depend on its meaning for a particular person. For example, a change of job might present as a threat for one person, but a challenge for another. Pregnancy could be a dream come true or an absolute disaster, depending on the person's wishes at the time and context of its occurrence.

Dichotomy corollary

> A person's construction system is composed of a finite number of dichotomous constructs. (Kelly, 1955, p. 59)

Out of a person's construing of 'replications', it is argued that one creates a series of *constructs*, which are dichotomous in nature. Examples of such constructs would be depressed versus happy; slim versus fat; hungry versus full; dead versus alive. It is important to stress, however, that these constructs are not the equivalent of dictionary definitions. For example, one client used the term 'sweet' as a very important construct, but it became obvious that it bore no relationship to niceness or sugariness, but was idiosyncratic in meaning to her and possibly her subculture. She knew what it meant, but she could not explain it to her therapist. Thus, while often using everyday language to label a construct, there is no guarantee that its meaning will correspond to general usage.

Kelly was at pains to stress the dichotomous nature of constructs, a feature that has proved to be one of the most controversial aspects of the theory. His point was that constructs emerge from our noting similarity and contrast. The contrast is seen to be as important to the construct as is the similarity. One of the important implications of this corollary is that what a person is not saying may be as important as what is being said. For example, when asked to describe family, some rather defensive clients (a not uncommon characteristic in anorexia nervosa) will strongly assert that they all get on well together. Their mere emphasis on this theme of 'getting on together' may suggest that they have construed the possibility of a contrasting state of affairs. Without the client's help we cannot be too sure what this is; it may be not getting on, falling out, breaking up, being angry and many other possibilities.

The identification of a person's constructs is a key feature of the clinical application of personal construct theory. To know and understand a person requires that we have some awareness of a person's constructs and we shall see later some of the ways we can go about this.

Organisation corollary

> Each person characteristically evolves, for his convenience in anticipating
> events, a construction system embracing ordinal relationships between con-
> structs. (Kelly, 1955, p. 56)

Our constructions do not just exist in isolation, but are interrelated and
organised. Kelly implied that there is a hierarchical aspect to this organisation. He argued that some constructs 'subsume' others. For example, a
construct such as good–bad may include a wide range of constructs: e.g.
intelligent–dull; kind–unkind; creative–dead; independent–dependent;
slim–overweight. In this case, the construct good–bad is a kind of overarch-
ing one that plays a superordinate one to the others. For someone with an
eating disorder, however, it may be that a construct such as slim–
overweight has a very superordinate position in the construct system. Many
things may be determined by whether or not you are slim or overweight.
Even being healthy or ill may be less important than slim–overweight. An
important implication of this corollary is that constructs do not stand in
isolation. To invite a person to construe themselves in a new way may have
repercussions throughout a whole range of interconnected constructs. Also
critical is that some degree of organisation of construing is essential for the
integrity of the person. Change may threaten the whole basis of a person's
ability to anticipate events.

Choice corollary

> A person chooses for himself that alternative in a dichotomized construct
> through which he anticipates the greater possibility for extension and defini-
> tion of his system. (Kelly, 1955, p. 64)

We have seen how constructs are meant to involve bipolar contrasts. It
follows that we can use either pole of a construct in any given situation. For
example, if the construct 'boring versus exciting' has meaning for a person,
then that person might opt for excitement as being generally something to
seek. But there may be times when there's too much excitement and the
person will settle for being bored for a while. The important point about
this corollary is that our choices are guided by the constructs we have
available. If fat–slim has become a major, if not the only, way of viewing
oneself and people, then most events will be construed in terms of a choice
between these two alternatives. Given the nature of the prevailing cultural
ideal, it is hardly surprising that most people opt for the slim end.

The nature of our choices will be influenced both by the possibility for
extension and definition of our construct system. Broadly speaking,

'extension' refers to an adventurous broadening out of our horizons, whereas, 'definition' involves staying with the familiar and going for more of the same. For example, an artist may choose boldly to change colour or mood (extension), but there is also the option to fill in some more detail (definition). An important clinical implication of this is that people do not necessarily make the choices we think they ought to. The alcoholic who continues to drink, the smoker who keeps on smoking and the anorectic who steadfastly stays anorectic, even though life may be in danger, all have made a choice that seems to them to offer greater scope for knowing where they are going. While therapy may be about creating the conditions in which the client can feel safe to move on, it should not be assumed that 'definition' is a bad thing. The choice to embark on major change may be followed by a prolonged period of fleshing out exactly what it means to go down a particular road.

Range corollary

> A construct is convenient for the anticipation of a finite range of events only. (Kelly, 1955, p. 68)

A construct's *range of convenience* consists of all contexts to which it could reasonably be applied. However, the idea that constructs are applicable only to a finite range of events seems to ignore the creative and imaginative aspects of our thinking. For example, a construct like 'sexy–not sexy' might have had a very limited range of convenience in Victorian days, but seems to have panned out into a whole range of areas these days, thanks in no small part to the media. Films, cars, computers, dreams, drinks, food and even books can be construed along the dimension. What Kelly was implying, however, is that a construct is more applicable in some contexts than others and indeed that it is particularly appropriate in some contexts (*focus of convenience*). It may be that some constructs could do with a narrowing of their range (e.g. slim–fat), whereas newer constructs could benefit from being tried out in a wider range of situations. For example, an overcontrolled person may need to try out a 'fun' construct in some new situations rather than seeing it as something that just happened as a kid.

Experience corollary

> A person's construction system varies as he successively construes the replications of events. (Kelly, 1955, p. 72)

Life continually invites us to reconsider our assumptions. Although we can usually have a rough idea of what to expect on a day-by-day basis, there is always the possibility of surprise, change, if not revolution. In the early 1980s, how many Eastern Europeans could have anticipated the 'new world order'? Such dramatic change can also occur at the personal level. A sudden bereavement, for example, can completely undermine the whole basis of one's existence. But it is likely that much change occurs on a more gradual basis. A series of experiences (or 'replications' of events) may eventually lead us to a new view of things, even though we may not necessarily be aware of it at the time. Psychotherapy is one structured way of trying to make use of new experience towards a more viable view of the world. Almost by definition, however, Kelly's view of experience is not of something that happens to us but as of the successive interpretation and reinterpretation of events. Moreover, we can choose to make experiences happen rather than waiting for 'life events' to descend upon us.

Modulation corollary

> The variation in a person's construction system is limited by the permeability of the constructs within whose range of convenience the variants lie. (Kelly, 1955, p. 77)

In this rather long-winded definition, the key word is 'permeability'. A construct that is permeable is one that is able to accommodate new experience. Here Kelly is qualifying the experience corollary by pointing out that not all constructs will be very adaptable. For example, a construct such as 'acid versus alkaline' might be highly useful for the chemist at work, but may be of little help in developing intimate relationships. While we need some permeability of our constructs, too much could be dangerous. For example, to one young man, who was preoccupied with the risk of catching AIDS, almost all situations were viewed as offering a direct threat to his vulnerability to the disease. Any personal contact was seen first and foremost, if not exclusively, in terms of whether he might catch the disease from them. Thus some variation in permeability seems necessary if we are to achieve a balance between too much and too little change.

Fragmentation corollary

> A person may successively employ a variety of construction subsystems which are inferentially incompatible with each other. (Kelly, 1955, p. 83)

Within our overall view of the world, we can be seen as having various 'subsystems', which apply to different contexts. The worlds of home, work and leisure can be very different and we could have different ways of construing in them. To an outsider our behaviour in these different situations may not seem to be 'logically' related. While this may appear to be so, we avoid disintegrating in Jekyll and Hyde manner by having more 'superordinate' constructs that reconcile the apparent differences. For example, you might turn to shouting when at home, which is a behaviour that would not be seen at work. Such apparent inconsistency, however, could be reconciled by your view that as a parent you need to exert discipline over your children, whereas work does not require you to act in such a role. The eating disorder client may similarly begin to learn that one can approach food quite differently in some contexts than in others; elaboration of relatedness to these varying situations may help to decrease any possible sense of fragmentation.

Commonality corollary

> To the extent that one person employs a construction of experience which is similar to that employed by another, his psychological processes are similar to those of the other person. (Kelly, 1955, p. 90).

This and the following corollary introduce Kelly's approach to the relationships between people. Having stressed the individuality of the person, it is here acknowledged that we are more than just individuals. We can and do share similar experiences, but more importantly it is here stressed that it is the similarity of *interpretation* of those experiences that is important. Thus people of apparently different backgrounds may have come to similar conclusions about the world. This is certainly true, it seems, for example, in the case of weight preoccupation, which seems to be becoming cultureless. Such apparent similarity of construing is important in the formation of relationships (Duck and Spencer, 1972) and has been shown to be a powerful element in group therapy (Koch, 1985). Thus self-help groups may play an important role in helping people to feel less alone. But we should also be wary of assuming too much on the basis of our constructions. Because we see people as having something in common with us does not mean to say that they share much in common from their point of view.

Sociality corollary

> To the extent that one person construes the construction processes of another, he may play a role in a social process involving the other person. (Kelly, 1955, p. 95)

Although some similarity of construing may be a prerequisite for the formation of relationships (see Duck and Spencer, 1972), this in itself may not be enough. We need what Kelly here calls *sociality*, or the ability to see things from the other person's point of view. Meaningful relationships require that we try to stand in the other person's shoes and look at how it might look from his or her perspective. This does not mean that we have to be able to understand a person completely. Such understanding is likely to be at best partial, even in the most sensitive of people. Thus, when involved with other people, our interactions become truly interpersonal if we go beyond being two individuals and strive for mutual understanding.

Button (1987) has argued that this kind of relating may be particularly deficient in the case of eating disorders. There may be a lack of such reciprocal relationships and more of a sense of an individual's own construing dominating. For example, Celia saw her mother as a very controlling individual who did not give her the feeling that she had any right to her own choices. She had to do what her mother wanted. Adult relationships are likely to flounder if based on such a premise. A major thrust of the therapist's work is to try to develop more understanding relationships via the therapy situation. It is the therapist's aim to try to understand the client's construing, but the client also needs to work towards understanding the therapist's construing. Bee and Mitchell (1984) use the metaphor of 'dancing' to describe such synchronised relationships. To dance really well seems to call for a good measure of sociality.

Emotional experience

A person is never completely static. There is always something going on, even when we are sleeping. From a constructionist viewpoint, we may see our personal construct system as never being completely at rest, but in a state of evolution. The way we see the world tomorrow is likely to be slightly different from the way we see it today. New experiences constantly invite us to reconstrue, but some experiences are more disturbing than others. When we face relatively major change in construing, our construct system faces a state of what Kelly called *transition*. Such transition is neither good nor bad per se, but it certainly will make its presence felt by the disruption and disturbance that comes in its wake. Being in love, for example, can be regarded as a state of construct system transition in which one or both partners anticipate the possibility of a major development through the emerging relationship. The excitement generated by being in love is unlikely to be accompanied by a period of settled, predictable behaviour. We are also likely to experience a fair amount of emotion and it has been suggested (e.g. Bannister, 1977) that emotion is at the heart of what Kelly meant by transition.

Love is but one kind of transition. There are many others and Kelly outlined a series of what he called 'dimensions of transition'. These should not, in my view, be regarded as a comprehensive range of transitions, but as some dimensions that might be useful as a way of understanding a person's experience of change.

Threat

> Threat is the awareness of imminent comprehensive change in one's core structures. (Kelly, 1955, p. 489)

Like all of Kelly's dimensions of transition, threat is a term often applied in everyday life. But he had a particular meaning for each of these terms. Threat is something we experience when we have interpreted evidence that there is about to be substantial change at the level of our *core*. The latter term is used by Kelly to refer to those constructions that are central to our identity and existence. Core constructs are of fundamental importance, as opposed to more peripheral ones that can be altered without serious consequences. Belief in God is likely to be an example of a core construct for a religious person. People will go to great extremes to ward off evidence that challenges those beliefs. For the anorectic client, the value of being thin may also be akin to a religion. Being thin and believing in the value of thinness is possibly at the heart of such a person's existence. To be confronted with the possibility of losing it could undermine the whole basis for existence.

Kelly wrote extensively about the importance of carefully managing threat in psychotherapy. Without being aware of threat, a therapist is highly unlikely to be able to enter into a fruitful therapeutic relationship with someone with an eating disorder, or anyone else for that matter. Managing threat will be elaborated upon later.

Fear

> Fear is like threat, except that, in this case, it is a new incidental construct, rather than a comprehensive construct, that seems about to take over. (Kelly, 1955, p. 494)

The difference is a rather subtle one, in that Kelly still sees core constructs as being involved. But the significance of the construct is rather narrower and simpler. 'What threatens us is that which we know a good deal about. What makes us fearful is that which we know less about' (Kelly, 1955, p. 494). Kelly gives us a fear example of someone driving a car and realising they are about to end up in a ditch. Realising one is about to knock over a child after a few drinks, however, might have such widespread implications that he would describe this as threat. Perhaps an analogy within the eating disorder field might serve to exemplify. Faced with having to eat apple pie and custard, an anorectic might encounter fear, but this would not perhaps compare with the threat of having to give up the whole world of being anorectic.

Anxiety

> Anxiety is the recognition that the events with which one is confronted lie outside the range of convenience of one's construct system. (Kelly, 1955, p. 495)

When we fail to make sense of a situation, we are likely to experience anxiety. The first day at school is a classical example of this, particularly if the child has not had the benefit of nursery education. It is also likely to be a strong feeling present when people have their first encounters with therapists, particularly in the strange world of mental health. The key to such experiences is of not knowing, of facing the difficult to construe. Kelly stressed that it is a *partial* failure to construe. Something totally unknown would not be construed as likely to lead to the experience of anxiety. Note that in contrast to threat and fear there is no stipulation that core constructs are involved. Relatively peripheral matters could thus make us anxious, provided we had difficulty making sense of them. For example, if one goes to a dinner party with strangers, we may feel distinctly uneasy until we can find some way into conversation that we can easily construe. People with eating disorders often avoid situations and I suspect that this both helps them to avoid contexts they cannot construe, but also serves to increase their inability to construe. It is only by interacting with people that we are likely to be able to develop constructs that enable us to anticipate them.

Guilt

> Perception of one's apparent dislodgement from his core role structure constitutes the experience of guilt. (Kelly, 1955, p. 502)

Our core role involves those fundamental constructs by which we maintain ourselves as an integral being. These constructs are not necessarily highly verbalised and indeed there might be a 'gut feeling' element to such construing. But we are talking about fundamentals rather than superficial aspects.

This is what Kelly means by core role structure. For example, I might have a construction of myself around being a psychologist that leads me to strive to be caring and understanding of people. Such construing, however, may be difficult to sustain and there might be times when I am faced with evidence to the contrary, for example, I am accused of being insensitive. This is what Kelly means by apparent dislodgement from one's core role structure. When we sense that we are not what we thought we were we can experience 'guilt'. We probably all know how painful such an experience can be.

An important aspect of this conceptualisation, is that guilt will be experienced only if a person feels that their sense of themselves has been invalidated. It helps to make sense of the fact that some people can commit the most apparently despicable acts (to an outsider), whilst feeling no guilt. At the same time, a person can feel enormous guilt about some apparently trivial indiscretion. Moreover, guilt thus defined can also be applied to 'positive' experience. Sometimes people eventually achieve something for which they had been striving for a long time, e.g. passing an exam or getting a new job. We can, however, feel most uncomfortable about this because it is 'not me', or not yet me. Faced with this kind of experience, it might feel safer to retreat to the old me.

It follows from the above that this can be an issue in psychotherapy. We are generally trying to help people to change. When they eventually see the possibility of that change becoming a reality, they may well develop 'guilt'. This applies as much to someone with an eating disorder as anyone else. Although appealing in fantasy, the world of being free of an eating problem may feel quite strange and it may feel more comfortable to stay with the 'devil you know'.

Aggressiveness

> Aggressiveness is the active elaboration of one's perceptual field. (Kelly, 1955, p. 508)

For Kelly, aggression was a positive state and not equivalent to hitting people over the head. By active elaboration he is referring to times when there may be a lot of development going on in a person's construing. The person is actively reaching out, questioning, challenging and perhaps precipitating him or herself into new situations. Kelly makes the point that such behaviour can be perceived as unwelcome by one's associates. Those who are seeking a quiet life may not take too kindly to the person who is constantly challenging, pestering and questioning.

In normal parlance, aggression is often seen as a 'trait'. But in Kellyan terms, we can pass through stages where we are more 'aggressive'. For example, adolescence is often viewed as a time of questioning, if not 'storm and stress'. At other times, however, we might be content to just tick over. In the psychotherapeutic context, such 'aggression' may be seen as an encouraging sign of movement. Take, for example, a client who had presented with anorexia nervosa. During the early stages of her stay in hospital, she had presented as very nice and conforming, perhaps typifying the good girl stance. After putting on weight, however, she became reconfronted with issues of becoming herself, particularly in relation to her parents. Her behaviour over many weeks changed to a rather rebellious stance, where she wasn't the most easy person to live with. She was seen standing outside her therapist's office with a rather angry look and deliberately dropping cigarette ends on the floor almost in a gesture of defiance. This is a rather mild example, but people can be much more expansive as they start opening up new horizons. In such circumstances, the therapist may be in for a very bumpy ride.

Hostility

> Hostility is the continued effort to extort validational evidence in favor of a type of social prediction which has already proved itself a failure. (Kelly, 1955, p. 510)

When faced with mounting evidence that we are wrong, we may go to extreme lengths to avoid changing our theory of the world. A mother heavily invested in the maternal role may find that teenage children are increasingly failing to adhere to her expectations. They may no longer wish to play the game of enacting child–mother expectations. Rather than face the inevitability of change, she may choose to try to force her children to conform to the old expectations. Trying to prove that they really do need Mum or enforcing rules about not staying out late might serve to temporarily stave off the inevitable.

The concept of hostility is very relevant to the concept of resistance. Faced with the risk of losing a very important set of beliefs, clients may resort to hostility. Classically, this would involve trying to prove that they cannot change and this might even involve having to get worse. Becoming suicidal could be an extreme way of warding off change, but it can be manifested in many less extreme ways. A person might seek to validate a belief that people cannot be trusted by not conforming in the therapeutic situation. For example, not turning up or being late may be ways of trying to prove that you will reject a client, thus confirming that you were not to be trusted. We should watch out for such signs of hostility in our clients. But it is not just clients who can be hostile. Therapists sometimes grimly hang on to an invalid theory. We sometimes might cajole patients by asserting something like: 'Well you didn't do what I asked did you? If only you'd have done your homework then you might feel better.' We too can get quite desperate in looking for any crumb to support our dwindling theory about how to help people.

Cycles and processes of construction

We have seen that our construing of the world is not static. In addition to the above dimensions of transition, Kelly described several other processes for charting psychological movement.

Dilation and constriction

> When, following a series of alternating uses of incompatible systems, a person broadens his perceptual field in order to reorganize it on a more comprehensive level, the adjustment may be called 'dilation'. (Kelly, 1955, p. 476)
>
> When one minimizes the apparent incompatibility of his construction systems by drawing in the outer boundaries of his perceptual field, the relatively repetitive mental process that ensues is designated as 'constriction'. (Kelly, 1955, p. 477)

These two opposing alternatives represent very different outcomes at the behavioural level. When dilating, a person will do things like jumping from topic to topic, seeing connections between a vast array of events. The manic patient represents an extreme example of this pattern of behaviour. At the other end of the spectrum, when constricting a person tends to withdraw, to batten down the hatches. By focusing on only a narrow range of events, the person reduces the likelihood of confronting further inconsistencies in construing. An extreme example of such behaviour would seem to be catatonic withdrawal, where the person seems to have virtually shut down all potential for construing. People with eating disorders also manifest such behaviours. One can view the avoidance of social eating as an example of constriction and the chaotic patterns often seen in bulimic clients as possibly reflecting a kind of dilation.

The C–P–C cycle

> The C–P–C cycle is a sequence of construction involving, in succession, circumspection, preemption, and control, and leading to a choice which precipitates the person into a particular situation. (Kelly, 1955, p. 515)

This cycle is concerned with the sequence that precedes choice and action. The first phase is what Kelly calls *circumspection*. Here we consider a range of possible ways of viewing a situation. Imagine a child in a room full of toys. The child is off school and has time on his or her hands. What are the possibilities? Jigsaws, colouring, building, cars, dressing up, playing a game? Maybe none of these . . . how about being a nuisance? Eventually a decision is made about the best option. This opting for one particular construction is what Kelly refers to as *preemption*. Let's say it is jigsaws. The last stage is deciding which particular jigsaw. This is what Kelly calls *control*. The cycle does not necessarily proceed through each stage in a neat, orderly manner. In some people, the circumspection stage is foreshortened or non-existent. Kelly calls this *impulsivity*. This is a pattern commonly seen in bulimic clients, who are often rather impulsive in their behaviour. Take eating, for example, and the way some clients throw food down themselves almost without stopping to breathe, let alone thinking about whether they are enjoying the food. At the other end of the spectrum, we find people who spend their life circumspecting, such that any real action is impossible. There are others who manage to choose the issue, but have difficulty in proceeding to action. The anorectic seems to have mainly pre-empted eating as the issue, but he or she may spend ages deliberating about what or whether to eat. In the therapeutic context, one may be often faced with issues of helping people to proceed through such cycles, such that they are neither overimpulsive nor frozen into inaction.

The creativity cycle

> The creativity cycle is one which starts with loosened construction and terminates with tightened and validated construction. (Kelly, 1955, p. 528)

Kelly's concept of 'tight' versus 'loose' construing has proved to be particularly fertile in the application of personal construct psychology to psychological disorder and well-being (see Winter, 1992). Broadly speaking, the concept contrasts more predictable and precise construing (tight), with less predictable and more imprecise construing (loose). For example, in the context of eating, tight construing would be exemplified by having rather rigid expectations of when, what and how much to eat (as typical of classical restricting anorexia nervosa). Loose construing of eating might be reflected by immense variability and lack of pattern to eating, perhaps approaching the kind of 'dietary chaos' (Palmer, 1979) associated with bulimia nervosa. It is important to stress that neither tight nor loose construing is superior. There may be a time and place for both and indeed well-being may be associated with the ability to move from one to the other in a cyclical way, as implied by Kelly's concept of the *creativity cycle*.

Kelly used the word 'creativity' in a very broad sense to refer to the process of change. In these terms, it is about making new constructions, but this has to be preceded by us questioning our original assumptions. Following a period of predictability, we may begin to doubt, to question, to rethink. The evidence does not fit any more. This can be disturbing, but we should be able to find a way of reconstruing and firming up on some new predictions. For example, a client with an eating disorder has come to think that fat people are unattractive to the opposite sex. This piece of construing has been well validated over the years, with the support of media images. The client's own experience has also supported the theory. He or she is fat and has not been invited out, whereas more slender friends have. Let's say that someone of the opposite sex shows considerable interest, the neat construction is brought into question. He or she might be thrown by this and try to avoid the situation, but let's say the interest persists. There is an increasing need to reconstrue. How to construe this is another matter. One possibility is that when people relate to each other closely and feel mutual validation, then narrow constructions such as fatness become irrelevant. The new construction might be about attractiveness being related to showing initial interest in another person. This will need to be put to the test in a number of situations. It may be that this formulation does not work, but hopefully in time the person will find a way of construing which works and validates his or her anticipations.

The management of loosening and tightening of construing is given a prominent place in Kelly's writing about psychotherapy and it will be looked at further in the following chapters.

4 The exploration of personal constructs

It should be clear by now that the nature of a person's construction of the world is the focus of a personal construct approach to problems. In the clinical application of personal construct theory, we will be wanting to explore how a person construes some aspect of experience that may bear on the problems presented. The basic unit of such exploration is the *construct*. The term 'construct' refers to a discrimination or contrast a person uses in the process of anticipating events. For example, in the context of writing an author might use a construct termed 'stuck' versus 'flowing'. At times the author feels stuck and cannot write anything, whereas there are periods where the ideas flow very easily. Using such a construct can help to chart progress in the writing task and helps to prepare for what lies ahead. Although this construct is particularly useful for making sense out of writing experience, it can be used elsewhere, so that it has a fairly wide 'range of convenience'.

Other constructs may have a more limited focus. For example, in tennis playing the same author might have use for the construct 'lob' versus 'drive'. Being able to anticipate a lob, for example, might prove very useful in playing tennis, but seems irrelevant to the experience of writing. At the other end of the spectrum, we also have constructs of very wide significance, for example feeling 'loved' versus 'unloved'. Thus we operate with a wide range of constructs, some applicable in rather narrow contexts and others of great significance in many situations.

In the examples given so far, words have been used to describe a construct, but it is important to stress that the words are not in themselves the constructs. The words can be seen as labels that can help to structure and communicate our understandings. But if we just take the words literally, we can easily misunderstand what the construct means for a particular person. Furthermore, many constructs cannot be easily expressed in words. The term 'gut reaction' perhaps symbolises this – we feel something, but we cannot be too precise about it. Certain situations or people can elicit such constructs, which can often have quite a profound effect on us. Kelly suggested that such constructs were often formed before a person had language. Thus, although words can play a very important part in communicating our constructs, we should recognise that there may be a lot more beyond the words.

An important aspect of Kelly's conceptualisation of constructs is of bipolarity. This was referred to under the dichotomy corollary, where it was stated that a person's construct system comprises a finite number of dichotomous constructs. This has proved to be one of the most controversial aspects of the theory, but taken literally it means that the exploration of a person's constructs should seek both poles. The problem with this is that people do not necessarily present their constructs in this way. They may just focus on one end of a construct and it might be quite difficult to identify what it is they are contrasting it with. Moreover, for any word or phrase describing a pole of a construct, there could be several possibilities for its contrasting pole. For example, if someone describes somebody as 'a thinker', the contrast could be something like 'in touch with feelings', 'a doer', 'just gets on with life', 'impulsive', or many other things besides. An awareness of the implied contrast may be crucial to understanding the person.

Elicitation of constructs

We can explore a person's construing in many ways. Indeed, everyday conversation often gives us a very good impression of another person's construing. But in our role as professionals, we may wish to explore a person's construing in a more formal and systematic way. The first stage in the formal elicitation of constructs is to decide on the context of a person's construing. If we are working with someone with a drink problem, then there could be a case for focusing on the construing of situations that may or may not elicit drinking. Similarly, for a binge-eater, we may wish to examine construing of events that could elicit binge-eating. Other areas to focus on could range from relationships with other people to stages in a person's life. Having decided on a context, the next step is to decide on a set of *elements*. We will need a reasonably representative set of items within the context chosen. If we were interested in relationships, the elements could include my relationship with my father, with my mother, with my boss, my partner, as well as my father's relationship with my mother and so on. The selection of which and how many elements will vary. Some investigators may wish to use a standard element set for a particular domain, e.g. a set of 'role titles' (such as a person you like, a good friend, a disliked person) for which the client has to supply the names of people for each role title. But you may alternatively wish to leave it up to the client, allowing maximum flexibility. Some combination of the two might be a possibility. There is no rule about the number of elements required but, as a broad guide, less than six would usually be insufficient and around ten to 20 is fairly typical.

The elements chosen could each be written on a small card, which might prove to be a convenient way of visually comparing elements. Having thus compiled the element set, we can then move on to the formal process of construct elicitation. There are a number of ways of going about this. The most popular of these is probably the *triadic* method, so called because it involves three elements. This was the original method described by Kelly (1955), which he termed the 'minimum context form'. Three elements are selected and the subject is asked to try to think of some way/ways in which two of the elements are alike and thereby different from the third. To exemplify, here is an excerpt from triadic elicitation with an overweight, bulimic client. When presented with the three elements: self, mother and father, Leanne came up with the following constructs:

- like a quiet life – volatile
- hideously untidy – extremely tidy
- very affectionate – hard to show affection
- can sit down and relax – cannot relax
- get tension headaches – does not get headaches
- take time to admit being unwell – hypochondriac.

In all the above constructs, the left-hand pole represented a similarity between Leanne and her father, in contrast to her mother at the right pole. This degree of consistency is not always the case and it would have been perfectly possible for her to see other constructs reflecting similarity between parents or between herself and her mother. The way she had sorted the elements, however, said a lot for Leanne's relationship with her mother. She added, after exhausting the constructs from this triad, that, 'she [mother] calls the tune, wears the trousers'.

The same process is repeated with a number of triads. The question of how many triads and when to stop is often asked. As with most aspects of construct exploration, there are no hard and fast rules. One way is to take random triads by shuffling the cards, a method which makes no assumptions about how the subject will group the elements. But one may alternatively prefer to pre-select which elements to group together in threes.

The number of potential triads is very large. For example, with ten elements there are 120 possible triads. It is thus impractical to work through all possible triads. Usually one would stop when the process results in the same constructs repeating themselves. The number of constructs one can expect can range from less than ten to 50 or more.

The elicitation by triads is quite a complicated task and it may often be preferable to use another approach, perhaps particularly with children or less intelligent subjects. One could, for example, elicit from *dyads*. In this case, pairs of elements are chosen and the subject is asked to identify similarities or differences. Alternatively, one may ask the subject to describe each element in turn. In cases where language may be a difficulty, a variety of procedures have been developed, e.g. the use of mime with deaf subjects (e.g. Baillie-Grohman, 1975).

There are many ways of eliciting constructs. The importance of self/person construing in eating disorders led Button to apply a systematic procedure known as SELF-GRID (Button, 1988a) in his research on self-image and psychological disorder. SELF-GRID will be used in many of the case examples that follow in Part III. Button's procedure should not be confused with Mancuso and Jaccard's (1988) SELFGRID, which focuses on a subject's construing of social interactions.

Illustration of SELF-GRID procedure

The elicitation of constructs using the SELF-GRID procedure can be illustrated in the assessment of Kevin, a 35-year-old man with anorexia nervosa of many years' standing.

Case example: Kevin

Kevin is an extremely introverted man, who has great difficulty communicating with people and clearly felt uneasy throughout our meeting. Although he was very slow in responding, he clearly thought very carefully about the task and we were able to elicit 30 constructs. I introduced the procedure to Kevin by explaining that I was interested in finding out the kinds of ways he viewed himself and other people. I added that I wished to do this because I had found that the latter was often relevant to understanding eating disorders. I told Kevin I would be asking him to compare himself with another person. Each time I would like him to tell me of any important similarities and/or differences between himself and the other person. I stressed that it was characteristics that were important to *him* that I was interested in.

In SELF-GRID, self is compared with five different people:

- mother
- father

- the person you feel closest to
- the person you least like
- the person you most like.

Where possible, the subject supplies the name of a person to fit the latter three 'role titles'. In this particular grid form, I record any similarities and differences as *unipolar* constructs. Thus, I do not ask for the opposite pole, but it is noted in parentheses if spontaneously provided. The following constructs were elicited from Kevin.

Self and mother Kevin described a large number of similarities between himself and his mother. They both:

- get on with things in a steady way
- think before speaking
- plan things beforehand (as opposed to 'let things happen')
- don't make many friends
- try to see other people's point of view (as opposed to 'view things from one side')
- hold things back
- like to travel/visit places.

The only difference was that mother was someone who 'liked their food'.

Self and father Kevin saw rather more differences between himself and his father. The following constructs were associated with father and not himself:

- self-reliant
- widely read
- like arguments
- finds it easy to communicate
- big and powerful.

But there were two similarities, both of them:

- prefer to do things themselves
- have no self-control.

Self and closest person Kevin chose his brother for this role. He began with two similarities, both being:

- introvert
- practical.

There were, however, more differences. His brother was someone who was:

- comfortable being angry (as opposed to 'bottle anger up')
- speak their mind
- live for the moment
- like animals
- do things on the spur of moment

- clear about what wants.

Self and least liked person   Kevin could not identify such a person, saying he did not know anyone well enough.

Self and most liked person   Once again he could not identify anyone. This shows just how much Kevin's world was constricted.

Additional constructs   After the above dyadic elicitation, I invite people to add any other characteristics of people that are important to them. Kevin was able to add the following:

- Caring for people (a valued quality)
- Interested in money/possessions (a quality he didn't like)
- Fit in with the world (something he felt he did not do, but would like to change)

Repertory grid technique

Learning something of Kevin's constructs tells us quite a lot about what are the important themes for him. We have also seen something of the extent to which he aligns himself with other people. But we may wish to take the process further and explore how Kevin applies his constructs to himself and others. The most common way of doing this is to complete some form of repertory grid. Repertory Grid Technique refers to a flexible methodology derived from the Role Construct Repertory Test contained in Kelly's *The Psychology of Personal Constructs* (1955). The main feature of a typical grid is that the subject is asked to sort all the elements in terms of all the constructs. There are various ways of sorting elements. For example, if the construct was 'good–bad', 'dichotomous' scoring would just allow for a simple all or none sorting of elements as either good or bad. With 'ranking', elements could be ordered from most good to most bad. Lastly, with 'rating', elements could be rated along a scale, such that some elements could be very bad, some moderately bad and some quite good etc.

An example of a grid using the SELF-GRID procedure can be illustrated with Kevin. In SELF-GRID an eight-point rating scale is used, in which the subject is asked to indicate how much of the time a construct applies to a person, ranging from always to never. Although the subject responds verbally, the response is recorded by the investigator as a number in a matrix or grid. The scale points are: always (7), almost all of the time (6), most of the time (5), often (4), sometimes (3), only occasionally (2), rarely (1) and never (0). The instructions given to subjects indicate that the therapist will be taking one construct at a time and asking them to indicate how much of the time they think the construct applies to each of the elements in turn. It is stressed that there are no right or wrong answers and it is their impression that is of interest. If they do not know or if the construct does not apply, they should say so.

Because the focus of SELF-GRID is particularly on self-construing, a number of different selves as elements to be rated are included. These allow the subject to say something about any change in self over time as well as whether they want to change. The six self elements are:

- me nowadays
- me when younger
- me a year ago
- me in the near future
- me in far future
- me as I would ideally like to be.

For the 'younger' self they are advised to think of some particular time in their life, which they see as 'when I was younger'. For the future elements, subjects are invited to try to imagine what they would be like. They often say, 'Is this how I'd like to be or how I think I will be?' The answer is, it is how they think they will be. It is as if they then enter a dialogue within themselves and often say, 'I hope I will be', taking an optimistic view.

In addition to these six self-elements, the five elements from which constructs were elicited are also included and they are invited to add one or two other important people in their life. In Kevin's case, not surprisingly he came up with no others and he was thus restricted to the self elements, his parents and his brother. The resulting grid is illustrated in Figure 4.1.

People are often bewildered initially when they see the mass of figures and wonder what an earth you do with it. There are three broad ways of looking at the data:

- to analyse the interrelationship between constructs
- to analyse the interrelationship between elements
- to examine the interrelationship between constructs and elements.

This can be done up to a point by just looking at it, the so-called 'eyeball technique'! For example, by looking at columns representing ideal self and mother, we can see that for most of the constructs, Kevin's mother is rated quite similarly to ideal self. In contrast, his father is rated rather differently from ideal self.

From the point of view of constructs, let us take the example of constructs 5 (make many friends) and 6 (like food). The pattern of rating is again very similar, which suggests that people who like food tend to make many friends, from Kevin's point of view. With a large grid, however,

Constructs	Me nowadays	Me when younger	Me a year ago	Me in near future	Me in far future	Me ideally	Mother	Father	Brother
						Elements			
1. Get on in steady way	1	3	5	1	3	7	5	5	3
2. Think before speak	7	7	7	7	5	5	7	3	3
3. Plan	7	4	7	7	5	7	4	1	0
4. Let things happen	1	2	1	1	3	3	3	5	6
5. Make many friends	0	0	0	0	3	3	4	5	3
6. Like food	0	1	0	0	3	3	5	7	5
7. Try to see other viewpoint	5	2	5	5	5	5	4	1	3
8. View from one side only	7	5	7	5	2	0	4	6	3
9. Hold things back	6	5	6	5	2	2	5	3	2
10. Like travel	3	5	3	2	4	4	5	1	3
11. Self-reliant	1	4	2	1	3	5	5	7	6
12. Widely read	1	2	0	1	3	3	3	7	3
13. Prefer do it oneself	5	3	5	5	4	4	4	7	2
14. Like arguments	0	0	0	0	2	2	4	5	2
15. Has self-control	0	4	1	0	5	4	3	0	5
16. Easy to communicate	0	1	0	0	2	5	5	7	5
17. Difficult to communicate	7	3	7	5	1	0	1	0	1
18. Big and powerful	0	0	0	0	0	0	3	7	4
19. Introvert	5	7	5	6	3	2	3	3	4
20. Practical	1	2	3	2	3	7	1	5	5
21. Comfortable being angry	0	2	0	1	1	3	4	6	5
22. Bottle up anger	7	6	7	5	5	3	3	1	3
23. Speak mind	0	0	1	2	2	3	6	7	4
24. Live for moment	0	3	1	1	3	3	4	7	7
25. Like animals	1	1	0	1	3	3	1	0	7
26. Do on spur of moment	0	2	0	0	3	4	5	2	4
27. Clear what one wants	0	1	0	1	3	3	5	5	5
28. Interest in money etc.	2	4	3	2	2	0	0	0	3
29. Care about people	1	1	2	2	4	7	7	3	5
30. Fit in with the world	0	2	0	3	4	7	5	5	5

Scoring Key
7 Always; 6 Always all the time; 5 Most of the time; 4 Often; 3 Sometimes; 2 Only occasionally; 1 Rarely; 0 Never

Figure 4.1: Kevin's grid

eyeballing is difficult and we will need some means of simplification. There are a number of computer programs that have been devised to facilitate this task. Before moving on to computer analysis, however, we will look at a hand method developed by Button (1993) for focusing on one particular aspect, namely self-esteem.

Button argues that a person's self-esteem should be measured in terms of his or her own personal constructs. One way of tapping self-esteem from SELF-GRID is to examine simultaneously the construing of 'me nowadays' with 'ideal self'. This method begins by identifying the value of each construct for the subject. Button operationally defines three types:

- 'positive' constructs are those where ideal self is rated at least most of the time on the construct
- 'negative' constructs are where ideal self is rated no more than only occasionally
- 'uncertain' constructs are where ideal self is rated as sometimes or often.

The therapist plots the ratings of 'me nowadays' and 'ideal self' in terms of these constructs.

In Kevin's case, this plot is illustrated in Figure 4.2. We can look at this as providing a profile of his strengths and weaknesses. Smaller discrepancies (say up to two points) can be considered as perceived strengths. For the positive constructs, Kevin is saying this about:

- plan things beforehand
- try to see other's point of view
- think before speak.

Under negative constructs, he is indicating that his strengths lie in:

- not being big and powerful
- not liking arguments
- not being interested in money/possessions.

Although he seems broadly satisfied on the above constructs, there are rather more constructs on which there are rather large discrepancies. These include his *not*:

- fitting in with the world
- caring about people
- being practical
- getting on with things in a steady way.

Moreover, he is also very dissatisfied on his negative constructs of:

- having difficulty communicating
- viewing things from one side.

	Always							Never
'Positive' constructs								
Plan things beforehand	0/X	–	–	–	–	–	–	–
Try to see other viewpoint	–	–	0/X	–	–	–	–	–
Think before speak	X	–	0	–	–	–	–	–
Self-reliant	–	–	0	–	–	–	X	–
Easy to communicate	–	–	0	–	–	–	–	X
Get on in steady way	0	–	–	–	–	–	X	–
Practical	0	–	–	–	–	–	X	–
Care about people	0	–	–	–	–	–	X	–
Fit in with world	0	–	–	–	–	–	–	X
'Negative' constructs								
Big and powerful	–	–	–	–	–	–	–	0/X
Like arguments	–	–	–	–	–	0	–	X
Interested in money etc	–	–	–	–	–	X	–	0
Introvert	–	–	X	–	–	0	–	–
Hold things back	–	X	–	–	–	0	–	–
View from one side	X	–	–	–	–	–	–	0
Difficulty communicating	X	–	–	–	–	–	–	0
'Uncertain' constructs								
Like travel/visiting places	–	–	–	0	X	–	–	–
Prefer do it oneself	–	–	X	0	–	–	–	–
Let things happen	–	–	–	–	0	–	X	–
Widely read	–	–	–	–	0	–	X	–
Like animals	–	–	–	–	0	–	X	–
Make many friends	–	–	–	–	0	–	–	X
Like food	–	–	–	–	0	–	–	X
Comfortable being angry	–	–	–	–	0	–	–	X
Speak their mind	–	–	–	–	0	–	–	X
Clear what wants	–	–	–	–	0	–	–	X
Live for moment	–	–	–	–	0	–	–	X
Has self-control	–	–	–	0	–	–	–	X
Do on spur of moment	–	–	–	0	–	–	–	X
Bottle up anger	X	–	–	–	0	–	–	–

Key: 0 = Me ideally;   X = Me nowadays

Figure 4.2:   Self-construing summary from Kevin's grid

There is also a group of constructs labelled as 'uncertain'. These are where the ideal self is less polarised. In Figure 4.2 this is reflected in the more central position of the zeroes representing the ideal self. These constructs could in some cases represent dilemmas. What is striking in Kevin's case is the large number of these. Most people generally have only a few such constructs. Maybe this reflects a high level of uncertainty about himself. While his rating of himself is extreme on most of these constructs and he would like to be less extreme, he does not wish to move too far towards the other pole of the construct. This includes 'like food', which he would like to do sometimes, but no more, it seems.

The overall picture presented here can be summarised by an index of self-esteem (Button, 1993). By taking the mean discrepancy between ratings of self and ideal self, we have a measure of how he evaluates himself in his own terms. In Kevin's case the score is 3.2. This is a very high discrepancy, even in psychiatric populations. In a comparison of a mixed group of 31 non-psychotic psychologically disordered subjects with 31 matched normal controls, the 'psychological' group had a mean of 2.3 and the 'normal' group had a mean score of about 1.2. (Button, 1993). Such simple measures can be calculated for other elements, such as his self in the past and future or his parents. For example, the comparable measure for Kevin's construing of 'me in far future' is 1.1, indicative of some degree of hope and anticipation of the possibility of change.

Computer analysis

The above procedure stays very much with the raw data as reflected by the subject's choice of ratings. Amidst the mass of ratings, however, may be hidden a structure and set of interrelationships that would be difficult to grasp by hand. Computer programs for grids have been developed using a variety of forms of analysis. One such method is known as principal components analysis. This is not presented as being the best form of analysis, but it is certainly one of the commonest in use. For more on the pros and cons of various forms of analysis, see Bell (1990) or Bringmann (1992).

Principal components analysis contains a number of features, but it generally begins with correlating every construct with every other. This in itself is a tall order. For example, in Kevin's case there are over 400 correlations generated by comparing all pairs of his constructs. We are thus likely to be selective in examining the resulting correlation matrix. We may be interested in looking at the correlations for particular constructs. Let's look at one of Kevin's constructs in this way, namely 'likes food'. Correlations are measures of the extent of linear relationship between two variables. They range from +1 to –1. High positive correlations reflect similar meanings, high negative correlations reflect opposite meanings and those near zero are relatively unrelated.

Perhaps a particularly important association to point out is the strong positive correlation with being 'big and powerful' (0.88). Given what Kevin has said about his dislike of big/powerful, we immediately see that there is an unacceptable consequence of liking food. But there are several other constructs that seem to carry difficult connotations for liking food. For example, people who like food don't 'plan' (–0.80), don't 'think before they speak' (–0.80) and 'like arguments' (0.95), all being constructs that Kevin has clearly indicated above that he does not wish for himself.

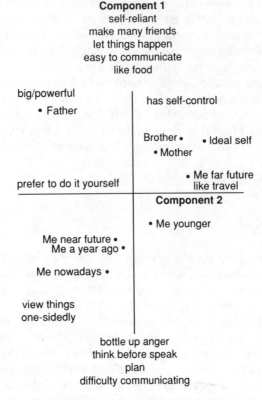

Figure 4.3:   Plot of elements in construct space from Kevin's grid

Such selective attention to correlations can be very useful, but it may be difficult to know where to look and principal components analysis offers a 'simplification' of the mass of intercorrelations. A common way of representing this analysis is by means of a two-dimensional diagram. The best way to explain this is by referring directly to the analysis for Kevin in Figure 4.3.

In Figure 4.3 we can see that the elements are dispersed as points throughout the two-dimensional space. This can be seen as somewhat analogous to a map, where the elements may be places plotted along west–east and north–south axes. In this case, however, the axes are not directions, but are groupings of constructs. The vertical axis represents the first component. This accounts for a great deal of the variability in the grid (59% in Kevin's case) and reflects a high degree of interrelatedness between many constructs. The second component is the next most meaningful (a further 18% of the variability) and is represented by the horizontal axis. Thus a

total of 77% of the total variation is accounted for by these two components, but this still leaves a further 23% to be explained. This is not atypical, so that a two-dimensional representation should be regarded only as a
rough approximation and the investigator may be advised to also examine
the third and other components.

For the first (vertical) component, we can see that Kevin's self in the
present, past and near future is isolated and contrasted with his parents,
brother and his ideal self. Whereas he is represented by constructs such as
'bottle up anger', 'think before speak' and 'plan', the others are seen as 'let
things happen', 'self-reliant', 'make many friends' and 'like food'. He is
saying that he would like to be at the latter end and anticipates moving
towards it in the far future. It is not uncommon for the first component to
largely define a person's evaluation of their ideal. It is also often the case in
the psychologically disordered to contrast their present and ideal self along
such a dimension, with the hope that they will move closer to their ideal in
the future.

The second component is less obvious. At the ideal end, we see 'like
travel' and 'has self-control' whereas the negative end includes 'prefer to
do it oneself', 'view things one-sidedly' and 'big and powerful'. At the
negative end, we see father isolated and contrasted with Kevin's ideal self.
Thus although father was construed positively on the first component, he is
construed very negatively on certain constructs. The construct 'big/
powerful' is particularly associated with father. This perhaps points to a
central dilemma for Kevin of how to achieve being the kind of person he
says he wants to be, without encountering the risk of being big and powerful, like his father.

Such diagrams can be illuminating in highlighting the broad contours of
a person's construing, but they should be treated with caution. As pointed
out above, a two-dimensional plot is only a partial description of the
analysis. If we examined the third and subsequent components, then the
picture may alter somewhat. There is also the important point that the
diagrams create an air of sophistication that may be more apparent than
real. The mathematical basis for principal components analysis makes
many assumptions and goes a long way from the original data. They
should best be treated as a rough sketch, a tentative representation that
may throw up hypotheses and be illuminating for therapist and client
alike.

These are the main stages involved in one form of grid. There are many
other forms of grid; see Fransella and Bannister (1977) or Beail (1985) for
further details of this kind of methodology. Ultimately the grid can be
tailor-made to suit the requirements of the investigation. First, however,
we will look at some examples of grids devised with specific relevance to
eating disorders.

Grids for investigating eating disorders

As we shall see below, much of my early personal construct research on eating disorders (Button, 1980) was conducted at London's Royal Free Hospital with Fay Fransella. I used a range of forms of grid during that time. My main focus was on investigating person construing and the grids I used reflected this. Self-elements such as 'me if I was at a normal weight' or 'me as other people see me' and non-self elements, such as parents and friends were included. Constructs were both elicited personally from subjects and I also used supplied constructs, thought to be particularly relevant to understanding eating disorders. For example, these included constructs relating to sexual attractiveness and being in control. Grids of this type, in which a selection of people elements (including selves) are the focus have been used extensively in personal construct studies of eating disorders. But grids do not have to be restricted to people construing and there have been several examples of non-people grids.

The first of these was something we used in the Royal Free studies. We called this the body grid and it consisted of a series of elements that were sketches of the female body ranging from very thin to very fat. The elements were presented in random order and subjects were required to rate each element on a seven-point scale using a series of supplied constructs, such as 'fat', 'thin', 'sexually attractive'. Unfortunately, although this technique provided useful insights into how subjects were construing their bodies, the resulting data and the details of the technique were never published.

This cannot be said, however, of a grid form published by Ryle and Evans (1991). Although also focusing on body construing, this is in fact something of a hybrid, including both body and self construing. The authors call it the Self and Body Image Grid (SBIG). As well as including five versions of self, there are also three versions of the body as a whole (normal weight, underweight and overweight) and six specific body parts. The latter consists of abdomen, hands, thighs, breasts, feet and inside my body. There are also 25 supplied constructs used on a five-point scale. The constructs were derived from clinical experience and current theoretical beliefs (e.g. I feel in control of, feminine, my mother approves of; assertive). I must admit to having some reservations about mixing self and body elements, given that they may not lie on the same 'range of convenience'. The authors mention, however, that subjects generally were able to complete the task. The grid was used by Ryle and Evans to test out certain hypotheses about eating disorders; the results of these will be referred to below. The technique may prove to be attractive, as the authors suggest, for refining our understanding of the personal meanings of eating and body weight. My main reservation, however, is that the exclusive use of supplied constructs may fail to tap into the more personal issues that a person may have about his or her body.

In addition to grids focusing on people or bodies, a third type of grid used in this context has centred on the construing of situations. Neimeyer and Khouzam (1985) and Coish (1990) have constructed grids where the elements have been situations. Coish developed her situations grids in the context of her study of bulimia. Following extensive pilot work, she devised grids in which there were ten supplied situations relevant to binge-eating. These were:

1. When I am tired
2. When everything has gone wrong
3. When I have an argument
4. When I am under pressure
5. When I am on a diet
6. When I imagine my ideal weight
7. When I feel bad about myself
8. When I feel good about myself
9. When I have eaten normally
10. When I have eaten more than I want

There were two forms of situations grids, one using personally elicited constructs and the other using eight supplied constructs:

1. Feel not guilty – Feel guilty
2. Am coping – Am not coping
3. Not preoccupied with food – Am preoccupied with food
4. Feel good about my body – Dislike my body
5. Feel calm – Feel angry
6. Feel relaxed – Feel anxious
7. Like myself – Dislike myself
8. Feel in control – Feel not in control

The situations grid is referred to again in the chapter on research (Chapter 6). There will also be reference to the Neimeyer and Khouzam (1985) paper, which used similar 'eating situations' and provided constructs drawn from the literature on binge-eating.

We have thus seen that several forms of grid have already been applied to studying eating disorders and it is possible to focus on a number of levels, including self, body and eating situations. There is, however, nothing to stop one from investigating other aspects of the context for a person with eating disorders. These could encompass specific foods, emotions, treatment and so on.

Although grids have proved to be the most popular of tools advocated by Kelly, there are a number of other techniques for exploring construing, but the most well known of these is his 'self-characterisation'.

Self-characterisation

The self-characterisation is, on the face of it, a fairly simple technique compared with the complexities of repertory grid methodology. Kelly's instructions for the self-characterisation were as follows:

> I want you to write a character sketch of (for example) Harry Brown, just as if he were the principal character in a play. Write it as it might be written by a friend who knew him very *intimately* and very *sympathetically*, perhaps better than anyone ever really could know him. Be sure to write it in the third person. For example, start out by saying, 'Harry Brown is . . .'. (Kelly, 1955, p. 323)

Kelly was very careful in his choice of words and his instructions reflect several aims. The use of the third person is partly to reduce threat. There is also a desire to get the person to stand back and look at him/herself from outside. The lack of detailed instructions about length and contents is designed to give maximum latitude for the client in deciding what will be shared with the therapist.

Here is an example of a self-characterisation written by June:

> It's very sad that June has these weights pulling her down as I know from when I knew her before she became ill how she used to love a social life and dancing and being with her friends. When I'm with her now, occasionally there will be a glimmer of happiness, of being able to share joy, but these moments are few. June always has something stopping her. In the silence, one can see her mind ticking away and what she is in contact with alarms her and changes her mood.
>
> Once, not so long back, June came up to a party. I was with several of my friends whom she didn't know. June stood there, not feeling at ease, not being able to join in the fun. She did not know what to do with her hands, her body looked so self-conscious. She obviously felt very inadequate. I find it difficult to understand why June has changed so much and still shows few signs of enjoying herself. It's all right when we're alone. She relaxes and can talk on many levels, but she tenses up if there is a third party, especially if they are attractive males or thin females. I can see her inadequacy or at least her felt inadequacy.
>
> For a less understanding and perceptive person than myself to meet June, unless she put on a fun-loving front which I have seen her do, they would perhaps be scared, or think her odd, sitting in her silence, observing, pensive.

I never can predict how I will find her. Always swinging in mood, rarely stable. When I suggest going out, part of her wants to so much, then she will start saying about nothing to wear, can't fit into most of her clothes, and feeling very fat. That's what is holding her back. Not like it used to be when she was a dancer, fit, slim and full of energy. That fluent machine has broken down and is being knocked about, deteriorating its working capability.

I only wish I could help, but it is up to June to let someone touch the scars that hurt and to help heal them. Even in hospital, her food problem has not been solved. I just have to be patient, I only hope her other friends and associates will be.

Kelly offers a number of suggestions for analysing self-characterisations. He suggests that one begins by examining the first and last sentences. The opening sentence can be seen as if it were a central statement of how the person views themselves now. In June's case her emphasis on 'these weights pulling her down' provides a powerful and ironic metaphor of how she sees herself. One wonders what life would be like without the weights to pull her down. Maybe they offer some safety?

The last sentence may be seen as an indication of where a person is going. June's emphasis on hoping others will be patient suggests that she anticipates the possibility of change, but that other people have to play a part. Maybe this is particularly directed towards her therapist and suggests that he has to be mindful of her expectation of his needing to be patient, perhaps to be allowed to 'touch the scars'.

At a more general level, the central theme seems to be June's difficulty in interpersonal situations outside of safe one-to-one relationships, such as with the writer. She implies that there is a link between this and her eating disorder, perhaps using her weight as a way of avoiding other than the more secure of relationships.

Self-characterisations do not have to be restricted to opening assessment. Indeed they can be usefully repeated at different stages. They can also be used as part of the therapeutic process of exploring movement. For example, one can ask the client to write one as they would imagine they would be if free of an eating disorder. The elaboration of what the client anticipates life might be like without an eating disorder could be a useful avenue to pursue rather than continuing the process of defining themselves as an eating disorder. Another way of using the self-characterisation is to use it as the basis for writing an alternative sketch, which the person would temporarily enact as an experiment. The latter procedure forms the basis for what Kelly (1955, 1973) called 'fixed role therapy'. This therapeutic technique is based on the assumption that a client could benefit from role-playing a different person for a limited time, say over a two-week period. For a more recent description of the use of this technique, see Epting and Nazario (1987).

Alternative ways of exploring constructs

Although grid technique and self-characterisation are undoubtedly the methods most associated with personal construct theory, we do not have to be restricted to them. Indeed, some authors (e.g. Dunnett, 1988) positively seek to de-emphasise the use of repertory grids. A major concern of authors such as Dunnett is the way in which the grid can be used and abused without reference to the parent theory of personal constructs. Its apparent air of mathematical sophistication and concreteness can clearly lead to it being used in a rather crude way, with all kinds of assumptions being made by the naive individual. Without wishing to 'throw out the baby with the bath water', we do not have to be restricted to grids and we are limited only by our own ingenuity.

A number of techniques have been devised by Kelly and others since for exploring personal construing. Perhaps, the most popular of these is *laddering*, a technique devised by Hinkle (1965) where the investigator wishes to elicit more 'superordinate' constructs. The procedure is as follows:

> For each bipolar construct (e.g. 'slim versus fat'), the subject is first asked which pole of the construct they would prefer. They are then asked why this is preferable. Let's say that 'slim' was chosen, the subject may say that being slim is preferred because 'people like you more', whereas fat people are 'looked down on'. The construct 'people like you versus people look down on you' is then regarded as a more superordinate construct. The procedure is then repeated with this construct, again asking the subject which pole is preferable. The subject might then say that 'being liked' is preferable because it makes you 'feel accepted', whereas if you're looked down on then you 'are worthless'. This process is repeated until such time as the subject can't go any further, when one has reached the most superordinate constructs.

Fransella and Dalton (1990), in discussing the use of laddering within a therapeutic context, suggest using a conversational style rather than just mechanically asking the question why. You might thus vary the questioning such as saying 'What is there about *x* which makes it seem preferable to *y*?' As they point out, laddering typically allows one to get into the most fundamental of constructs to a person, their ultimate values and maybe life and death issues. Such superordinate constructs are also likely to be those most resistant to change.

A similar procedure, but going in the reverse direction, can also be applied to investigate the hierarchical aspects of construing. This technique, called the *pyramid technique* (Landfield, 1971), may be particularly useful for clients who have difficulty in moving from generalisations and need to move to a more concrete level. Rather than moving to more superordinate levels one is seeking to reach more subordinate levels in their personal construct system. Let's say a client wants to be more 'loved'.

You might ask the question 'What kind of a person is loved?' They might reply that someone who can 'accept affection' is likely to be loved. You might go as far as seeking specific behavioural examples, such as by saying 'How do you know when someone is accepting affection?' They might, for example, say that 'allowing a friend to touch me' would help. You might go even further and ask in what circumstances one might allow a friend to touch you, and so on.

One further technique, known as the *ABC technique* (Tschudi, 1977) allows one to investigate what Hinkle (1965) termed 'implicative dilemmas'. The initial construct, perhaps representing a problem, would be called A (A1 being the present pole and A2 being the alternative, desired state). The subject would then be asked what are the disadvantages of A1 and the advantages of A2. It is the next question that seeks to identify the dilemma that is leading to resistance to change. What are the advantages of A1 and the disadvantages of A2?. Fransella and Dalton (1990) exemplify this procedure with an unhappy overweight client, who wanted to move from being fat (A1) to slim (A2). The disadvantage of A1 was looking unattractive (B1), whereas she thought being slim would make her look attractive (B2). The disadvantage of being slim, however, was that she would be likely to be raped (C1), whereas being fat meant she was unlikely to be raped (C2). This is perhaps a very potent example of the power of such techniques to identify important and sensitive dilemmas, but Fransella and Dalton caution that they should be used carefully at the right time and in the right context.

In all the above examples, the use of words have figured prominently. There are many other ways of eliciting the client's constructs in words, such as poems, essays and diaries. For some clients, however, there might be difficulties in verbal expression and other modalities that can usefully be explored include art, music, dance and mime. A musical bent, for example, might lead a therapist to particularly explore musical constructions and to explore their parallels with person construing (see, for example, Button, 1988b). For some of the more guarded clients, for example, music can be used as a way into their world. Catherine was extremely wary when it came to self-disclosure. But she had indicated that listening to music was one of her main sources of pleasure. It seemed to her therapist that exploring her musical construing might offer a relatively safe way of relating more comfortably. But when she was asked what kinds of music she had she would only say that it was 'broad-ranging'. Giving specific examples was far too risky for her and even with friends she would be reluctant to share her musical tastes. She was therefore unwilling to talk about particular pieces of music with her therapist. Some months later, however, she had loosened up somewhat and told her therapist of a friend visiting and of letting her see her record collection. Although very apprehensive about this, she had felt sufficiently reassured by this experiment in sharing to go so far as to extend the sharing with her therapist. Other sharing seems to have followed in its wake.

Ultimately, there is no limit to the range of ways we can explore a person's construing. We are not tied to one technique and we should not forget one very basic clinical technique – listening and watching. By tuning in to the client's sighs, gestures, posture, tone and pace of voice we can potentially learn a lot about a person's construing.

5 A personal construct approach to therapy and change

A central theme of modern psychology is that people show features of both continuity and change. On the one hand, we seek to preserve stability, to confirm our identity, but in other respects this is not sufficient. Whether through sheer boredom or as a result of pressures from outside, it is pretty difficult to go through life without making changes. Some of these changes may be superficial, but others may run deep. Change may be sought after or resisted, it may be pleasant or painful, but is probably inescapable. For most people, change comes about through everyday experience and relationships. To learn to drive, to move jobs, to fall in love are just some of the numerous avenues to change. For those who have not been too successful at utilising such experiences for beneficial change, psychotherapy or counselling may be on offer. People with eating disorders are no different from anyone else in this respect. They can change, whether through everyday experience and/or through professional help. But it is also likely to be the case that for some, the risks or costs of change will be so great, that they will have to stay where they are. My concern in this chapter will be to outline an approach to working with people with eating disorders, which respects the right to stay the same, but also attempts to open up the possibility for change, which is meaningful and acceptable to the person concerned.

Personal construct therapy

Kelly (1955) outlined a psychotherapeutic approach to helping people, which has since become known as *personal construct therapy*. In some respects, his approach can be construed as an 'orienting framework for clinical practice' (R.A. Neimeyer, 1987, p. 4), a kind of theory about therapy in general. Indeed, compared with some forms of psychotherapy, the personal construct approach can be regarded as relatively content-free. Fransella (1985, p. 278) makes this point: '... the therapist and client have to work closely together to build a unique structure for understanding the problem. This structure has to be built *from scratch and couched in the client's own terms*'. Thus, although Kelly presents a detailed conceptualisation of the process of psychotherapy from a personal construct theory standpoint, there are no 'prescriptions' and relatively few specific techniques. Indeed, a personal construct therapist may draw upon a range of techniques, whether from other therapies or from his or her own imagination. As Fransella continues: 'All the therapist can do is try to understand the client's view of the world, and thereby the problem, and so go hand-in-hand with the client exploring possible alternative ways of viewing the world, which will ultimately lead to reconstruction and a more useful slant on the problem area.'

Kelly viewed the therapy room as a kind of psychological laboratory in which therapist and client collaborate in experimenting with constructions. In his view, the task of therapy was 'not to produce behavior, but rather to enable the client, as well as the therapist, to utilize behavior for asking important questions' (Kelly, 1969). For those who are interested in finding out more about the personal construct approach to therapy, there are a number of useful books (e.g. Epting, 1984; Neimeyer and Neimeyer, 1987; Fransella and Dalton, 1990), as well as, of course, the original source (Kelly, 1955).

A personal construct approach to eating disorders

Here, I would like to describe my personal approach to applying the principles of personal construct theory to trying to help clients with eating disorders. I shall begin by outlining some of the general principles and assumptions within which I approach the task of working with such people.

General principles

People have the choice   It is ultimately a personal choice whether to seek psychological help. I have no desire nor right to seek to impose change on another person. However abnormal or ill a person's behaviour may seem, I make no assumption that this equates with the need for help or treatment. It is my view that people have the right to live in whatever way they choose, provided they are not posing a threat to others. This is a particularly important issue in anorexia nervosa, where a person's life can become endangered. However well intentioned the action may be, I suspect that forced treatment may in the long term be counter-productive and certainly not conducive to a therapeutic alliance. I thus make it very clear to clients that I am prepared to try to help, but only if they wish to change. I make it clear that there is no rush and that I expect them to very carefully consider the matter before making up their mind. Once they make up their mind, they can also change their minds at a later date – the time has to be right for change.

Change is possible   When presenting for help, clients are often doubtful whether anything can be done to change their situation. The most common question I am asked at the end of an assessment interview is 'Can anything be done to help me?' Behind this question may lie the expectation that eating disorders are incurable, in much the same way as people can present with alcohol or drug dependence. It can be useful to explore the basis for such constructions, which could potentially have an important influence on the scope for change – such expectations can become self-fulfilling prophecies. Once I have clarified the client's expectations, I set out to put over my view as derived both from the literature and my own clinical experience. Broadly speaking, my message is that one *can* let go of eating disorders and that most people with eating disorders improve in time, although some do not. The message is thus hopeful and we know that hope is a very important ingredient for psychotherapy, but I try to avoid being unrealistically optimistic or grandiose.

Change is difficult   My caveat to the message of hope is that change is likely to be difficult, at least in part. Again, I think a realistic message is important to give and will help the client to anticipate what lies in store. I point out that when we have been used to something for a long time, it is usually difficult and painful to let go of it. Moreover, that letting go of weight and eating control is likely to involve needing to face things that might be uncomfortable and difficult to handle. I add that I will try to help them to manage the difficulties associated with change.

We're in it together   This is very much the stance taken by Kelly in his approach to psychotherapy. The kind of relationship I try to create is a collaborative one, in which we work together to explore alternative ways of dealing with the difficulties experienced by the client. While acknowledging my expertise in the field of eating disorders, I do not claim to have the answers to the client's problems, nor the ability to 'cure' them. They are the experts on themselves, but I am prepared to work with them towards trying to find alternative ways of dealing with their difficulties.

Assessment

I see a thorough and careful initial assessment as an important part of the process of therapy. A hurried or skimpy assessment runs the risk of leading client and therapist into an inappropriate and unhelpful relationship that can hinder the overall prospects for change. In working with clients with eating disorders, I have been gradually evolving a fairly systematic approach to assessment that is both structured and flexible. My aim is to both obtain a reasonably good initial picture of the kind of person I may be working with and to have some understanding of the nature of problems experienced. In terms of the latter, as well as hearing of problems in the client's own terms, I make use of standard measurement instruments. Ultimately, in terms of any psychotherapeutic work to be done, it is the former idiographic information that is most relevant. But it is also useful to have information about how clients compare with others, particularly if one is concerned, as I am, with trying to evaluate one's work.

The initial meeting   The chances are that the client is rather nervous and unsure at the first meeting. It is important to try to make the client feel reasonably at ease. After introducing myself and explaining broadly what is involved in the first meeting, I enquire whether they have any immediate concerns or anxieties they would like to express or questions they would like to ask. I spell out the fact that this is very much an assessment meeting, that nothing definite has to be decided today. It is presented as a chance for me to find out about the client and vice versa.

Once any initial concerns have been dealt with, I ask the client to say in their own terms what, if anything, they see as the problem. It cannot be assumed that the client perceives there to be a problem. They may well have come along under pressure, a feeling of obligation or just simply because they lack the assertive ability to express their views. Usually, however, most clients I see for assessment do perceive there to be a problem, but the problem may not be the same as that presented in a referral letter. Among other things, the situation may have changed by the time they arrive. In view of the common experience of heavy demand for psychological help, delays of several months are not uncommon. Since presenting to the referrer and/or deciding on wanting help, the wheels of change may already be in motion.

Identifying the client's view of the problem is important at a number of levels. It highlights the client's own priorities, e.g. one might discover that the main issue is not that there is an eating disorder, but there is an imminent threat of losing a job or an important relationship. The client's initial formulation will also give an early flavour of the kind of constructs the client uses and perhaps of the way that his or her anticipatory processes are operating. For example, a client I recently assessed referred to turning to food as a way of trying to deal with 'stuff' that comes into her head. She was rather vague about what this stuff was, except that it was unpleasant. She went on to use the same word many times during the interview and provided some early clues that her construction of 'stuff' would be an important therapeutic issue.

Having identified the client's view of the problem in an open-ended manner, I move to a more focused part of the interview, where details relevant to eating disorders are sought. This includes detail of the client's weight history, as well as his or her preferences in this respect. For females, details of menstruation would be sought and for all clients I now use a structured clinical interview focused on the various symptoms of eating disorders. Within the team I now work with, we use CEDRI (Clinical Eating Disorders Rating Instrument; Palmer et al, 1987). Behaviours and attitudes, such as dietary restraint, vomiting, binge-eating and attitude to 'normal weight' are all rated on a 0 to 3 scale with three indicating the most severe response.

In the next phase of the interview, I enquire about more general aspects of a person and his or her life, including health, educational experience, interests and social pursuits. A major focus of this part of the interview is on self-image and important relationships, including family. Having taken quite a wide overview, I end by asking the client their views on the future and the issue of change. This again is very important in getting some kind of indication of their anticipations and expectations of the possibility of change. Finally, I ask whether they have any questions.

This initial interview usually lasts about an hour and a half, depending on the client. By this time, both of us may be quite exhausted and need time to reflect. I invite the client to go away and think about our meeting and offer the opportunity of a further assessment interview. Most clients take up this option. In the meantime, I would ask them to complete a battery of questionnaires, which gives further breadth to the assessment process. Currently this includes the Eating Attitudes Test (Garner and Garfinkel, 1980b) and the Eating Disorders Inventory (Garner, Olmsted and Polivy, 1983), both of which provide an element of measurement of the level and nature of eating disorder. I also use the Rosenberg Self-esteem Scale (Rosenberg, 1965) and a measure of general psychological well-being. Currently I and the team I work with use the SCL90R (Derogatis, 1977).

The second meeting   I would usually see the client for their second meeting a week or two later. During this period, they will have had time to reflect on their first meeting. They will also have had the opportunity to talk with other people about it. After briefly asking them about the questionnaires, I would enquire about what kinds of thoughts they had been having. Reactions vary from having been busy and not thought or talked about it, to very intense reflection and deep conversations with a significant person. In my experience, most people will express some desire to do something about it, but will be unsure as to how possible this will be. At this point, I would offer them an outline of my perspective on eating disorders and what can be done about it.

The main theme I wish to put over to them is that I see their eating problems as a reflection of their attempt to deal with some very important issues in their life. Weight and eating control is presented as a common strategy, particularly among young women, when they are faced with difficulties and uncertainties in their experience of themselves and in relation to others. I go on to describe some of the psycho-biological consequences when a person tries to overcontrol their biological needs. This leads to the view that their efforts to control one problem leads to another problem, namely the control of hunger. Moreover, that the further they go along this track, the more isolated they become from other people and the deeper and deeper they become enmeshed with the struggles associated with hunger. In turn, this makes it likely that they are no longer dealing with the original issues, which they will have to learn to face if they ever are to have any chance of recovering. The overall message is, thus, that if they are to overcome the eating disorder, they are likely to have to find new ways of dealing with food, but also that they will also need to find new ways of dealing with the broader issues. The general direction this is likely to take is outlined, with emphasis on eating behaviour likely to need to take precedence in the early stages and the broader issues increasingly coming to the fore in the later stages. It is pointed out that this process can take quite some time and that it is unlikely to be easy to let go of their way of life. I add that people sometimes make this journey by their own steam and with the help of friends/family, but that professional support and guidance is often likely to be necessary. I point out that I would potentially be prepared to work with them to help them along this road, if that is what they wish.

Most people indicate that they feel this all makes sense to them, but they may have reservations about the extent to which they can put it into practice. The idea of life without their eating preoccupations may seem like a very distant unknown quantity. Some people may be reluctant to enter into a therapeutic relationship and others feel they would prefer to try to work on it on their own. For some people, the very idea of coming to depend on another person is anathema to them, even though I emphasise the collaborative nature of the relationship. Where there are marked doubts, I would usually suggest another meeting some time ahead, say a month or three months' time. This will give them enough time to try out things in the light of what they may have learned from the assessment, in a sense testing out whatever theory they are entertaining. If they decide they do not want help, then I would leave it at that, but stressing the option to return to me at a later date if they change their mind. Where they agree to help, I would usually suggest having an initial series of weekly meetings, usually ten or twelve. Where there are some doubts about the client's ability to make use of psychological help, I might suggest a trial six sessions. I would tell them that at the end of this initial series of sessions, we would jointly review what had been learned from the sessions. I inform them that at that point a decision may be made to extend the sessions or to stop there.

The early stages of therapy

The agreement to enter treatment may sound like a neatly packaged arrangement, but at this stage it is likely to be no more than a very hazy idea for the client. I try to help the client prepare for this by pointing out that we are going to need time to get to know each other, as in everyday relationships. At an early stage, I would nowadays usually introduce SELF-GRID (Button, 1988a) assessment (see Chapter 4), as part of that process of getting to know the client. In introducing SELF-GRID, I re-affirm my view that the eating problems need to be viewed in the context of the person they are. Knowing more about how they see themselves may help to throw further light on issues that may be relevant to the eating problems.

I will not reiterate the process of completing the SELF-GRID, except to add that people vary considerably in their reaction to it. There are some who react very defensively as if they feel very threatened by the exercise. Usually, I find that these are people at the anorectic end of the eating disorder spectrum. For example, Gwenda reacted rather dismissively to the exercise, saying that all her family were the same, not wishing to make comparisons. Larry was also very irritated, an emotion he expressed more after the interview than during. He commented that he could not see the point of it, seeing it as stupid and a waste of time. More often than not, such reactions give a pretty good indication of what is to follow. They provide a good test of the extent to which the client is likely to be open to exploration and experimentation in different experiences. Both the latter clients, for example, proved to be very defensive and reluctant participants in the therapeutic process. At the other end of the spectrum, however, there are clients who react very enthusiastically to the procedure, saying that it really made them think or that they had become aware of something new by reflecting on their responses.

I would normally feed back the 'results' of the grid assessment at the next session, mainly focusing on the 'self-esteem profile'. This would highlight important constructs, their perceived strengths and areas of possible dilemma. In some cases, I would also show them the results of principal components analysis, although there is a danger of over-bombarding the client with too much complex information. As well as feeding back some of my observations, I am keen to elicit their views and ask them what they make of it and whether it throws up any questions. The resulting dialogue could be the prototype of what therapy might be like. Out of this discussion may come some preliminary ideas about issues that need to be worked upon or explored further.

The second procedure that I usually introduce early on is on the face of it at the more behavioural end of the spectrum. This is the eating diary, a much-used tool in the treatment of eating disorders, particularly where there is a cognitive-behavioural emphasis. The eating diary involves the client keeping a daily record of the pattern of eating and any of the associated behaviours, notably vomiting and laxatives. For me, the most important element of this is them writing down notes about the context of their eating, such as what they were thinking and feeling in association with eating. This will create the opportunity to explore their constructions of eating and associated events. Some clients are reluctant to do this, for example, seeing it as an intrusion. Another common concern is that they might have difficulty being honest, a response that tends to indicate an expectation of being judged, of having to do well. I point out that the exercise is primarily to facilitate communication and help throw further light on the problems – they certainly will not be told off for having a bad week. I stress that it is not compulsory, but I would like them to try it out for a while, consistent with an atmosphere of experimentation that I am trying to create. If they are adamant, I would certainly not push it, but point out that this might limit our ability to deal with the eating difficulties.

Within the first few sessions, there will thus be some preliminary exploration of both the person and their eating. Important issues will often come up in these first few sessions and one of the most important of these is motivation to change. This is often revealed initially by difficulty over keeping appointments and there may be lots of plausible excuses, but I usually raise the question of doubts about treatment early on. Their theory that they want to change may prove difficult to realise when they actually put it to the test. For some people, they may be used to taking on a listening/helping role for others and they might have fears about placing themselves in a dependent role. By being alert to the signs of such concerns early on, one can explore them with the client and often allay any anxieties. It is sometimes necessary to reiterate that this is a collaborative relationship and that nothing is going to happen without discussing it with the client.

I encourage them to let me know if there is anything they are concerned about or if they feel I am pushing them into something they feel uncomfortable about. Although such uncertainties can often be ironed out, there are others for whom the issues concerned are too sensitive for them to handle. For example, Daphne had great difficulty acknowledging her bulimic behaviour. Whereas she had been relatively comfortable presenting anorectic and other psychological symptoms, she regarded the bulimia as a sign of weakness that she was unable to show others, even a previous therapist whom she had been seeing regularly for many years. Her strategy was to submerge herself in work, which was all-consuming in terms of time. We had a few sessions, which I had arranged late on a Friday afternoon to accommodate her busy job, but even then she failed to consistently make it and soon dropped out, ostensibly with the reason that she was too busy in her job. This might be true, but it said a lot about the degree of priority which she ascribed to changing her eating behaviour.

Thus, quite a number of people drop out within the first few sessions, and in such circumstances I would keep the door open for them to return at a later date if their motivations changed. As I have said before, the time has to be right and I think it would be counter-productive to push when a person was not ready for it.

Although there will be clients who will go through the motions for quite some time before acknowledging the impasse, most people who have lasted the first few sessions will have made some commitment to the therapeutic relationship. If they can feel safe with you, the chances are that one will have been able to make some tentative steps towards change in these early stages. This may involve changes in eating behaviour or other aspects of life.

Sometimes changes are made before one has formally got into the therapeutic process. For example, with Andrea it became obvious in initial assessment that a major factor contributing to binge-eating was the destructive relationship she was having with her boyfriend, with whom she was living. He had been physically violent to her on many occasions, particularly after drinking alcohol, which was adding to the negative feelings she had about herself. Without any prompting on my part, she had decided to leave him and return to her parents before we had completed our assessment. This led to an immediate improvement in her eating behaviour and, although her boyfriend continued to pester her and plead with her to give him another chance, she remained resolute in her decision not to go back to him.

Changing eating behaviour

As discussed above, most clients will be keeping eating diaries in the early stages. I will also give them some general recommendations about how they might approach changing their eating patterns. In similar vein to most treatment approaches to eating disorders, I will point out that moving towards having regular balanced meals is a necessary prerequisite for change. Having regular balanced meals will help the anorectic to put weight on and counteract the effects of starvation. For the bulimic client, it will help to reduce the likelihood of binge-eating, as well as move towards greater regularity and stability. This sounds easy in theory, but of course is rather more difficult in practice. A gradual approach is, therefore, often required. Thus, with a severely anorectic client who is hardly eating anything at all except for food like yoghurt and lettuce, it may be a matter of taking one meal at a time, such as breakfast and suggesting introducing one or two items that would previously have been 'forbidden'. Initially, the client may be very fearful of the consequences. My colleague Pamela Marshall (1988), for example, has shown that anorectics often have very unusual beliefs, such as the idea that one biscuit would result in a weight gain of a couple of pounds. Often they are amazed to find that this is not the case and can be gradually reassured by evidence that weight change is much smaller than anticipated. It is very important to find a way of trying to help such clients manage their need to feel that things are not going out of control. They may, for example, fear that if they give in to their need to eat that all hell will break loose and they will not be able to stop eating and putting on weight. These are quite understandable and not entirely unrealistic fears and I let them know that from my experience it may well come to feel like they are going the other way. I point out that is often the case with any behaviour that has been suppressed, that we may well go to extremes for a while, but that gradually things tend to balance out once the initial novelty has passed. Reassurance is also given that I will try to help them through such a phase, rather than expect them to sink or swim once they had started to eat regularly.

With bulimic clients, moving towards regular balanced meals will often, in itself, produce a dramatic and early reduction, if not termination of binge-eating. But often this behaviour persists, sometimes because the client is not fully adhering to the regular meals. The pattern of binge–avoid eating–binge etc. may be very hard to break and the slightest aberration may lead the client to skip meals again, so ensuring that subsequent eating will be construed as binge-eating. With such clients, one can reflect back to them the consequences of such patterns, but one may have to prune one's expectations to a rather gradual approach to change. It may also be that they are uncomfortable about the perceived consequences of regularising their eating behaviour. This could be linked with the anticipation of weight gain or perhaps they may have negative constructions about life being too regular and ordered.

With most bulimic clients, some binge-eating will persist, but the eating diaries will usually reveal some variation in the behaviour within and between days. This may be a simple matter of time of day. Very often it is evenings that are the most vulnerable times, perhaps because the client is alone, with nothing to do. By exploring possible alternative ways of dealing with evenings, one might plan trying out something new. This might entail, for example, planning to have something to do that will involve someone else, such as going to visit a friend. By planning the way one organises the day, the doors may open towards some new avenues, rather than just reacting with the familiar pattern of binge-eating. In addition to such patterns within days, there might be variations across days, with weekends often being a difficult time, perhaps because they are unstructured and the client is out of a routine. Once again, exploring some new possibilities for how weekends are spent, for example as an opportunity to visit somewhere new or as time to recharge our batteries after a hard week, may create new possibilities.

Such broad patterns are not the only source of binge-eating. Diary entries will often reveal more subtle signs of a person's construing being channelised into an eating/weight track. Typically, an event has occurred that has been construed in such a way that the person feels unhappy or ill at ease. Generally, this will involve another person, for example a comment that might be seen as criticism or lack of appreciation of the client. Rather than deal directly with this experience, perhaps by confronting the person or sharing the feelings with someone else, the client has kept it all to himself or herself. In order to comfort or distract from the feelings, eating may be the chosen response, which leads to further eating and the construction of a binge. Now the focus can be turned away from the original source of discomfort and into providing further evidence for the eating-disordered construction of self. Although this might feel bad, it is at least familiar and possibly easier to construe than dealing with the original problem.

Not everyone writes everything down in their diary. Sometimes one has to winkle out the underlying constructions. By enquiring about what was going on on a particular day, the client begins to remember things that may have been undermining them. On further exploration, often it becomes clear that something quite important was going on. As trust develops in the therapeutic relationship, the client might gradually feel more comfortable about sharing such constructions.

Although the underlying constructions often relate to situations involving people, there is also a need to work on constructions of food and eating.

An important aspect of this is the actual act of eating, to be able to move away from seeing any deviation from a narrow set of expectations as a binge. A typical construction imposed by the client might be 'I'm being greedy' or 'I shouldn't have this'. While there may be no shortage of supportive evidence for such construing from peers and the slimming media, I would invite them to consider alternative constructions. These could include more positive ones, such as 'I *need* something to eat', 'I deserve to have something nice', or 'Other people eat sweet things, why not me?' My aim would be to get them to try another, more positive way of construing it, in which enjoyment, fun or stimulation might play a part. I point out the great importance of food in our society and that we all use food at times for reasons other than hunger. Linked with this idea is of exploring possibilities for enjoying food as having social meaning. It is not uncommon for the bulimic individual to be avoiding eating with other people, except by eating salads or other diet food. I invite them to think about situations where they might eat with others in a pleasurable way. This usually involves thinking about people that they may be more comfortable eating with. In my experience, movement towards more sociable eating in which the client stops eating just diet food is usually a major pathway to change. For example, Ursula had been bingeing daily. But she began experimenting with going out for meals with her close friends and found that she could eat and enjoy foods, which if eaten on her own she would construe as a binge. After a while, a very clear pattern emerged of binge days being confined to those days where she was on her own at home with nothing to do. Whether she 'chose' to stay on her own on these days was perhaps questionable, but she began to realise that she could do something about it. I suspect that for her it was a matter of accepting that she needed to depend on others, rather than maintaining a façade of strength and independence.

Reconstruing self and relationships

It is my view that at the heart of therapy in general is the need to reconstrue self and one's relationships with other people in such a way that one becomes more free to creatively engage in living. This also applies to the treatment of people with eating disorders. If all that was necessary was a change of eating, then professional help would hardly need to go beyond the services of a nutritionist. But anyone who has any experience of people with eating disorders knows that there are complex psychological issues that hinder a simple eating re-education process. The initial work exploring possible changes in eating behaviour is thus typically a prelude to the main work. In some cases, in fact, it may be appropriate to modify the approach of beginning with eating work. A recent client of mine, for example, made it very clear that she felt that she needed to sort out the issues concerning her low self-esteem before she could hope to make headway on the eating front. Although such expectations can mask a wish to avoid fundamental change in eating behaviour, there is nothing rigid about the idea of working on eating first. The two will interact and come in and out of focus at different points in time.

Before elaborating further on the process of reconstruing self, it seems appropriate to outline some of the assumptions I make about *self*. The first of these is that self is *constructed*, i.e. we create our own view of self, rather than self being God-given or carved in stone. As something that we ultimately construct ourselves, it can also be *reconstructed*. Much as the sculptor has the power to change the sculpture and the writer has the power to change the nature of a character in a novel, so we have the potential to change ourselves. In similar vein to the artist, we may suffer from a limited range of materials or, more importantly, inspiration, but the potential is there. We may also be reluctant or even fearful of changing ourselves, but the fear does not have to prevent change. At different points in time, we may be more or less open to changing ourselves, indeed at some points being quite satisfied with what might appear to be the finished product, perhaps being content to give it the odd polishing and sit back and admire it. But who knows when that might change? Like the sculpture, we or someone else may want to come along and take a hammer to it.

The second assumption I make about self is that it may be useful to think of *selves* rather than a single self. Some years ago Miller Mair (1977) proposed the idea of a *community of selves*, a concept I have found very useful. Within each of us there may be many different selves, which exist alongside each other, much in the same way as individuals exist in the community. For example, for me there may be Eric the psychologist, Eric the father, Eric the husband, Eric the son, Eric the musician, Eric the neighbour, and so on. Within the many contexts within which we operate, we may thus construct a different self, each in turn being appropriate to that context. The kind of person I choose to be when with my mother may be quite different from the part I choose to play as a psychologist. This of course places self very much in the context of roles and relationships and broadly speaking this is the position I generally take. From this standpoint there is thus not one single fixed self, but the potential to become different people at different times. Some people would find such an idea frightening, but it could also be construed as liberating. We are, perhaps, more free than we think. Each relationship perhaps has the potential for a new adventure, to create something quite new, rather than assuming that we have to simply act out a part wherever we go. In suggesting a *community* of selves, Miller Mair is pointing to the nature of the relationship between our selves. The term 'community' seems to imply some sort of interrelationship, a living together. Without this quality, we may be left feeling fragmented, perhaps akin to the notion of multiple personalities. To be able to feel comfortable with these different selves thus requires that there are links between the selves. This is where our construction system comes in. Hopefully we will have superordinate constructions that enable us to integrate the varying aspects of our experience. For example, the very existence of constructs that enable us to anticipate the differences in our behaviour and experience depending on who we are with will help to ensure that we are not left feeling confused and disintegrated.

Linked with the idea of a community of selves, is the assumption that there are many different *perspectives on self*. We can look at ourselves from many different standpoints. The current view of self we have does not have to be the only one. The bereaved person, for example, might be all-consumed by the experience of the loss of validation of self through the lost loved one. In time, however, the chances are that other perspectives on self will emerge and the person will feel free to engage once again in the process of living and elaborating their view of self with other persons. An important feature of this *perspectivist* position is the acknowledgement that other people are likely to have different views of oneself. Thus, in addition to my view of myself, there is my mother's view of me, my father's, my children's, my partner's, my boss's, etc. We do not have the monopoly of perspectives on any particular self. It is my assumption that none of these views is right or wrong, but they reflect different perspectives and different experiences with a person. I remember, for example, at the time when Prime Minister Margaret Thatcher was being vilified in some sections of society for her appearance of being hard and uncaring. Political friends would come forward to her defence and assert that she was really a very caring person. Notwithstanding the cynical view that politicians are good liars, I take this as evidence of perspectivism. The chances are that the political friends were experiencing a rather different, perhaps private face of her than the public were more inclined to encounter. The acknowledgement of these different perspectives on self is I think an important aspect of becoming freer to be oneself. But it is important to stress that the perspective on self is not a reality, but merely a construction, which presumably has some utility in helping the construer make sense of their world. People can, for example, feel quite trapped by what they see as their parents' construction of themselves. By coming to understand the meaning of that construction for the parent, the person who is the object of the construction may be able to see that they are not defined by it.

My fourth assumption follows on directly from the above and concerns the experience of emotion or what Kelly preferred to call transition. At times our construction of self will reflect transition, as we become aware of change in our experience of ourselves. Although much of the time we validate our view of ourselves in a quite predictable way, sometimes we sense that things may not be quite what we anticipated. This may take many forms and could become labelled as love, anger, fear, threat, etc. Even in writing this book, I am laying myself open to the possibility of invalidating my existing view of myself. This could be exhilarating or devastating. At times, for example, I have felt rather hopeless, when I have construed myself as having less that is worth saying than I had anticipated. I have also at times felt the excitement of really getting somewhere, as if I am articulating some new aspect of myself. The prospect of an evolving as opposed to a static self is thus not for those who are seeking a quiet life.

These are the main assumptions I make about self and perhaps will help make sense of the way I approach the task of trying to help people change themselves, or perhaps more correctly their construction of themselves. I hope I have also highlighted the fact that I do not see self as in isolation. Our construction of self is inextricably linked with our construction of other people. Indeed, it has been pointed out that we have a construction not of self, but of self–other (Bannister and Agnew, 1977). In construing ourselves, we are contrasting ourselves with others and, moreover, the construing of ourselves in no small part derives from our construction of ourselves in relationship with other people. The understanding of self seems to be virtually inseparable from the understanding of relationships, hence the heading above.

As already argued, the person with an eating disorder usually seems to have some difficulty in their construction of themselves. This can vary in degree and kind from those who have virtually no sense of self, except as someone thin, to others who have quite extensive elaboration of self, but with some uncomfortable inconsistencies. Wherever the client is on this spectrum, I aim to try to help them elaborate and define themselves in whatever way seems meaningful to them. They may fear that without their bible of thinness, they may be left with nothing or that no-one could possibly like them. If they are ever to move beyond being trapped by such fears they will need to put such assumptions to the test. One place to do so is in the relatively safe environment of the therapy room. If they can come to feel safe with me, then maybe they can take some chances with themselves.

There seem to be two basic tasks to work on if one is to attempt to move beyond an eating focus. These are to uncouple self from a weight-dominated construction and to facilitate the development and elaboration of self in other terms. It is likely that weight and eating constructs play a large part in defining self and in setting the parameters for the ideal self. To let go of such construction is likely to be no easy task, particularly when the client's world has been constricted to an extreme degree and over a long period of time. But even with the most chronic of clients there is likely to be at least some residue of a self beyond weight and eating. I aim to identify such constructs and explore the possibilities for their further elaboration. Where the person has a fair amount of positive constructions of self to work with, this may prove to be a relatively straightforward task. It may often be in such cases that a degree of self-doubt and lack of confidence has held the person back previously, particularly in certain contexts. There may be a number of contexts within which the person can function quite well and feels good without having to resort to constructs about weight etc. This could be in any area of life, but the strengthening and further validation of such constructions is an important part of the initial development of self. It may well be that such contexts have fallen in abeyance or are underutilised, perhaps because of negative feelings related to eating behaviour. A change of focus towards areas of life in which one is succeeding can help to shift the balance away from the construction of failure and weight domination. For example, with Sonia (see below) it was spending time with children and being with her sister. She felt good with children and had a comfortable relationship with her sister. By shifting the focus from thinking she had to lose weight at all costs, she began to feel better about herself and her confidence to take the plunge and try out more adventurous things began to grow. Previously she had withdrawn further and further into herself, eaten more, put on weight and felt she had to avoid people.

Although Sonia was able to begin moving forward, she was needing to confront areas of life that were difficult for her. Like many clients, a lack of confidence in certain areas, particularly in encounters with the opposite sex, had held her back. This is not an uncommon issue, perhaps a particularly female one. In encounters with men, many female clients seem to assume that the most important thing is to please men by having the right looks, being the right size and conforming to what the man wants. This is a well-trodden piece of social behaviour, but seems to lead to rather unsuccessful relationships with the opposite sex. In exploring this area, I encourage the client to look at it more in relationship terms, which means taking the construction of both parties into consideration, but importantly to explore the nature of the relating and communication between them. When working with a female client, my relationship with her offers a very good starting point for reconstruing such relationships. I aim to give the client a sense of feeling comfortable with me, of not feeling obliged to act in a particular way and being an equal partner in the therapeutic process. I encourage the client to speak up and let me know her point of view and to challenge me if she thinks I am going off in the wrong direction. This in itself can be a very good learning experience for someone who has limited experience of power with the opposite sex.

In moving towards everyday encounters with the opposite sex, I would spend some time exploring the possible constructions held by men when relating to women, including the potential effect of being in a group of men. I will generally encourage the client to try to find out for herself, but will also prompt by offering possible constructions, such as those relating to trying to impress. I will also try to help the client see that the man is not just a man, but a person with his own possible doubts and anxieties, in spite of his apparently confident behaviour. In such ways, I try to help the client experiment in the way she would communicate with the opposite sex. I offer a model of relationship development requiring maximum communication, in which both parties share their constructions and move towards a possibly better understanding of each other. I hope to open the client's eyes to the possibility that good relationships are more likely to develop when both partners construct systems, are freely elaborating and share some common constructions.

More pervasively negative constructions of self often are associated with particularly negative experience of parents. Such relationships can form the blueprint for subsequent relationships, which can further validate a highly negative construction of self. Although there will often be some area of positive self construction that can be built upon, it is not uncommon for quite considerable work needing to be done in the area of parent construction. My approach to this is to try to help clients make sense of their parents, to move towards an understanding of a parent's behaviour through exploring possible constructions underlying the behaviour. There are many ways of going about this, which might actually include the client asking his or her parents how they saw their role as parents and maybe what their experience of their own parents was. One might also encourage the client to imagine what it would be like to be their parents and perhaps role-play this during a session. Such explorations may not necessarily take away all the negative feelings they have about a parent, but on making sense out of the behaviour this might go some way towards freeing up the person's construing of themselves. For example, Chris (see below) had considerable negative feelings towards her mother, who she considered as domineering. By exploring how her mother seemed to approach her role, it became clear just how central and tightly defined was her mother's view of her role. Mother seemed to have a very considerable need to rule the family, almost to the exclusion of everything else. She seemed most content when her children related to her like a child, but clearly found it difficult dealing with Chris, who did not fit into those kinds of expectations. Gradually Chris began to see that her mother's expectations did not have to rule her, that she could still be free to be herself in spite of it. Her mother's constructions of her did not have to be completely validated all the time, nor completely invalidated for that matter. I put it to her that there might be a time for going along with her mother's constructions, e.g. at her parents' wedding anniversary, but that Chris was free to be herself in general if she chose to be.

A problem with this kind of reconstruction is that the client might be used to seeking and expecting approval (or what Kelly called 'validation') and experience repeated disappointment when not receiving it. The client's anticipations of other people are likely to have a major bearing on the eating behaviour and construction of self. When people fail to conform to expectations, then it is not uncommon for the client to shy away from such people, perhaps turning further inward on the eating track. Often such experience is based upon an assumption about the other person that has not been tested out. Instead the client has interpreted an event as conforming to a familiar construction of herself, e.g. 'People don't like me', 'I get trodden all over', 'He didn't like me being fat', etc. I encourage people to explore alternative possibilities, much in the same way as a cognitive therapist would do. But there is no assumption that there is a right or wrong way of construing events. It *is* possible that someone may not have liked the client because of fatness, but one cannot know that without further evidence. Even if it was the case, I encourage the client to consider what they think about a person who construes in such a way. Rather than just seeing it as further evidence of the importance of controlling fatness, I would invite the client to consider whether he or she would want to get too close to such a person.

The key point to this kind of process is that I am inviting the client to explore possible constructions held by the other person, which take into consideration that person's perspective as reflecting a need to make sense out of their own experience. As such, other people have their own agenda, which might be quite different from the client's, not meshing in any sense. It may be that the client has become accustomed to social contexts within which one just complies with other people's expectations. There are many social contexts that can validate this position: schools in which pupils are expected always to do what teachers expect, rather than showing their own initiative; parents who expect their children to be seen and not heard; husbands who expect to dominate their wives into fulfilling a subservient role. In many ways such contexts can have advantages for people. They can create fixed expectations, which make life predictable. Like one of my clients said about his army days, at least you knew where you were then! Many rather abusive relationships can also be preserved because life can become predictable within them – maybe anticipated abuse is easier to handle than when it is unpredictable. Needless to say, these are not the kinds of relationship that I am seeking to foster in psychotherapy.

In the process of developing self beyond a narrow eating focus, I find that relationships with friends often play an important part in getting things moving. Although the client may feel uneasy in many kinds of relationship, it will often be the case that one or two friends can create a feeling of being comfortable. They may feel a mutual sense of understanding and acceptance. Usually when time is spent with such people, this can create the potential for avoiding binge-eating and experimenting in social eating. Sometimes, however, the relationships can be limited by a lack of honesty from the client. They may be wary of giving too much away in case the person rejects. Also, they can sometimes put themselves in difficult positions because they are not sufficiently open. For example, Amy frequently got herself into difficulty by inviting friends round to have dinner and creating an expectation that she would have to prepare a really nice meal. Invariably, however, she could not cope with this and in the preparation phase would get into a continuous binge, often having to make excuses to back out at the last minute because of the resulting physical and emotional pain. On exploration, this had resulted out of an assumption that she had to reciprocate. In exploring alternatives, we came up with the need to let such friends know that she found preparing food difficult and in future the friend would come round and join in the preparation. The result was an enjoyable and relaxed social occasion, with no lessening of the appreciation of it in the friend.

If a few such trusting relationships can develop, the process of exploring difficulties within such relationships can help to generate principles that can be applied towards extending and developing relationships into more difficult areas. Hopefully, they will have learned that if they let people know more about themselves – how they view the world – then social encounters are more comfortable and less likely to generate problems. By the same token, they will hopefully have discovered the importance of finding out about the other person's view of things and whether they share a common agenda. They may thus come to see certain other people as having the potential to play an important role in the development of themselves, not primarily as a threat.

Such a process seems to be occurring with Carol, an overweight, bulimic young woman, who was extremely closed in and withdrawn. In her family, no-one showed emotion or affection and social encounters were very superficial. She had come to avoid all but the most superficial of communications with people. This extended to her encounters with me, in which she was initially very wary of expressing herself. We worked a lot in the early stages on issues such as asserting herself in the work situation, being able to tell people if she did not want to do something, for example. Having for years allowed people to walk over her, she had learned that she could speak up and have more control over events. In her social encounters, however, conversation was often restricted to casual joky talk, without really saying what she meant. She eventually was able to say to me that food was not the problem and it was more of a response to a great yearning and emptiness, loneliness, a longing for closeness. She thus is beginning to open up the agenda towards deeper levels of communicating and relating.

We have recently begun experimenting in such communicating. She indicated how she wanted to be able to tell her friend how glad she was to see her, but could not. I introduced the Gestalt technique of the empty chair, in which she imagined her friend was sitting in a chair in our consulting room. I suggested she try to say something to her friend in the chair. This she found extremely difficult and I suggested she try it in her head. This she did and commented that if she could do it in her head she could say it, which she proceeded to do. This small step forward showed just how difficult such issues were for her. But I felt that she was beginning the process of moving towards communicating some of her more 'core constructs' in her most important relationships.

I have tried to illustrate above how one can approach the task of moving away from an eating focus and towards developing self and the ability to form meaningful relationships with other people. As the client's confidence in themselves and their ability to get on with other people increases, the chances are that they will be able to put weight and food issues in perspective and allow them to take a back seat. With more chronic clients, however, it is possible that only relatively superficial and slow development can occur, so extensive is their reliance on weight control. Even when they eventually begin to realise that they could function without putting all their efforts and energy into weight control, this realisation can leave them with an immense feeling of loss. This was very much the experience of Chris, who at almost 40 years of age resented all the lost years and opportunities. Having discovered that she was really a likeable person, she realised she could have avoided the years of destructive behaviour. Moreover, she understandably saw her options in terms of career and being a parent as increasingly narrowed. Perhaps, as in bereavement of a loved one, she too had to go through a kind of mourning process before she could really move on and seize the opportunities that were increasingly coming her way.

Ending and moving on

The therapeutic relationship has to come to an end at some point, but this varies considerably in terms of duration and style of ending. With some clients, the end comes very quickly and unsatisfactorily, perhaps symptomatic of the client's difficulty in handling relationships. Optimally, I see ending as a jointly negotiated process and usually in a gradual manner, rather than the sudden death approach of some schools of therapy. I see therapy as continuing while there is useful work being carried out. Like decorating houses, some will need more extensive work than others. For some, where the paintwork is basically intact, it may just be a matter of a quick job covering over the cracks. But where the plaster is crumbling away, major renovation, if not rebuilding may be required. As in decorating, you can always find more work to do, but at some point you need to leave it alone and get on with something else. In my therapeutic relationships, I tend to build in a series of reviews, which help to focus one's attention on where one is going and on future needs for help. Often, breaks such as holidays offer a good opportunity for testing out the client's ability to function by his or her own steam. For some clients, a fair degree of dependent feelings can develop and this needs to be mutually shared. The time has to be right for letting go of the leash and I think that it is important to introduce spacing out of sessions as soon as possible. But this needs to be done with the client. Sometimes, I find they take the initiative, whether directly or indirectly by telling me when they want to get on with it more on their own. Whatever the timescale, I prefer a flexible approach where one can if necessary increase frequency, perhaps where readiness to terminate has been overestimated. Underlying this process is the parallel need for the client to have built up a range of people who can be depended upon for different needs. The greater are their resources, the less likelihood they will need to see the therapist as necessary for their continuing functioning. When the end does come, I emphasise that it does not have to be all or nothing. As in most relationships, there can be a case for keeping in touch and reporting back to base, at least for a while, until other relationships take over in meaningfulness.

At the end of the formal therapeutic relationship, I hope that the client will have learnt something about themselves and other people that enables them to get on with their life without feeling stuck and bogged down by weight. The ability to be open to a wide range of perspectives on people and life should help, but it is over to them as to what direction they take.

6 Personal construct research on eating disorders

One of the key features of personal construct theory is that it has generated a fair amount of research, particularly in the area of psychological disorders (see Button, 1985a; Winter, 1992). Although the personal construct research literature on eating disorders is relatively small in quantity, it does make a contribution to our understanding of these disorders and helps to substantiate the theoretical position taken here.

In common with over 95% of personal construct research (Neimeyer, 1985), some form of grid technique has invariably been the favoured methodology, beginning with two case studies from London's St. George's Hospital (Fransella and Crisp, 1970; Crisp and Fransella, 1972). In both cases the authors used a repertory grid to illustrate how a client with an eating disorder might resist change. In the first of these (Fransella and Crisp, 1970), an obese person seemed to be resisting permanent weight loss in the belief that life was more meaningful as an overweight person than as a normal weight person. In the second case (Crisp and Fransella, 1972) with two anorectic young women, it was suggested that clinical change did not occur until weight was no longer of central importance in defining the self. Fransella and Crisp (1979) later went on to extend the use of grid technique to an empirical comparison of anorectic, neurotic and normal control subjects. One of the intriguing findings from this study was that, for the anorectics, being thin was less favourably construed than being normal in weight. One of the hypotheses put forward to try to explain this unexpected finding was that the anorectics may have been suffering from what they called the 'if only' syndrome. In other words, they were idealising what life might be like 'if only' they were not anorexic.

A theme that ran through all these studies was that one could usefully explore the meaning of being eating disordered using grid methodology. Fay Fransella went on to extend this work at London's Royal Free Hospital. She sought to test out the hypothesis that weight change may be resisted, in part, because life may be more meaningful at a particular weight. This was an extension of analogous work by Fransella (1972) with stutterers in which she had shown that stutterers may resist fluent speaking because life is more meaningful as a stutterer. It may be that other people with long-standing complaints may resist giving up these complaints because life is more meaningful with something you know well. In the case of eating problems, Fransella argued that the obese and the anorectic may both resist changing to becoming normal in weight because life was more meaningful being fat or thin respectively. A research project was initiated by her to test this hypothesis and I worked on the project as a research assistant between 1973 and 1976. It was this period of working with Fay Fransella at the Royal Free that provided the foundation for the ideas expressed in this book. Although the project focused on both obesity and anorexia nervosa, I shall only present the results here in relation to the latter disorder, which is based on 20 consecutive anorectic in-patients. The main research tool was a form of implications grid (Hinkle, 1965; see also Fransella and Bannister, 1977), a type of grid in which there are no elements and the subject is asked directly to indicate the connections or 'implications' between constructs. Full details can be found in Button (1980), but essentially for all poles of all bipolar constructs the subject is asked a simple question: 'If all you knew about a person was construct x (e.g. "slim"), would you also expect that person to be construct y (e.g. "popular")?' Each time the subject indicated such an expectation, this would be called an 'implication' and recorded in the grid as a tick. For any particular grid, the total number of implications was operationally defined as a measure of meaningfulness.

In order to test out the above hypothesis, two types of grid were constructed. In one of these, the *thin* grid, constructs were first elicited by comparing 'me as a thin person' with a series of other people. In the *normal weight* grid, in contrast, constructs were elicited comparing elements with 'me at a normal weight'. In this way, it was hoped that the two types of grid, although similar, would be measuring the construing or 'meaningfulness' of two different worlds: on the one hand being thin and on the other hand being normal in weight. If the hypothesis was correct, there should be more implications in thin grids than normal weight grids. Results were, however, not totally in line with prediction. Thus, there was no difference in meaningfulness between the two sorts of grid. But it was found that for both sets of grid subjects on their first admission to hospital had significantly higher numbers of implications. One possible interpretation of this is that those patients who had been in hospital several times had generally less meaningful construct subsystems for construing people. Thus, while the particular methodology chosen failed to demonstrate that being thin was more meaningful than being normal in weight, there was evidence of increasingly impoverished social construing as a person goes further and further into the anorectic world. There was also evidence that measures of meaningfulness were relevant to outcome. Those patients who showed relatively higher meaningfulness scores for normal weight grids on admission to hospital showed better weight maintenance at follow-up. Moreover, there was also a non-significant trend for increases in meaningfulness of being normal weight and reduction in meaningfulness of being thin to be associated with better outcome.

Following on from the above study, a second grid study was carried out at the Royal Free using the more conventional form of grid, in which a set of elements are sorted in terms of a series of constructs. It was felt that a lot of questions had been left unanswered by the first study and the rated grid offered the opportunity for greater ease of administration and analysis, the implications grid being very cumbersome and difficult to analyse in my experience. A rated grid also allowed the possibility of detailed examination of the way anorexics construed significant people in their lives, as well as a number of versions of 'self'.

The subjects were a further 20 anorectic in-patients, who were assessed on a maximum of four separate occasions: on admission, at discharge and on two follow-up occasions within a year of discharge. The grids consisted of up to 12 personally elicited constructs and nine supplied constructs. There were 20 elements, including a number of versions of self as well as other persons. The elements were rated for all constructs on a seven-point scale. Full details of the methodology can be found in Button (1980) and the main results are summarised in Button (1983a). The aims and hypotheses of this study were much broader than the earlier study, but the overall aim was to achieve a better understanding of the construing of anorexics and the relationship of such construing to the process of treatment and outcome.

First, the construing of the group as a whole was examined, using one of Slater's (1977) computer programs for summarising the construing of a group of persons using the same or similar grids. Although this averaging process can mask important individual differences, it can often throw up a rough picture of the typical construing of a group of people. Using principal components analysis, the most striking initial finding was of a sharp contrast on the first component between the elements 'me at thinnest' and 'ideal self', with 'me at normal weight' positioned towards the ideal self. This thus replicated the Fransella and Crisp (1979) finding of thinness being curiously construed negatively in anorexics receiving treatment. The finding also held up when supplied constructs were excluded and analysis was restricted to the subject's personal constructs. As well as being construed more negatively than being normal weight, 'me at thinnest' was also construed more extremely, which could be expressed alternatively as more meaningfully. Thus, using a measure different from that used in the implication grid study, there was support for the original Fransella hypothesis that life as a thin person for the anorectic would be more meaningful than at 'normal weight'.

Although these anorexics, on the face of it, were paradoxically construing life at normal weight as more favourable than being thin, the picture changed somewhat when one examined the lesser principal components. Specifically, on the third component, ideal self was at the opposite pole to several elements, one of which was 'self at treatment weight'. The full wording of the latter element was 'me at the sort of weight I imagine the treatment team want me to be'. The significance of this is best clarified by examining individual patients' grids. For example, one patient preferred to be 'inconspicuous', but saw herself at treatment weight as becoming more 'conspicuous'. This suggests that when presenting for treatment, anorectic clients may portray an overall picture of wanting to be normal weight, but when one looks beneath the surface, there may be certain important constructs on which there could be very negative consequences of weight gain.

The relationship between various measures and clinical outcome were also examined. Those clients who on admission to hospital had a more unidimensional construct system and construed themselves more extremely tended to fare poorly at outcome. Consistent with these findings, a smaller distance between the elements 'self now' and 'self a year ago' predicted poor outcome. This all suggests that more fixed construing, particularly of self, is associated with resistance to change. Moreover, when examining changes in construing over time, those clients who did well began with looser construing and went through a cyclical process of tightening and loosening. The resistant clients, however, tended to stay with tighter construing.

There was also further evidence of the importance of the construing of normal weight and thinness. In general, it was found that at discharge from hospital, clients' view of themselves was far less clear compared with on admission. Those clients, however, who had a more definite view of themselves at normal weight soon after leaving hospital showed better weight maintenance in the longer term. At the same time, after discharge, it was found that a decrease in meaningfulness of the construct 'thin–fat' was associated with good weight maintenance.

Taken as a whole, the above studies provide ample evidence that both the structure and content of construing of anorexics is relevant to the resistance to weight change and their response to in-patient treatment geared at weight restoration. But none of these studies demonstrate what is peculiar about the construing of someone with anorexia nervosa. Several studies have aimed to compare anorexics with normal controls and other groups. Mottram (1985) used repertory grid technique to compare 15 female anorexics with 15 psychologically healthy female students. There was a significant structural difference in construing, with anorexics both using more extreme ratings and having more unidimensional construing. There was also a difference in content of construing, with anorexics having a greater distance between self and ideal self. Mottram also found that the anorexics' ideal self was more isolated from other elements, which he suggests could reflect perfectionist tendencies.

Several studies have investigated eating problems akin to anorexia nervosa in subclinical populations. Munden (1982) used repertory grids in a comparison of 17 female students who construed themselves as having an eating problem and 16 female control students. Once again, those with an eating problem had a more negative view of themselves, as reflected by the distance between self and ideal self. Those with an eating problem also indicated that they thought that being slim would make them closer to their ideal self, whereas the control group did not envisage any significant change if they were slimmer. There was no evidence, however, of structural differences in construing between groups. Batty and Hall (1986) also found evidence of negative self-construing, but not of 'tighter' construing, in a small study of a mixed group of students with anorectic/bulimic symptoms attending self-help groups. Unfortunately, however, there was no control group.

Neimeyer and Khouzam (1985), however, did find evidence of structural differences in construing between people with and without eating problems. They used Bieri's (1955) concept of 'cognitively complexity' in a grid study of 68 female students, some of whom showed evidence of eating restraint. High eating restrainers were less cognitively complex than low restrainers, i.e. they construed in a less multidimensional way. High restrainers also viewed themselves more negatively on the supplied 'affective' constructs. It should be mentioned that the form of grid chosen in this study was somewhat different from the other studies in that it focused on the construing of eating situations rather than on people.

Heesacker and Neimeyer (1990) also used a student population in their grid study of the role of both 'cognitive structure' and 'object relations'. A total of 183 undergraduate females completed a grid and a measure of object relations (Bell, Billington and Becker, 1986). The grid was focused on person construing and once again low differentiation of construing predicted disordered eating. There was also evidence of disturbed object relations ('insecure attachment' and 'social incompetence') predicting disordered eating and the authors suggest that rigid cognitive structures may develop out of disturbance in early relationships.

The overall theme of these studies, investigating people at various points along the anorectic dimension, is that such individuals are inclined to have more negative views of themselves and less multidimensional construing. But what of the bulimic person? Many of the above studies were carried out before the concept of bulimia nervosa had been formulated and reached its current high profile in the research literature. Surprisingly, little work has been published so far. Weinreich, Doherty and Harris (1985) used grids in a comparison of 17 bulimics with 9 anorectics, 13 normal controls and 12 psychiatric controls. The focus of this study was primarily on self-construing and within a meta-theoretical framework known as 'identity structure analysis' (Weinreich, 1980). The most interesting finding in this rather small-scale study was that the bulimics showed evidence of 'sustained identity problems', i.e. seeing themselves in negative terms both now and in the past. In contrast, the anorectics showed evidence of 'plummeting identity crises', in which they were evaluating themselves more negatively than when younger. This was the first indication that bulimics may be somewhat different in construing from anorectics, a theme to which we will return.

The most substantive personal construct study of bulimic eating disorder to date was carried out by Coish (1990). In her doctoral thesis, she sought to test out a number of hypotheses using two forms of grid. She proposed that bulimics have relatively few constructs for interpreting their worlds and that those constructs would be more rigidly organised; they would use more constructs concerned with food and weight, and they would have a more extreme and negative view of the world. The subjects were 52 bulimic women, defined by their scores on the Bulimia Test (Smith and Thelen, 1984), and who participated in a 12-week treatment programme. There was also a control group of 20 normal women. This study is complicated by the fact that four types of grid were used, investigating the construing of people and situations and with both elicited and provided constructs. It is not possible in the space available to do justice to all the results and there was a fair amount of inconsistency across the different types of grid. There was some evidence, however, in support of all the hypotheses, at least for some of the grids. Thus, on some of the grids, bulimics tended to be more extreme, less differentiated, less positive and use more eating and weight constructs. This study provides some evidence that the kinds of deficit in construing found in anorexia nervosa may also extend to bulimia nervosa. But, there are a lot of questions unanswered from this study. Most significantly, there was no control group of people with other psychological disorder, so that it is not clear to what extent differences reflect bulimia per se or more general psychological disturbance.

Ryle and Evans (1991) have recently published results of a study in which they compared a mixed group of bulimic and anorectic subjects with a normal weight comparison group. The authors took the view that there were a lot of similarities between the two eating disorder groups and thus pooled them together. Twenty-seven people fulfilling DSM111 (American Psychiatric Association, 1980) criteria for eating disorders (19 anorectic and 8 bulimic) were compared with 20 normal-weight females using the self and body image grid (Ryle and Evans, 1991), described above. The study focused on the content of construing, rather than structural features, and once again found greater negative self-image in the eating disorder group. Not all results were consistent with prediction, but one finding seems particularly pertinent to the above studies. The eating disorder group were characterised more by their identification of a negative self-image with average and overweight body images, rather than by their positive identification with the underweight body image. This is consistent with the above studies, in which thinness was not positively construed in anorectics, but where 'normal weight' was in some respects construed negatively. Unfortunately, however, the value of this study is clouded somewhat by the mixing of the anorectics and bulimics, whom it cannot be assumed construe in the same way.

The above studies provide some insight into the construing of people with anorectic or bulimic disorder. It is not clear, however, if there is anything specific about their construing over and above being psychologically disordered in general, nor is it clear whether anorectic and bulimic persons differ from each other in construing. There thus seems to be a strong case for a study to investigate differences in construing among four groups, namely anorectics, bulimics, the generally psychologically disordered and normal controls.

Recent grid data

I have used SELF-GRID (Button, 1988a) in a comparison of a sample of females from the above four groups. Preliminary findings have been reported in Button (1992) and the study is not complete yet, but the pattern of results is proving to be quite consistent. To date (early 1993) there are 26 anorectics (AN group) and 31 bulimics (BN group), all of whom fulfil DSM111R (American Psychiatric Association, 1987) criteria for eating disorders. The latter seems important as previous grid studies have not been too precise on the extent of disorder. Data was also available from a separate study (Button, 1990b) on 26 normal female controls (NORM group) and 17 females presenting with general non-psychotic psychological disorder (PSY group). A comparison has been made using measures similar to those used in Coish's (1990) study. Findings obtained so far suggest the following.

Differentiation/integration of construing

I have used a number of different measures of construct system structure, including several that focus on what might be called differentiation/ integration of construing. Based on my earlier research with anorectics (Button, 1980) and my subsequent clinical experience of eating disorders in general, I hypothesised that anorectics would show less differentiated construing. The results have been in line with this prediction. Although there has been some variation in level of significance, depending on which measure has been chosen, comparisons between anorectics and bulimics consistently show evidence of less differentiated construing among anorectics. For example, on the total percentage of variance contributed by the first three principal components, there is a highly significant difference (AN mean = 84.8%; BN mean = 79.4%; PSY mean = 78.1%; NORM mean = 79.5%; F [3,96] = 5.04, p = 0.003). The anorectic group scored higher than all three groups, indicative of less multidimensional construing. In short, they seem to have less avenues open to them for construing themselves and other people. Thus, while once again we see that less multidimensional construing is implicated in anorexia nervosa, this is apparently not so in the case of bulimia nervosa.

Extremity of construing

This measure was based on the use of the various points on the rating scale, with higher scores indicating more use of extreme responses, such as 'always' and 'never', when construing self and others. Lower scores, by contrast, reflect more use of mid-way rating such as 'sometimes' and 'often'. There is, in fact, no significant difference between groups and the two eating disorder groups scored very similarly.

Positivity/negativity of construing

Several measures of positivity/negativity of construing were used and for none of these was there any significant difference between anorectic and bulimic groups. Not surprisingly, however, all three psychiatric groups showed much higher negativity than the normal controls. In terms of specific elements, the most marked difference between anorectics and bulimics was in the construing of 'self when younger'. The percentage of 'negative ratings' of 'self when younger' (see Button (1992) for details of the measure) differed significantly between groups (F = 3.45, p = 0.019). Whereas bulimics (mean negativity = 19.4%) scored similarly to psychiatric controls (mean = 23.9%), anorectics (mean = 11.4%) were indistinguishable from normal controls (mean = 11.6%). In the case of the construing of 'self nowadays', however, all three psychiatric groups scored much more negatively than the normal control group. Thus the anorectic group construe themselves much more negatively than when younger, whereas the bulimics share with the general psychological group a more persisting negative self-image.

This tendency of anorectics to see themselves less favourably nowadays than when recalling their younger self is reminiscent of Weinreich, Doherty and Harris's (1985) study, which suggested that anorectics suffer from 'plummeting identity crisis', whereas bulimics have 'prolonged identity crisis'. Although the results are consistent with the idea of a 'plummeting identity crisis' in anorexia nervosa, it cannot be said that their perceived younger self is any more perfect than healthy females. Moreover, one should qualify these findings by pointing out that the construing of 'self when younger' was retrospective and thus cannot be taken as indicative of how these women construed themselves at the time. This would need a prospective study of the kind being undertaken with adolescent girls (Button, 1990a).

Number of constructs

The number of unipolar constructs elicited by SELF-GRID was compared between groups and there was a significant difference ($F = 3.85$, $p = 0.012$). The anorectics had fewest constructs (mean = 18.8%), differing significantly only from the normal controls (mean = 24.5%).

Content of constructs

In similar manner to Coish, the number of constructs that could be categorised as relating to weight, eating or appearance were counted. These 'eating disorder constructs' were relatively small in number, but bulimics came up with more (mean = 7.3%) than anorectics (mean = 2.6%). The overall difference between groups was highly significant ($F = 7.56$, $p = 0.0003$). All three psychiatric groups produced more such constructs than healthy controls, consistent with the view that women with psychological problems in general are more likely to construe themselves in terms of appearance/weight. Clients with eating disorders, however, do have other constructs for construing themselves, but bulimics present such constructs more than do anorectics. Whether this reflects a different psychological agenda between these two groups or whether it is another example of anorectic denial is open to question.

Self-esteem

The pattern of self-image between the groups was compared on a number of measures and in terms of their present self, anorectics and bulimics were quite similar to each other and to the general psychological disorder group. All three psychiatric groups showed a fair amount of negativity of construing and much more than normal controls. For example, on my self-esteem measure (Button, 1993), all three psychological groups were highly significantly different from the normal control group ($F = 9.91$, $p = 0.00005$; AN mean = 2.40%, BN mean = 2.47%, PSY mean = 2.25%, NORM mean = 1.33%). Thus, low self-esteem does not mark out eating disorder clients as different from others with psychological disorders.

But this negativity of self-construing was not absolute among eating disorder clients. In terms of the principal components analysis, for example, both groups saw themselves as having a mixture of positive and negative characteristics. Common positive constructions tended to refer to what I have called 'tenderness towards people' and includes constructs such as 'loyal' and 'caring about people'. This is also reflected in a perceived absence of what might be called 'negative social behaviour', e.g 'I am not conniving' or 'not controlling'. On the negative side of things, both groups often referred to problems with emotion, e.g 'fly off the handle', 'afraid of affection'. They also see themselves as lacking in social ability, e.g. 'cannot make friends', 'lack of confidence'.

Summary

The above studies point to quite a number of similarities between anorectics and bulimics. Both groups tend to construe their recent self relatively negatively, in similar vein to others with psychological disorder. My research also points to similar themes of interpersonal and emotional difficulty. Perhaps surprisingly, people with eating disorders came up with relatively few weight/appearance constructs in construing people, but bulimics presented such constructs more often than anorectics.

The main difference between these two groups is the greater tendency of anorectics to construe in a less multidimensional way, what might be called 'tight' construing. Moreover, they tend to have fewer constructs for construing people. One aspect of the construing of anorectics that could not easily be quantified was their response to the repertory grid task. Quite often, they reacted in a somewhat prickly manner, being rather wary and critical of the exercise. Several anorectic clients who were approached to conduct SELF-GRID refused to do it, saying they could not do it or did not know what to say. Typical of this type of reaction was Gay, who was extremely defensive and wary of it. After several attempts to present it differently, she made it very clear that she would not cooperate, forcing the task to be abandoned. Her reaction was to prove a foretaste of things to come in unsuccessful efforts to engage her in treatment. This is not a kind of reaction found among bulimics, who often show a fair amount of interest in the exercise. If one could tap the construing of those anorectic clients who refused to do the grid, the differences between groups might show up even further.

The other major difference is that anorectics tend to construe their younger self relatively favourably compared with bulimics. This may suggest that their construct system has proved less able to handle the events of life in recent times compared with when younger. It may well be that their limited way of construing of the world worked quite well with the more simple demands of childhood, perhaps validated by significant others such as parents. When faced with the more complex and variable construing to be found in the wider and adult world, however, such limited construing as they have available is likely to be inadequate. It is perhaps not surprising that they constrict their world in search of greater predictability and control.

Although structural deficits in construing seem to play a greater part in the development of anorexia nervosa, for eating disorder clients in general, a focus on negative constructions of self is likely to be important therapeutically. Moreover, there is no firm evidence that women with eating disorder are too different from other young women with psychological disorder, except in their choice of symptom.

Part III

THE EXPERIENCE OF PERSONAL CONSTRUCT THERAPY: SOME THERAPEUTIC STORIES

Introduction

Having outlined in broad terms my approach to working with people with eating disorders, it seems to me that the best way to flesh out what this means in practice is through the medium of clients. In this part of the book I shall therefore present a series of case studies of clients I have worked with. It is important, I think, to stress the context of this work, particularly for those working outside Britain. All the clients have been seen for psychological help within the context of the National Health Service, rather than in private practice. They are thus not fee-paying and are drawn from a reasonably wide cross-section of the population, although I have little doubt that those of higher socioeconomic status are more likely to have the ability to access this kind of specialised service. This is particularly so when 'experts' on eating disorders are likely to be thinly spread around and there is a heavy demand for help.

In each case I shall focus primarily on personal construction as it seems to bear relevance to the problems with eating. This is clearly a biased approach and I make no apologies for this. Each person, when taking on the role of client, will present and be presented partly in terms that are meaningful to the particular therapist. A psychoanalyst would undoubtedly describe the following clients and the work done in terms quite different from my own. At a less extreme level, another personal construct therapist would be unlikely to handle the clients in exactly the same way. While they may use similar language, construct therapists are ultimately unique persons and have different emphases and styles. Thus each of the clients will be open to alternative interpretation. I would be very surprised if readers do not bring their own creative constructions to bear on the clients. My hope, however, is that my constructions will enthuse others as to the potential value of focusing on the significance of personal construction and theorising in people with eating disorders.

The selection of these particular client examples from among the hundreds of people I have worked with was not the easiest of tasks. It would be very tempting to just select those clients I had been successful with, and indeed there will no doubt be unconscious processes that will push me towards a broadly favourable self-presentation. As far as possible, however, I have tried to offer a realistic cross-section of clients, which will include those in whom there was little or no progress. This is consistent with my experience and, I believe, that of psychotherapists in general. In addition to aiming for a cross-section of clients, another consideration has been the availability of information on clients. This has led to a bias towards more recent clients, during a period when I have been more systematic in the way I assess clients and monitor progress. There will also be a couple of examples of earlier work that have already been documented elsewhere. A further bias is that all the clients are female, which is a realistic reflection of my practice. I would have dearly loved to have included a detailed example of a male client, but at the time of writing there was no male whom I had worked with over a sufficiently long period of time. Although this partly reflects the bias towards females suffering from eating disorders, I suspect it also says something about me.

As well as being selective of people, the stories that follow are selective in time. They are chapters in people's lives, rather than their whole story. I hope that they have many more interesting chapters to follow. Indeed, in a number of cases, I have been able to follow up people some years after our work together and learn something of later chapters. For most people, their life seemed to have moved forward, but it cannot be assumed that it will stay that way. Those who have progressed can slip back into old familiar ways and those who are stuck may one day move forward in a new direction. In my approach to working with people, I make no claims to make them 'well', but I do offer to give time to exploring possible ways ahead. In some cases, we seem to have developed fruitful relationships, which have created the safety to explore and move ahead. In other cases, little change has occurred. Moreover, one piece of therapy is not necessarily the whole story as far as change is concerned. Although I aim to help open up new avenues in a person's life and thus free the person to move on, earlier work may have paved the way for my contribution and I hope that later experiences will continue where I have left off.

The clients described in the chapters that follow have all been given fictitious names and personal details have been changed to help preserve their anonymity. In some cases, the individual concerned has been a very active participant in this book. I felt it was important to make use of the voice of the client wherever possible and excerpts in the client's words are often included. In certain cases, moreover, the client was specifically asked if they would like to write something of their experience for possible inclusion in this book. I am very grateful for their contributions, which I have found deeply illuminating. I hope their experiences will bring home my theme of needing to try to understand the client's perspective.

7 Anna

Anna seems like a good person to begin with. Chronologically, she was the first case study I have detailed on eating disorders. I wrote about her (Button, 1980) at a time when my ideas on eating disorders were first developing. Although I run the risk of being overly dependent on selective memory, I am helped by the fact that she was documented in detail as part of my doctoral thesis. It also feels right to me to go back to my beginnings, in the same way as a client's construing can be meaningful when viewed in a historical context.

Anna is somewhat different from the other clients to be described in that I was not her principal therapist. Most of the important initial therapeutic work was done by a former colleague of mine (whom I shall call David). After he had moved on to a new post, however, I was involved with Anna for some time as a kind of transitional therapist between him and independence from treatment. While my therapeutic involvement was not continuous, I had, however, known Anna as one of my research subjects for the whole of the time she was in treatment.

At the age of 23, Anna was admitted to a specialised psychiatric unit with a diagnosis of anorexia nervosa. She had been transferred from a medical ward at another hospital at a weight of 5 st. (70 lb) at a height of 5'2". Anna's previous weight had been steady at around 8 st. (112 lb), so that she had lost almost 40% of her previous body weight. In addition to self-induced weight loss, Anna fulfilled all other requirements for a medical diagnosis of anorexia nervosa.

Anna was one of three children brought up in a close-knit Jewish family. Although not orthodox Jews, social links were almost exclusively with Jewish people and there was an implicit expectation that any boyfriends would be of her faith. Her reflection on her childhood was full of unhappiness:

I hated my childhood. My father's a very dominant man – a strict disci-
plinarian. You always had to have good school reports and if you had a bad
report he would always quiz us and we were very frightened of Daddy. He
was the sort of person who completely took over everyone, including my
mother. I remember things like every Saturday afternoon we had to go over
to my Grandmother's for tea. He was very close to her and used to say to my
mother. 'This is how my mother does it. You ought to be like her.' At our
grandmother's, all my cousins and aunts and uncles were there and he would
look at me and say, 'Anna!' and up I would jump and help to make tea . . .
and 'Anna!' and that look again and it was time to get the coats. On the way
home in the car he would quiz me and my mother about why we did or did
not say this or that.

This theme of having to please her father was very prominent and it
seemed that pleasing people was a construct she took into other relationships. For example, at school she referred to trying always to model herself
on someone. It also applied to the sexual relationship she developed prior
to the onset of the eating disorder. When at university she met a young
man, Alan, who was 'everything I'd never known before', being non-Jewish
and from quite a different family background. She was immensely taken up
with him and could not believe that she was going out with him, given that
he was attractive, popular and much sought after as a boyfriend. She 'fell
head over heels' for him and spent all her time trying to please him in her
endeavour to keep him. It was around this time that she began cutting
down on food, thinking that she had to be slimmer in order to keep Alan,
despite his protestations to the contrary.

Although her relationship with Alan appears to have been pivotal in
the development of anorexia nervosa, there were other factors at that
time that Anna thought were relevant. One factor was the desire for
achievement, which had always been very important. Although doing
quite well academically, she was desperately striving for excellence, such
as wanting to do 'the most fantastic thesis ever'. Unfortunately, everything she considered did not seem good enough and weight control was
one desperate way in which she felt a sense of achievement. An additional factor was concern about her parents, who had never got on well
and Anna had played the role of peacemaker. Now that she was far away
from them at university, she felt there was little she could do to control
the situation. She also felt guilty about her relationship with Alan, which
had remained secret.

During the next few months she got deeper and deeper into the weight
control issue, to the point where her boyfriend eventually gave up on her
and she had to return home without completing her course. Following a
brief psychiatric encounter, she improved somewhat and went on to take
an administrative job. Once again she became obsessive about her work
and withdrew from social and sexual relationships. Eventually the drive for

thinness took over again and took her to the point of no return physically, where admission to hospital became a necessity.

Change in construing and treatment

Soon after arriving in hospital, I saw Anna for assessment, as part of my doctoral research on anorexia nervosa. This involved assessment on a number of different measures, including a repertory grid. I also had asked her to write something about what life had to offer her. This is what she wrote:

What life has to offer me
This question seems to me to imply some sort of expectation from the future. This I cannot do as I expect nothing from anyone. Every time I have put my hopes to something or the future, things just fall through. I suppose, trying to answer this as best as I can, I expect that life could offer me a little more success with people. I try so hard to get on with others – to help people where I can – not to speak badly of anyone – yet I can never keep friends – or have great difficulty meeting new people. It just seems to me that at 23, there must be more to life than just working – weekends and evenings too. I invariably just stay at home or work through nothing else to do! Life now should be going out – having a good time – meeting people before I settle down. I would really like to have a steady relationship soon. Perhaps life will offer me that one day!

This sad statement seems to convey a sense of disillusionment in her experiences with people. The girl who has tried so hard to please her father seems to have failed in her efforts to relate to people as an adult. It seems to be not for want of trying, but maybe she tried too hard. The end result seems to have been a giving up in the social domain, as if social construction was no longer possible.

Anna had also completed a repertory grid focused on person construing. A mixture of personal and supplied constructs had been included in this grid. The elements consisted of ten personally important people, a number of 'self-elements' and both parents. Elements were rated on a seven-point scale and the completed grid was analysed by means of the Ingrid programme (Slater, 1977). This uses principal components analysis which, as we have seen above, can produce a two-dimensional diagram offering a crude representation of the subject's intrapersonal world. A simplified version is displayed in Figure 7.1. Anna's grid analysis is also described in Button (1985c).

The first (vertical) component contrasts, in particular, the constructs 'Jewish', 'close to family' and 'can be attached' versus 'non-Jewish', 'separate from family' and 'can't be so attached'. On this component, 'me now' stands at the Jewish end in opposition to her former boyfriend Alan.

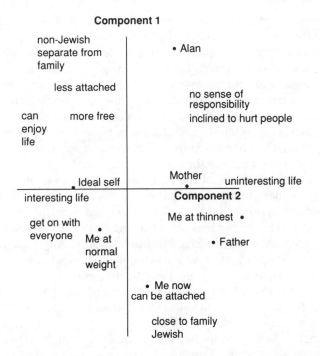

Component 1

non-Jewish
separate from
family

less attached

can   more free
enjoy
life

• Alan

no sense of
responsibility
inclined to hurt people

. Ideal self

interesting life

Mother
•   uninteresting life

Component 2

get on with
everyone   •
Me at
normal
weight

Me at thinnest •

• Father

• Me now
can be attached

close to family
Jewish

Figure 7.1:   Plot of elements in construct space from Anna's pre-treatment grid

Perhaps not surprisingly, father is seen as most similar to her on this dimension. The neutral position of 'ideal self' on this component suggests that Anna is unsure about the close family aspect of Jewish life. Inspection of the loadings of some of the other constructs on this component seemed to provide some clues to the nature of a possible dilemma. Although Alan's way of life has the advantage of being more free, it also may mean you 'can't be so attached', have 'no sense of responsibility' and are 'more inclined to hurt people'. In contrast with this uncertain construing, on the second (horizontal) component, however, ideal self is more clearly defined. In contrast to life at her thinnest, she envisages her ideal as being 'interesting', 'can enjoy life' and 'can get on with everyone'. She imagines that 'me at normal weight' would be close to her ideal self. Thus, as we saw above, life as an anorectic is not construed rosily by Anna, but we have also identified an area of surrounding uncertainty in construing, which may help to explain why it may be safer to be anorectic.

Anna was in hospital for about four months. During this time her weight had increased to around 7 st. 12 lb (110 lb), but slipped back to 6 st. 11 lb (95 lb) when she was discharged. Her eventual discharge from hospital was actually preceded by an earlier unsuccessful discharge when she quickly returned after an overdose at her parents' home. The following two months of her stay in hospital were characterised by almost consistent unhappiness and pessimism about the possibility for change. She also displayed considerable anger and rebelliousness towards both family and members of ward staff. It became clear that further time in hospital was achieving nothing. Her construing on discharge revealed a very negative construction of herself as very wary of life and lacking in understanding of people. Inpatient weight restoration had thus not led to more positive self-construing; if anything, the opposite was the case.

During her stay in hospital she had, however, begun seeing my clinical psychologist colleague and Anna's therapist's main therapeutic direction was towards trying to help her become more independent of her family. Instead of returning to her parents, when she finally left hospital she went to stay with a cousin, which seemed to work out well. Although her weight continued to drop again, there was some improvement in her self-construing when I followed her up a month after discharge. But this proved to be somewhat short-lived and there continued to be instability in her construing for some time, in particular focusing on the issue of being separate/dependent on family.

During the next 18 months, however, she managed to hold her own and gradually climbed her way forward. She was well on her way to recovery when she was referred to me on the departure of her therapist. My work with her focused mainly on helping her to consolidate and build upon her gains, as well as coming to terms with the loss of her therapist. She had, in fact, somewhat idealised him and putting him in perspective seemed like an important challenge to her black–white construing. By about 18 months after her admission, she had substantially improved and we agreed to terminate treatment.

She kept in touch, however, and I was able to follow her up some four years after her initial admission to hospital. On this occasion I was concerned to find out how she was construing her world, as well as her views on the process of change. One of the most noticeable things about our meeting is that, despite referring to a number of aspects of herself about which she was not entirely happy, she did not describe herself in terms of her weight. Issues that concerned her included her emotional vulnerability, not having a steady boyfriend and a continuing need for approval. Although identifying room for improvement, she appeared to be relatively accepting of the limitations in herself and her family. More importantly, she did not see weight control as a solution to these problems. She did, however, describe a very recent period of a few weeks in which she got 'very down' after difficulty in finding a new job. She remarked, as if to reassure herself, that she had not stopped eating, but 'all the warning signs were there'. It may be that we can never be completely sure that we have left something behind.

I would like to elaborate on Anna's view of herself at follow-up, first through the 'self characterisation' she produced shortly after our meeting:

Twenty seven, 5'2", brown hair and brown eyes. She is rather a home-bird at heart. Not the 'parental nest' – that is one place she realises she would never go back to living in. But she is one who would choose to stay in rather than go to clubs etc. Anna is by no means a shy, reserved creature: socially she relates very well with others. Her work involves her speaking to and entertaining businessmen daily and this she does with relative ease. Work to Anna is a very large part of her life. Although still doubting her capabilities, she is not half as self-doubting as she was a few years ago – she has I feel gained the ability to seek help – something in the past she found of great difficulty. The lengthy hours she still, to a small extent, uses in terms of excusing her from her own personal social dates. It is not that Anna is lacking in friends, boy-friends – like most single people this is a see-saw affair – busy going out for weeks and then nothing much. Anna without a boyfriend does not exactly push herself to go out much – but I reckon she looks upon life as fated – if she is going to meet someone, it will happen. Anna is basically a warm person who wants, needs approval. Do not get the idea she sticks herself on her own – No, she is too aware that this is not good for her.

Parents to Anna are better 'seen from afar'. Aware of her father's some-what overbearing affection and her mother's neuroses, Anna is at least aware that she is better stepping out of the situation – not necessarily permanently, but choosing her time to step in and say help. In fact, she probably gets on better with them now than she ever has done before. As for her brothers, she simply worships her younger brother Martin.

In terms of moods, I would not exactly call Anna a 'moody' person as such. When she does feel 'low' though – stay away! She clams up inside and creates a real atmosphere around her – a real pain – it passes as quickly as it comes and she is usually full of apologies. Her biggest fault most definitely is that when she does have a problem – something in her mind, she will not talk things over so it bubbles up inside. Sense of humour – yes – a touch on the dry side appreciating people like Woody Allen, the Marx brothers.

To sum her up then she is not really too complex a character – still a touch on the insecure side and personally I reckon a 'nice steady relationship' would sort that out. Her home and friends mean a lot to her and luckily she has good people surrounding her. She is very aware of how lucky she is and I think her anorectic past made her a stronger character all in all. I doubt if she would appreciate herself and her life without it.

Unfortunately, I had not asked her to complete a self-characterisation prior to treatment, but comparison with her statement about her life at that time reveals quite a contrast in theme. On admission to hospital, her main theme seemed to have been about invalidation of her construing in the social sphere. People were not living up to her expectations. This theme is not evident in the above sketch. Moreover, there are several statements indicative of change:

she is not half as self-doubting as she was a few years ago – she has I feel gained the ability to seek help

[re parents] in fact she probably gets on better with them now than she ever has done before

I think her anorectic past has made her a stronger character all in all

Although Anna feels she has changed, the picture she presents is by no means all rosy. She is clearly aware of vulnerabilities, such as her need for approval, but she seems broadly optimistic about herself and the role that other people can play in the development of her life.

I was also able to repeat her original grid. This presented a much more favourable view of herself as very close to her ideal. The main contrast between herself and her self at her thinnest was in terms of the construct 'has a good understanding–poor understanding of people', seeing herself as having moved towards a good understanding.

As well as repeating the original grid, it seemed appropriate after all this time to re-elicit a fresh series of constructs, given that there may be new themes to her construing. A summary of her construing is revealed in Figure 7.2. Here we see that her present self is relatively neutrally construed on the first (vertical) component. She has a clear view of her ideal self: contented, believe in self, secure, don't need approval, etc. Her self at thinnest, in contrast, is construed negatively along with parents and her

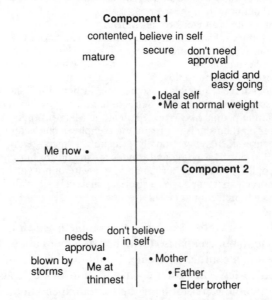

Figure 7.2:   Plot of elements in construct space from Anna's follow-up grid

elder brother. Her more neutral construing of self now reflects a mix of characteristics, including a tendency to often being 'blown by storms', as opposed to being 'placid and easy going'. It is interesting that a slightly different picture had emerged with these re-elicited constructs in contrast to repeating the original grid. It perhaps indicates that the removal of old complaints (as reflected in her pre-treatment grid) is not synonymous with the absence of complaints. If you ask a person about only previous complaints, then you might miss out on some new ones that have emerged. Although Anna does not idealise herself, the correspondence between actual and ideal self is, however, fairly positive and in keeping with greater psychological well-being.

A retrospective construction of the process of change

We have seen how Anna seems to have managed to move quite a way from her anorectic way of life. When I went along to interview her some four years after her admission to hospital, I was interested in her views on how this had come about. The following is based upon a structured interview we had together:

ERIC: What do you think helped you to emerge from anorexia nervosa?

ANNA: First and foremost – David, the first person who did not focus on weight. He did not start probing straight away . . . just listened. That started it – an outlet to all the things that were happening to me. Somehow all sorts of things, things I had been asked about a thousand times by doctors about my past etc. . . . I got asked all sorts of questions that were different and unusual. He played a big part. Very slowly, without really realising it, my weight was going up. He was aware and I was that I was very weight and calorie conscious, but it was not so much of a preoccupation. It is more than just weight. We just wrote down lots of things and he met my parents a few times. He was just a very sane person to have and he was very gentle.

ERIC: How did his being like that help?

ANNA: He gave me a belief in myself. He did not actually tell me what to do . . . he somehow prompted me, suggested things, like work, where to live. He was the one who gave the impetus to a lot of things, which in a sense all built up my belief in myself . . . slowly I built up that inner confidence.

He made me see – I must have done a lot myself, but I think he put me in the right direction in terms of seeing my parents as they are – before I had always wanted to change my parents. He made me see that my parents would never change – you can change your attitude to them, but you cannot fundamentally change them. I think he tried to, but after talking to my father for a couple of sessions realised there was no way you could do anything with a man like that! Some people are better left as they are . . . because they really are quite happy. So the approach and change of attitude had to come from myself.

I think the other thing that helped was Anorexic Aid*, because I met a couple of people who had actually *recovered*. I spent a lot of time at the hospital, meeting people like 'R' and 'J' who came back and forth into hospital and my total belief was based on my contact with people who had not recovered. With Anorexic Aid, for the first time I met people who said, 'I have had it and I am married with two children'.

A little bit of competition – 'M' at one stage was ahead of me – competitiveness in terms of actually getting better. One wanted to be as well as 'A' who had made it . . . We would talk about, for example, calorie counting and laugh at it and I suppose really ultimately how I got over it was just through living. I mean when I had a stable job, suddenly life started slotting into place. Without ultimately thinking I am going to give up anorexia nervosa – at one point I said I must get better. Very slowly, I did not *need* anorexia, food, calories because I did not have the time. It was a very natural happening. I did not wake up one day and say – 'Isn't it fantastic!' In the same way as I drifted into it I drifted out of it.

ERIC: You seem to imply that you actually needed to be anorectic?

ANNA: I needed anorexia because life was so awful. It gave me calorie counting, my scales, control of my family – social situations. It would give me lots of things (I would avoid parties, boyfriends, meeting people). Then as life slotted into place these things came back but I was more able to handle them.

ERIC: What helped you to be more able to handle these things?

ANNA: Confidence in myself – the ability to know your limitations – that I am not going to climb Everest. Before, I could never fail or do anything badly. If I did something I had to be very good, whereas now I know that I am not going to be top dog – number one. Some things I am quite good at, other things I am not. Basically now I like myself . . . the perfection is not there any more.

ERIC: Why do you think perfection was so important to you?

ANNA: It was this failure thing . . . there are only two sides to an anorectic – you are either perfect or a failure. My personality was very black and white.

---

*A self-help organisation; now superseded by The Eating Disorders Association, Sackville Place, 44–48 Magdelen Street, Norwich NR3 1JE, England. Telephone UK +(603)621414.

People either loved me or hated me. There was nothing in between those – that is how I viewed life.

ERIC: Do you think you approached things like that even before the anorexia nervosa developed?

ANNA: No, I was very wishy-washy . . . a very nice girl, not particularly attractive, not a sparkling personality. I was just good plain Anna – just an ordinary child.

ERIC: So, you had not always been like that?

ANNA: No, all that was very much as the anorexia came out. Before, my ideal was very much to please my father – to be a good girl. But it was not *drastically* important. I mean *food* was not drastically important. I did not like myself as a child. I did not think I had many friends. I never thought people liked me. I liked them but it never occurred to me that they might like me.

ERIC: So the control was part of a broader attempt to find some sort of . . . *(Anna answered before I completed the question)*

ANNA: Yeah. You see to me life was very mediocre. I never managed to do anything outstanding. My father was the only outstanding person. When I discovered the thing called diet – all of a sudden I was a top dog in my own little world – it was fantastic! . . . because everything else was just Anna being plain Anna, but here in my little world I could do all the things no-one else could do.

ERIC: You say when I found it – it is almost as if you feel that was an accident, that you happened to find it.

ANNA: I think it *was* actually, because when I put myself on this grapefruit diet I never perceived what was going to happen . . . I suppose really as an ex-anorectic, the most important thing to me was that control. I really think that is very much a key part of the whole thing of anorexia . . . everything was out of control and that little bit inside you says, 'I am in control . . . I can do it for myself'. If no-one else likes you . . . In my own world I was in total control of my food situation . . . my parents . . . that was the feeling that most kept me going.

ERIC: And maybe now control is not so crucial?

ANNA: You see, before I did not like myself, so what people thought and said was very important to me. Now . . . it does not matter, because fundamentally I quite like myself and how people see me is hopefully nice and, if it is not . . . well not everyone gets on with everyone.

Comments

What struck me about this interview at the time was how clearly Anna had formulated a meaningful view of her experience and how she had changed. Whether she is right or wrong is less important than the fact she seems to have a reasonably workable theory about herself and her troubled past. In considering recovery, it is quite clear that Anna found it necessary to talk about her previous difficulties and we might summarise her construing as contrasting illness versus recovery. The main constructions seem to be:

Illness		*Recovery*
Wanting to control my parents	versus	Able to accept them as they are
Having to always please my father	versus	Not always having to please father
Not free to be myself because of parents	versus	Can be myself in spite of parents
Not liking myself	versus	Liking myself
Seeking perfection	versus	Can accept my limitations
Black and white approach	versus	Can tolerate in-betweens
Crucial what people think of me	versus	Tolerate people not liking me
Need to control	versus	Don't always need everything kept under control

I felt that control was the central issue. In the context of increasing diffi-culty in making sense of social feedback about herself, Anna seemed to have constricted her world so that she was able to extort evidence that she was 'top dog' within the world of her weight control. Although being hopelessly ill-equipped to deal with the world of people, she seems to have reached the point where she was open to change. Her therapist appears to have provided a relatively safe context within which she could gradually begin to reconstrue. Her relationship with him seems to have been crucial in providing a platform from which she was able to begin social experimen-tation and question her previous assumptions. Her recovery was a bumpy road, but gradually life started 'slotting into place'. While there were still difficulties in her life, she no longer came over as 'stuck'. Her thinking was not characterised by complaints, confusion or circularity, but seemed to be taking her forward in the continuing journey of life.

Anna highlighted several things for me:

- that it was possible to relate to someone with anorexia nervosa as a person, without getting hopelessly bogged down in issues of weight and eating
- that such a person could loosen their grip on weight and eating as a prime means of control
- that behind the superficial features of anorexia nervosa, there often lies considerable fragility.

Life for Anna after anorexia nervosa was clearly no easy path and some of her old constructions, such as the need for approval, could not easily be abandoned. Anorexia nervosa is no trivial matter. But if you take time to get to know and understand the person behind the symptoms, a more fruitful relationship can develop. This is what I am continuing to strive for with all my clients with eating disorders and we will see how this has developed with a number of people with whom I have had the privilege to share something of their lives.

Postscript

It was 12 years after this case study was completed, that I was writing this book. I heard indirectly that Anna was now 39, married with three children, eating regularly and no longer watching her weight. I managed to get in contact again by phone and Anna seemed pleased to hear from me and was happy for me to include her as a case example. Her initial message was a positive one, stressing how good her family life was and that she wanted to say that 'there *is* life after anorexia'. She did, however, want to see this chapter, which I sent her and we did talk about the possibility of meeting up rather than her *writing* something for the book. Not unexpectedly, receiving the chapter stirred her up and she soon rung me up to talk about it. She was very keen for a 'reunion' and we met up about ten days later. I think we both found this to be a valuable experience, both from the point of view of checking out where she was, but more importantly to explore the issues raised by my chapter. I cannot do full justice to this interview, but I will try to pick out what seemed to be the main themes and issues.

What struck me most was the sense of continuity. Talking to Anna again was very easy. We soon picked up the threads and our session felt full of warmth, feeling and humour. I did not attempt to ask her detailed questions about weight and eating, but they did emerge within the interview. Thus I did not ask her about her weight, but she looked slim (I would guess around 7 st. 7 lb – 105 lb) and later mentioned that she would not allow herself to go beyond 8 st. (112 lb), which it will be recalled was her pre-anorectic weight. Anna began by describing her reaction to the chapter:

ANNA: The underlying question within me of how far have I moved on? . . . that terrible feeling of where I was now, trying to place myself . . . it left me very unsettled. I think it's not the unsettled food feelings, but it's certainly the unsettled emotional feelings.

ERIC: What does that focus on?

ANNA: Certainly the highs and lows . . . it's funny because you were talking about this cry for pain when I can't talk things out and I'm still exactly the same. I still find it very, very difficult to say I'm hurting inside . . . And in a way now the difficult thing is that I can't use my weight or the food thing. I'm not saying I'm not conscious of what I look like, but I don't think more than most girls/women.

ERIC: That's sometimes a bit disconcerting isn't it, when we see bits from our past which we thought we had moved on from and they sort of pop up again for one reason or another . . . I'm not surprised that effect was there.

ANNA: Really?

ERIC: I think there is a lot of continuity with us as people, there are lots of things we carry forward through our life, themes, our personality, our way of thinking, our way of relating . . .

ANNA: Yeah, it's this feeling of thinking I had moved forward so much, but I hadn't . . . obviously I have in terms of the outer side of me, like all that's physically showing . . . the children, the husband, the really nice house. But deep down inside there's all the other emotional things, which you wonder, is that always going to be me? . . . Will I always have these self-doubts?

ERIC: . . . I expect there to be a lot of doubts in people, uncertainties, although on the surface we might act as if things are OK . . . neatly sort of packaged together and so on . . . It seems to me a healthy thing to have some doubts . . . I think the fact that you have moved on from the food thing doesn't stop you from having areas of your life you feel vulnerable about.

ANNA: . . . In a way that's quite reassuring because maybe that's the bit of me that's striving to be Miss Perfect still and one has to turn round and say it actually is all right to have all these doubts and someone to say to you it's all right . . . and that it's normal . . . You can lose sight of what is normal . . . I'm obviously someone who still has this feeling of needing to be in control. And it was that which allowed me to be four and a half stone *[63 lb]* or whatever. So although that's gone, that feeling of being in control hasn't gone.

ERIC: I think we need control, perhaps some people deal with it differently from others . . . but clearly like anything you can go to extremes can't you?

ANNA: Oh yes, my anorexia was my extreme, my life now is very much middle of the road, but just being aware of knowing when to put the brakes on and allowing spontaneity and just rolling with it . . . I can so easily see now why I was anorectic. It couldn't have been drink, that would have been letting rip on something, but something I had to abstain from and do without and deprive myself of and that feeling of being so hungry but knowing I'm in control was . . . You know intellectually you'd never want to go down that road again. It was too painful and nothing was achieved from it. But it was your own little statement, your own way of saying to someone I'm unhappy when you can't verbalise it . . . It's just a road you physically go down, because now I am hungry and you just can't deny those feelings any more. But sometimes it has the appeal of 'help, notice me' that you just can't use any more.

ERIC: So now you can look back and see it's handy to have that physical demonstration of things.

ANNA: It was for when it happened, because I was so screwed up that I had to go through it. You have to ask the question: Am I justifying eighteen years out of my life of having anorexia? . . . but I would never have got here, as self-doubting and questioning, as insecure as I am. I would never have got to this stage if I'd not had anorexia

ERIC: So how do you think the anorexia thing helped you to get to this stage?

ANNA: It focused on me as a person. It made me look at moving on from where I was 21, 22 so on, to help me move along, move me from my parents, see them in perspective, see myself a bit more in perspective. . . . The question we then get to is, where we started from, is have I done my growing now, have I got to accept the way I am or have I got more to go?

ERIC: What do *you* think?

ANNA: *(pause, sigh)* I suspect there's a little more to come. I think I've got to accept me a bit more as I am . . . I think I've still got to let go of being a perfect person.

We spent some time further elaborating on issues surrounding coming to terms with her imperfections, which she had been reminded about by my chapter. Later on we moved on to the subject of letting go of anorexia nervosa and treatment.

ANNA: It reminds me I've also stopped smoking and I had to . . . it was almost like a friend . . . a cigarette was a friend and not eating was like a friend . . . It's like leaving a friend that you're completely addicted to seeing and completely part of your day and part of that regime. That's the hard thing of letting go of your regime which you feel safe in. I know you're right that the only way you can do that is by giving you lots of other opportunities. And I think probably with me, um, it was probably seeing my world open up made me not want that friend any more.

ERIC: So how do you see the role of treatment, experts in this process of moving on from it?

ANNA: Well I think certainly the way they did it in hospital was totally wrong. The emphasis they put on weight . . . I think it has to come from the psychological side. I don't see how else it can do because what you're talking about is someone replacing one thing with another. And until you realise what's behind it all, then you're never going to move forward.

ERIC: You said earlier on that you were still worried about weight to a certain extent, can you say a little bit more about that, how you see that?

ANNA: I would always see myself as big. I know intellectually I'm not, but I would always see myself as having a big stomach. I can't help it, um, and Jonathan *[her husband]* would say that I eat with control. I'm not so sure that I do, I just don't think I have a huge appetite. I still rigidly stick to eating three meals a day. . . . It is important to me what I look like. I don't think there's anything wrong with that. I just don't want to be a fat person . . .

ERIC: So still an important part of you is what you look like, isn't it? And you are quite clear you don't want to be seen to be fat and in a way you've got a degree of distortion of your view of yourself.

ANNA: Oh yes and I don't know if that's true of other anorectics or people who have had anorexia?

ERIC: . . . I think it's common that people who've had anorectic problems are left with that kind of concern with their bodies. It's difficult to let go quickly, but again it's a matter of how in perspective that is, whether controlling your weight is the be-all and end-all of everything at the centre of your life, ruling your life or whether it's *part* of your life.

ANNA: I think for me now it's *part* of life because now I've got other things to replace it. I have the work, the children, the husband, the love that comes from all that, but it is *part* of my life, whereas perhaps the reason why I was anorectic was that it was *all* my life . . . now it's *part* of me and it's not out of control, it's not destructive and it's seen in perspective against everything else. I mean the most important thing in my life is Jonathan and the children and nothing would ever come between that . . . the weight thing is *part* of me, but it's not a big issue, most of the time (99.9% of the time) and I could never let it get out of control.

This was not the end of the interview, but it seems like a suitable place to end this chapter. Although Anna now seems to have a very full life 'beyond anorexia' and has moved on a lot, she is all too aware of her emotional vulnerabilities, her perfectionist tendencies and her need to control her weight. Maybe she will never completely lose these particular 'friends', but Anna and her family seem to have grown and hopefully will continue to do so.

8 Jenny

Jenny was referred to me when she was 20. She had approached her family doctor for help, having heard about me from a friend who was a former client. The referral letter described a 'long, unhappy history of bulimia' and it seemed from the first letter that the family situation was of some relevance. The doctor's first contact with Jenny had been over three years ago, when her parents complained that they thought she was stealing food, but could not confront her. Jenny's doctor was able to help bring out the family problems and her compulsive eating, but the problems recurred and she was eventually referred for psychiatric help. This was not successful and about a year later, after further pressures at home, she was referred to me.

Treatment

At our first meeting, Jenny described her main problem as about finding it 'very difficult to communicate' and that she would like to do so. She added that she got 'very stressed up', which both caused eczema and made her eat a lot. When under stress, she found it hard to admit it, even to people she was close to, such as her mother and her fiancé, Mark. Jenny's presenting complaint provides some encouragement for the would-be construct therapist. She had moved beyond a primary focus on eating or weight, which characterises many eating disorder clients. Her focus on communication is psychological in nature and her reference to needing to learn how to communicate, hints at an anticipation that change is possible.

Having heard her initial formulation, I enquired about when the problems had started. She was a bit hazy about this, but thought it was when her aunt died, when she was 16. They had been very close and her death left a 'big hole'. The effect of this was that Jenny 'just closed up' and was unable to communicate the considerable upset she was experiencing inside. She felt unhappy and irritable and started to have eating binges. Although about four years had passed since her aunt's death and Jenny had now accepted the loss, the problems in communication had persisted and she felt they might even have become worse. Jenny's upset at this bereavement is quite understandable, but the persistence of communication difficulties suggests that deeper problems may have prevented her from moving on. A taste of this is provided by her description of her family relationships. Her mother was described as a 'controlled anorexic', whom Jenny 'thought the world of ... *but*'. Jenny said that she and her mother saw the worst in each other, but that 'ideally I'd like to be as slim as her'. Her relationship with her father was described as different from that with her mother: 'I don't talk to him in the same way ... I don't think he really understands.' She broke into tears when I asked her whether her family was a happy one. She went on to say that Mum and Dad were drifting apart and she wondered whether she was trying to bring them together. Although she felt Mum admitted a problem, Dad was described as shelving it, because he found it difficult to admit things were less than perfect. Jenny implied some personal responsibility for this state of affairs, feeling that she'd caused them a lot of arguments and had not been easy to live with.

In spite of the above difficulties, Jenny was not without personal resources, having a fiancé, close friends and a wide range of interests. Her self-image, however, was not too positive, describing herself as mixed up and not liking herself. 'I come across as very confident, but I'm not inside.' Her motivation for change was quite strong and she stressed that it was *her* decision, whereas previously when referred for help she hadn't wanted to talk. She wanted help from me, because she had heard from a friend that I was 'easy to talk to'. Thus in spite of her difficulty in communication, she was prepared to work at it and face overcoming this difficulty. Her expectation from help was to be able to accept herself as she was – to be able to say 'sod everyone else' and to become more confident and able to talk without being afraid.

After this initial interview, I asked her to complete a battery of questionnaires and invited her back for a second interview before making any commitment to treatment. She agreed to return the following week, at which time she completed the systematic assessment of self–other construing I have devised, known as SELF-GRID (Button, 1988a). A simplified section of the grid focusing on self-construing is shown in Figure 8.1.

It can be seen that her unipolar constructs are predominantly 'negative' (defined by position on ideal self), outnumbering 'positive' ones by two to one. This is consistent with my findings (Button, 1990b) of a negative emphasis to construing in psychological disorder in general. The distance

	Always							Never
'Positive' constructs								
Countrified	0/X	–	–	–	–	–	–	–
Patient	0	–	–	–	X	–	–	–
Calm and steady	0	–	–	–	X	–	–	–
Skinny	–	–	0	–	–	–	X	–
Easy to talk of feelings	–	–	0	–	–	–	X	–
Confident	–	–	0	–	–	–	X	–
'Negative' constructs								
Town person	–	–	–	–	–	–	–	0/X
Intolerant	–	–	–	–	–	–	–	0/X
Pushy	–	–	–	–	–	–	–	0/X
Shy	–	–	–	–	X	–	0	–
Gullible	–	–	–	–	X	–	0	–
Fiery	–	–	–	–	X	–	–	0
Resent parents	–	–	–	–	X	–	–	0
Tough time at school	–	–	–	X	–	–	–	0
Worry	–	–	X	–	–	–	0	–
Had share of problems	–	–	X	–	–	–	–	0
Hang-up about food	X	–	–	–	–	–	0	–
'Uncertain' constructs								
Perceptive of people	–	–	–	0/X	–	–	–	–

Key: 0 = Me ideally;   X = Me nowadays

Figure 8.1:   Self-construing summary from Jenny's pre-treatment grid

between ratings of self and ideal self gives an idea of where her perceived strengths and weaknesses lie. On the positive side, for example, she is 'countrified' and not a 'town person', as well as not being intolerant or pushy. There are many large discrepancies, however, particularly with regard to 'hang-up about food'. She also emphasises such things as a lack of confidence, lack of ease in talking about feelings, lack of skinniness and worrying. Her initial therapeutic hopefulness, however, is reflected by the fact that 'me in the future' brings her much closer to her 'ideal self'. As far as other elements are concerned, her mother is seen rather negatively, father more favourably and her fiancé and friends are seen very favourably. This well reflects the above interview data, which suggests that much of the locus of her difficulties with people is focused on her mother. Indeed, one might speculate that the nature of the mother–daughter relationship was the key precursor to the disorder. On this front, it is worth mentioning that Jenny was an adopted child.

I gave Jenny some preliminary feedback about assessment. I also outlined my therapeutic approach as not guaranteeing answers or solutions, but as about working together in exploring possible alternatives to her present stance. I asked her whether she would still like to proceed. She had no hesitation and seemed keen to try. We agreed to an initial ten-session contract, to be followed by a review. Although my therapeutic approach is grounded in my theory of deficient person construing, as I have indicated above, I also focus on reconstruction of situations relevant to eating behaviour in similar vein to Coish (1990). Jenny's initial homework was to be aware of the circumstances surrounding her eating behaviour and to consider alternatives. Here follows a brief description of the main themes of each session.

Session 1

We went through her diary and she became quite tearful and distressed at times. She was facing her difficulty in communicating her feelings, but she was clearly concerned at the prospect of 'giving in'. I used support and encouraged her to experiment with communication. In particular, I suggested she focused on whether she was putting herself over to other people. Kelly's concept of sociality is very much at the heart of my therapeutic strategy and I was trying to encourage her to communicate her construing to others.

Session 2

Jenny reported on a positive experience of increased communication. For example, on holiday she had been tense at first, but it improved after she shared her concerns with Mark. Although there was also successful experimentation with asserting herself in various contexts, the superordinate construct of 'giving in versus coping' reared its head again. I made no attempt to challenge this construct, but did raise the possibility of developing others, such as 'accepts limits', which might be used to help avoid getting over-stressed.

Sessions 3 and 4

There was a report of increasing success in speaking up, particularly at college. For example, she had actually argued with someone in a seminar. She was beginning to realise that her theory of being 'trampled all over' by others could be invalidated only by speaking up. Otherwise she would say nothing and get angry. Along with improvement in communication, she had also stopped bingeing.

Session 5

As so often happens, after a period of successful experimentation, she returned with a tale of several negative events. There were a couple of specific negative events, including someone who didn't keep an appointment and in both cases the 'trampled over' construct had been re-awakened. A more serious problem was arising in her relationship with her mother, whom she felt was cutting her off by not communicating. In each case she was encouraged to try to find out more about other people's perspectives, rather than stick with her initial interpretations.

Session 6

She returned happier, having sorted out and reconstrued the specific situations. She had met her parents, however, and received a lot of negative feedback. They seemed to be complaining about her neglect of them and there were strong signs of their discomfort at her growing independence. This caused considerable distress and she reported that she had occasionally gone 'mad' with her eating. She was determined not to be pulled down by it, however, and she was now not bothered about her weight.

Session 7

She had sorted out some things with her parents. There was an 'exchange of views', with Jenny asking to be treated like an adult and her parents requesting that she act like one!

Session 8

Her cat died and we discussed the bereavement experience, which included some useful comparisons with the death of her aunt. Good progress was being made in her eating and her work.

Session 9

Work was going reasonably well, but she was still somewhat troubled by her mother, who occasionally went on about Jenny's weight. Jenny referred to thinking 'I should do something about it'. I raised the question of what she *wanted* to do about it in contrast to what she *ought* to do.

Session 10

The above sessions were spread over about six months and we had come to our review. Jenny said she felt she had progressed a lot in her confidence and ability to stand up for herself. Food was more in the background. In spite of these gains, however, she was still having continued problems with her mother's non-acceptance of her (Jenny's construction), especially with regard to weight. She requested more sessions to see if she could work on it, as it was knocking her confidence.

Further Sessions

Following a few more sessions, Jenny eventually made a breakthrough in her relationship with her mother. They had a very long talk, in which she was able to learn that when her mother was cold to her, it was often because her mother was having difficulty coping with her own problems. This seemed to bring them closer together and brought much greater understanding. We were also able to extend such discovery to other difficult people in her life. By this time she was progressing well, but she still requested seeing me as a 'back stop'. After a couple more spread-out sessions, however, Jenny felt happy to let go of our relationship. As well as the improvements in her family relationships, she was successfully losing weight (in a controlled, sensible way). It was as if, having dealt with the issue of self-acceptance, she was now able to tackle her weight, perhaps without encountering the construction of 'giving in'. After 17 sessions spread over ten months, she was now ready to let go of treatment, being quite happy with the way things were going and having a positive attitude to the future. Her improvement was also reflected in formal assessments, with normal scores on all questionnaires, such as the Eating Disorders Inventory (Garner, Olmsted and Polivy, 1983).

A repeat of the SELF-GRID (Figure 8.2) also showed dramatic strengthening of her self-image, with far less discrepancy between self and ideal self. On my measure of self-esteem, she now had a mean discrepancy of 0.9, typical of psychologically healthy subjects (Button, 1993) and quite different from her pre-treatment mean of 2.7. Although not illustrated here, there was also a fair amount of change in her construing of others. We can also see that she added two new 'positive' constructs, namely 'respects other's feelings' and 'understand people from their point of view', both of which suggest increased sociality. In reflecting on the process of therapy, it is worth noting how her progress waxed and waned. It does take time to reconstrue and it would appear that change in construing of herself in relation to family and mother, in particular, was necessary before she was

'Positive' constructs	Always							Never
Countrified	–	O/X	–	–	–	–	–	–
Patient	–	–	O/X	–	–	–	–	–
Calm and steady	0	–	X	–	–	–	–	–
Skinny	–	–	0	–	X	–	–	–
Easy to talk of feelings	–	O/X	–	–	–	–	–	–
Confident	–	O/X	–	–	–	–	–	–
Respects others feelings	0	–	X	–	–	–	–	–
Understand people from their point of view	0	–	X	–	–	–	–	–
'Negative' constructs								
Town person	–	–	–	–	X	0	–	–
Intolerant	–	–	–	–	–	–	O/X	–
Pushy	–	–	–	–	–	–	O/X	–
Shy	–	–	–	–	–	–	X	0
Gullible	–	–	–	–	–	O/X	–	–
Fiery	–	–	–	–	–	–	X	0
Resent parents	–	–	–	–	–	–	X	0
Tough time at school	–	–	–	–	–	–	–	O/X
Worry	–	–	–	–	X	–	0	–
Had share of problems	–	–	–	–	–	X	–	0
Hang-up about food	–	–	–	–	–	–	X	0
'Uncertain' constructs								
Perceptive of people	–	–	–	0	X	–	–	–

Key: 0 = Me ideally;   X = Me nowadays

Figure 8.2:   Self-construing summary from Jenny's post-treatment grid

able to more fully let go of her preoccupation with weight. Jenny's verdict was that the most important therapeutic factor was my approach of helping her to talk things through and discover solutions to problems. From my standpoint, I see no particular formula, just a matter of working together towards greater understanding of herself in relation to others and working hard and patiently to find alternative ways ahead. I was helped by Jenny's obvious potential to relate to people and her ability to comfortably work with me. It doesn't always work so smoothly!

Note: My account of Jenny is based upon a case example included in my chapter in *Advances in Personal Construct Psychology* (vol. 2). Edited by R.A. Neimeyer and G.J. Neimeyer. (1992) Greenwich, CT: JAI Press.

9   Angela

I came to meet Angela in circumstances different from many of my clients. She had heard about me from the Anorexic Family Aid Centre (a self-help organisation concerned with eating disorders) and she wrote to me with a detailed letter requesting my help. Angela communicated a lot to me in writing. I think the following extracts from her letter give quite a good introduction to the themes and style she adopted.

I am a twenty-four-year-old student and suffer from bulimia nervosa and have done for over two years. I have attempted on numerous occasions to bring an end to this disease, but have inevitably failed. At times I have felt absolutely desperate. I am constantly forcing myself to be sick and often take packets of laxatives; last year I managed to prevent myself from doing so up to three or four days at a time but now I cannot restrain myself from taking one or the other routes to rid myself of excess food at least once each day. I desperately want to stop myself because it is ruining my whole life; my college work is suffering due to the amount of time I spend in the bathroom. I always feel exhausted and depressed. My relationships with others also suffer. I find I am forced to treat people badly so that they will leave in order that I can be sick or before I am forced to spend hours in the toilet. I am unable to socialise properly for the same reasons. My greatest regret is that I would dearly love to be able to participate in a close relationship with a boyfriend but as soon as it becomes intimate I must back off before he discovers how fat I am and hates me for it. The only time I can really be happy, can really be myself, is when I am working. I work behind a bar and therefore the bar and the excuse that I am working provide an excellent barrier for me and I am able to be myself, to feel confident and even to thoroughly enjoy myself. I find that in this situation I am extremely popular and everyone seems to love talking to me, and I have made many friends in this way but it is when they want to become more than just friends that I begin to feel intense fear and put up my defences.

I have never told anyone about my problems because I am sure they will be as disgusted with me as I am with myself. However, at the beginning of the year

> I went to see my doctor and explained to him what I was doing. The problem is that the doctor refused to acknowledge that I had bulimia – he told me I was depressed because I hated myself and had suppressed all my anger in the past and offered to put me on antidepressants, which I felt was pretty pointless if I was only going to be sick anyway. . . . As I said, I cannot bare to tell anyone else, I could not put myself through that again but I feel desperate and I need help. I cannot cope with the pressure of bulimia. . . . I know I must get help from somewhere. . . . Please help me if you can.

If there was any doubt about the degree of desperation expressed in this letter, it was reinforced by a further letter after I had sent her a letter of appointment. In this, she referred to being encouraged by my letter, but was also extremely worried by 'the change in my personality and the feeling that I can't be bothered with anything any more'. She went on to say that she was feeling very depressed and that everything was an effort and she felt she was going backwards. I think these early feelings conveyed something of the person I was to meet: someone with very strong feelings and a great deal of volatility; a sense of frequent desperation and crisis; and a willingness to work and explore her problems psychologically.

Treatment

At our first face-to-face meeting she described her main problem as that she didn't like herself, mainly physically. She wondered why and thought it was stupid because she got on well with people. It felt like there was something inside her bothering her. She couldn't put her finger on it, but thought it may have to do with her parents; her Dad had been quite violent and that's why she left home. Angela had felt close to her father when young, but at around the age of 13, he had become violent when drunk, and as well as hitting her mother he had sometimes hit Angela. She was so frightened of him that she had three bolts on her door. She said that it was around this time that she started eating a lot and got very fat. As a young child she had been skinny and wouldn't eat and remembered being taken to the doctor about it. Her teenage years were thus very unhappy and she recalled being very fat and being treated very badly because of it. She said that as she grew older she began to hate herself and until she was 20 never left her room unless she had to go to work because she was so ashamed of people seeing her. When she was 21 she went on a diet and went from 12 st. 10 lb (178 lb) down to 8 st. 2 lb (114 lb). She said she was very pleased but was left with an unsightly bulge that she needed to get rid of and turned to 'bulimia', namely vomiting and using laxatives. She felt that at first she was in control and indeed around that time for the first time in her life she felt confident enough to enjoy herself, having started college and met lots of friends through a bar job. But increasingly she began to feel that food was controlling her and she was hating herself and avoiding going out again.

In the context of this disturbed past, it was clear that Angela had gradually developed a quite typical and severe pattern of bulimia nervosa. As we have seen, she binge-ate several times a day on average and regularly induced vomiting. Her weight at presentation was within normal limits (9 st. 7lb – 133 lb – at a height of 5'7"), but she was constantly struggling to prevent it from going up and during the past few years her weight had been very volatile. She put her ideal at around 8 st. 9 lb (121 lb). The extent of her eating disorder was confirmed by her high score on the Eating Attitudes Test (80) and she scored highly on several scales of the Eating Disorders Inventory (drive for thinness, bulimia, ineffectiveness, interpersonal distrust, and interoceptive awareness).

In spite of all her difficulties, Angela had been able to make some progress in her life. Having not achieved much at school and left home rather precipitously, in the last few years she had been putting a lot of effort into improving her education. Following a lot of hard work she had got herself on to a degree course, which seemed to be offering her a more creative outlet for herself. Her intelligence came over in our first meetings. She was keen for help. She wanted to change the way she felt about her body and hoped that talking to somebody could help her sort herself out.

Angela was one of the first people with an eating disorder on whom I applied SELF-GRID (Button, 1988a) as an assessment tool, which we completed at our second meeting. She seemed to enjoy this task and had no difficulty in producing quite a large number of constructs. In fact, the following week she spontaneously produced a further set of constructs that she had elicited and written down. This was an early indication of her willingness to grapple with the business of construing people. The most striking thing about the elicitation of constructs was the virtual complete contrast she was making with her mother. On eight of the nine constructs that emerged when comparing herself with her mother, she saw a difference. In all cases her mother was construed unfavourably (e.g. doesn't show emotions, critical, doesn't listen). For only one construct did she construe similarity, namely 'fat'. The position with regard to her father, however, was reversed, with predominant similarity between him and Angela. With the other elements, however, there was a more mixed picture of both similarities and differences, perhaps reflecting a more balanced form of construing in contrast to the more polarised construing of her parents.

When it came to completing the grid it was striking how extreme Angela was in her construing of herself. This in itself has not proved to be specifically pathological in my research, but it was perhaps characteristic of her desire to be sure about things. Her construing of the other people in the grid, however, was more moderate. In Figure 9.1 I illustrate her evaluation

	Always							Never
'Positive' constructs								
Concerned about learning	O/X	–	–	–	–	–	–	–
Friendly	O/X	–	–	–	–	–	–	–
Care about hurting others	O/X	–	–	–	–	–	–	–
Tell the truth	O/X	–	–	–	–	–	–	–
Understanding	0	X	–	–	–	–	–	–
Accept others	0	X	–	–	–	–	–	–
Listen to others	0	X	–	–	–	–	–	–
Sense of humour	0	X	–	–	–	–	–	–
Caring	0	X	–	–	–	–	–	–
Can be themselves	0	X	–	–	–	–	–	–
Show emotions	–	0	X	–	–	–	–	–
Intelligent	0	–	X	–	–	–	–	–
Interest in world affairs	0	–	–	X	–	–	–	–
'Negative' constructs								
Concern about material things	–	–	–	–	–	–	O/X	–
Resent people doing better	–	–	–	–	–	–	–	O/X
Say what people want to hear	–	–	–	–	–	–	O/X	–
Difficulty with people	–	–	–	–	–	–	X	0
Use people to get what want	–	–	–	–	–	–	X	0
Critical of others	–	–	–	–	–	X	–	0
Just switch off	–	–	–	–	–	X	–	0
Fat	–	–	–	X	–	–	–	0
Lack confidence	–	X	–	–	–	0	–	–
Try hard to seem confident	–	–	X	–	–	–	0	–
Negative about life	–	–	X	–	–	–	–	0
'Uncertain' constructs								
Sensitive	–	X	–	0	–	–	–	–

Key: 0 = Me ideally; X = Me nowadays

Figure 9.1: Self-construing summary from Angela's pre-treatment grid

of herself in her own terms. This shows a predominantly positive evaluation. For her 'positive' constructs, for example, there is very little discrepancy between present self and ideal self. She emphasises many positive qualities, of which concern with learning, being friendly, caring about hurting others and telling the truth are her greatest perceived strengths.

With regard to 'negative' constructs, however, the position is more mixed. On the one hand, she is pleased that she is not concerned about material things and not resentful of others doing well. But there are also quite large discrepancies, indicating negativity about life, lack of confidence, trying hard to come across as confident, and fat. There is only one construct that I categorise as 'uncertain'. This is 'sensitive', a construct that she seems to see as prominent in her and she would like to be less so. Her rating of her ideal as 'often', however, suggests that there are also advantages for her in being sensitive.

The overall mean rating discrepancy between self and ideal self of 1.5 points is somewhat on the borders between what is typical of healthy people and the psychologically disturbed. The corresponding figure for her self when younger, however, was 3.24, indicating that she sees herself as having improved a lot. On several constructs, there were large changes from younger to nowadays. Most notably, she was finding it much easier to be herself and to get on with people. While there are several areas of negative construction about herself, I regarded the large number of positive constructions of her persent self as an encouraging sign that she had something positive to build upon. Angela was aware of her emphasis on positive characteristics and she commented after doing the grid that maybe she was conning herself. She also felt bad about criticising others, saying 'I shouldn't, should I?'

A principal components analysis was also carried out and the first two components are displayed in Figure 9.2. The main contrast is represented by the first component along the vertical axis. The main elements representing this contrast are her ideal self versus mother, in particular, but also father and several other people. Broadly speaking she is seeing recent and future self at the positive end. The main positive constructs are: friendly,

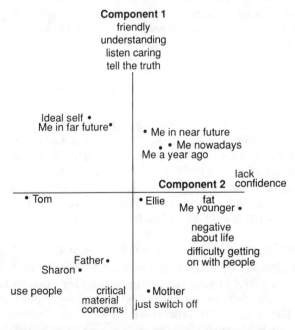

Figure 9.2: Plot of elements in construct space from Angela's pre-treatment grid

understanding, listen to others, caring, and tell the truth. At the negative end we see: use people, concerned with material things, critical of others, and 'just switch off'. We can see that Angela's construing of self when younger is also towards the negative end, so that she sees herself as having improved on this dimension. The second (horizontal) component mainly contrasts herself when younger with Tom, her 'most liked person'. This component is rather lopsided and negative in definition, focusing on younger self, which lacks confidence, is fat, negative about life and finds it difficult getting on with people. Not surprisingly, her ideal self is at the opposite end, perhaps implicitly referring to confidence etc. But at that end, we also see Sharon, her least liked person, and we could speculate that there might be some risk of Angela taking on board some of Sharon's characteristics, such as use people. Such combining of confidence with uncaring qualities is not an uncommon dilemma in clients.

After carrying out this preliminary assessment, I presented my view that her eating disorder seemed to have arisen as an attempt to deal with issues arising from her relationship with her parents, but that subsequently her eating behaviour had affected her relationships with other people. I suggested that psychological help would need to tackle both the relationship issues, but also her eating, particularly in the beginning. She accepted this idea, but was clearly quite emotionally volatile and upset inside. She accepted an initial contract of ten sessions. We agreed to begin by aiming for regular meals.

Session 1

We began by examining her diary. The day after coming to see me she had got up determined to be 'good', because she knew she was getting help and felt she owed it to me to make a real effort. She consequently ate proper meals and resisted the urge to binge by making herself busy and talking to people at work. She even managed to have a couple of apples as a snack because she felt 'peckish', but didn't mind. At the end of the day, she felt really pleased with herself and felt it had been a really good day.

Not uncharacteristically, however, this was not to last. The next day started well, but in the afternoon she went to her sister's and she had bought Angela a box of sweets from holidays. Her other sister was also there and she said that both of them sat and talked continuously about food. She had wanted to talk about other 'more important things' because she wasn't there for long, but she felt they didn't seem interested. Consequently, she felt 'frustrated, upset, disappointed, alone' and once again binge-ate and vomited afterwards, the end result being a considerable feeling of guilt. These kinds of unpleasant feelings seemed to carry on for the rest of the week and she binged, vomited/ purged on every subsequent day. By the end of the week she recorded in her diary feeling a failure and not being able to be bothered to try to make the effort any more.

It seemed that the trip to her sister's had been the turning point and this formed the first detailed therapeutic focus. We examined this occasion in some detail. She had gone to see her sister Ellie, who knew about Angela's problems and whom she got on with quite well. Also present, however, was Ellie's husband who she said viewed Angela as a bad influence on his wife and he was inclined to be argumentative and tried to wind people up. Also present was her younger sister Rita, whom Angela described as very concerned with her own image. It seemed in retrospect that Angela had not anticipated Ellie's reaction at this visit. Angela had been keen to tell Ellie about her visit to see me, but she felt that Ellie did not want to know, that they were laughing at her and did not want her to be there. She now regretted telling her about it. The predominant construction was of being 'let down' (by Ellie). Such failed anticipation of people is a common precipitant of negative feelings and binge-eating. My contribution was to try to explore with her a little more about the context she found herself in that day. She had come with a particular expectation, but how were the other people viewing the situation? It seemed possible that the context of being with her sister and husband had modified Ellie's behaviour and she may have been unable to focus on Angela's concerns. I therefore suggested that her main task for the week was to try to put right the communication with Ellie. I also suggested she made notes about positive and negative thoughts and feelings that can affect eating behaviour.

Session 2

During the week she had heard from Ellie, who had apologised for not being able to talk properly the previous week and they subsequently met and had a good talk. She realised from this that she was too ready to think that she had done something wrong and blame herself. I pressed home the principle that when people don't behave as we expect, we need to try to consider how the other person may be construing the situation – that other people may have their own agenda, which doesn't necessarily complement our own.

Her week had been generally much more positive, having had three binge-free days. She reported on several positive events, all of which involved positive communications with other people. On the negative side, however, she found being taken notice of difficult – people getting too close. She felt that people did not know the 'real me'. This was particularly difficult with her own age group. Out of this, I raised the idea of different selves. It seemed to me that there was, for example, her younger self, when she was hidden away from the world. Then there came her self at the pub, which had formed a very important role in helping her to move out of the home situation. And now there was her self at college, which although promising, was perhaps less certain and when faced with difficulties, she was inclined to turn back to the earlier safer selves. In summarising this session, Angela felt that it was her feelings that were more important, not food. We decided to stop the eating record, but that she would make notes about her feelings.

Session 3

The previous week had not been particularly good or bad, but Angela was expressing a 'can't be bothered' feeling. There was 'nothing or nobody to do it for' and she couldn't do it herself. She also referred to people judging you because you are fat and not giving you a chance. Maybe this was a sign that she was beginning to confront her need for more intimate relationships, something which at assessment she had admitted to shying away from. I tried to acknowledge her need for people and suggested that maybe she needed to explore new places and people. She had in fact removed one potential obstacle to this in giving up an early morning job in a baker's shop, which as well as exacerbating the food problems also tired her out, thus reducing her motivation for seeking out people.

Session 4

She had been thinking a lot during the week and felt she was trying to capture her lost youth and wondered whether the people she was mixing with were too young. She felt she needed to mix with people with whom she could both be serious and have fun. We discussed the fact that she was needing to 'move on', but also that this was scary. In particular, this applied to relationships with the opposite sex and she mentioned a young man she liked and that she felt she knew it was leading up to something, but that she knew she would put up a barrier. I suggested that she view it as natural to be nervous in such a situation, particularly since she hadn't had much experience with men. I invited her to consider the developing relationship as something to explore, rather than it being *the one*, which everything depended on getting right. She seemed to be able to make good use of this alternative perspective.

Session 5

Things were going well with this young man, but the issue of being let down was very much to the fore. For example, one night she had expected him to come to the pub, but he hadn't turned up and she binged afterwards. Although she realised the connection and managed to stop this earlier than previously, she realised that being let down was something she had felt a lot in her life, particularly from her father. My approach to this was to acknowledge the feelings that arise, but also to help her try to construe what may be going on in such situations. As with the earlier example of Ellie, I suggested that she needed to try to go beyond her own needs and try to make sense out of other people's needs. In any interaction, I suggested that both parties' constructions need to be considered if one is to make sense of the situation.

Session 6

Immediately as Angela entered my room, her facial expression communicated that she was feeling bogged down again. She was finding it difficult to find alternatives to eating as a way of dealing with feeling let down. She felt that her present situation was exacerbated by feeling tense owing to pressure of college work. In this context, it seemed that she needed a break from her pub work to be able to relax, but she was wary of asking for time off for fear of letting down the manager. Once again, thus, the 'let down' construct was in play, this time the roles being reversed, but the construct was clearly all-important. It seemed that she had created an image of herself to them as always being able to rely on her. We explored this idea in detail and I think it came home to her how entrapping such constructions are.

Session 7

She had asked for a break from work and to her surprise they had not minded. Once again this was used as an example of how we can move on from our sometimes negative anticipations of others. A similar approach was taken during the session to a new issue that was looming in her bar job. There was also concern around, however, about feelings of panic that were at times arising. I put to her the possibility that such an emotional response could reflect the fact that she was moving on from a food response and left in a transitional state without her old prop. She felt that this made sense and we were able to discuss some of the ways we could learn to manage such feelings.

Session 8

The panic feelings seemed to have subsided and she had successfully dealt with another problem at work. Although communicating about the latter had been painful, it took a lot off her mind to resolve it. She felt that she was learning that facing up to things was more constructive than just worrying about it. She was also enjoying things more and learning that people do actually care. On the eating front, she was feeling stronger and gave an example of a friend giving her a bar of chocolate, which she enjoyed and managed to eat without feeling guilty.

Session 9

Angela began by talking of her increased awareness of the importance of friendship, realising that friends were more important than food. Communicating with people seemed to be working better for her than something less social, such as reading.

This led into focusing on a 'let down' example again and this time there was more of an overt expression of feeling angry. This led to a discussion of the way anger was dealt with in her family. At one extreme, her mother was regularly angry, whereas her father was angry only if he'd had drink. This led to a fruitful examination of different ways of dealing with anger and I suggested to her that the earlier communication of concerns might help to prevent strong feelings of anger building up. All of this seemed to crystallise Angela's concerns about her parents' marriage and her difficulty understanding why they stayed together. She now felt she couldn't face going to their home, which created feelings of guilt. We agreed that it might be necessary to have some space from them while she was actively in the process of trying to deal with the eating problem.

Session 10

The summer vacation had come to an end and she was back at college. This coincided with the time to review the ten sessions we had had. Angela felt she had learned it's not all food and was more aware of issues involving other people. She felt she was coping better with difficult situations and was less negative. But she also thought she needed to build on positive thoughts and start doing things rather than dwelling on things. Perhaps as a reflection of this stance, she expressed a desire to go it alone now. She felt I had done all I could for her and it was now up to her. I did not challenge her intention, but suggested meeting for a follow-up after five weeks, to which she agreed.

Session 11

At this follow-up appointment, the impact of now being at college was very evident. Having put a lot of energies into her pub friends over the summer, she was now feeling that she neither belonged in one camp nor the other. I presented this as very much being a settling in matter, quite typical in my experience among students presenting with psychological problems. I used this session mainly in a consolidatory and supportive way encouraging her and reinforcing some of the notions that perhaps had slipped from her awareness during the gap.

Session 12

We built on the theme of belonging and Angela reflected that perhaps last year (the first year of her three year course) she had tried too hard and hadn't really fitted in. Now, however, she was beginning to realise that certain people were important to her rather than thinking that she had to get on with everyone. She could not see the point in being hypocritical towards people you do not really get on with. At the same time as this improvement on the social scene, her eating was much better and she was allowing herself to eat more without construing it as a binge. But she still had bad days. She felt she could stop it if she set her mind to it and could see a time ahead when she would stop.

Session 13

By joint agreement, we had now moved to meeting much less frequently and perhaps as a reflection of her continued need to communicate with me Angela sent me a letter prior to this session. This was a very person-ally revealing letter and was in many ways generally positive in tone. She referred to a number of positive developments, such as asserting herself more, eating socially and allowing herself to get closer and more affectionate with friends. A most significant development had also oc-curred in that Angela had met a man with whom, to her great surprise, she had immediately felt comfortable and at ease. Quite quickly the relationship had developed into a sexual one and Angela felt for the first time she had been able to feel safe, secure and relaxed in a sexual rela-tionship. The only complication was that this man, Dean, was married (albeit unhappily) and it had crossed her mind that this had attracted her by creating an expectation of eventual rejection and in so doing to avoid the hurt. In the context of all this, she felt much more balanced and stable, but at the same time she was perplexed that her eating had got out of control again.

By the time of seeing her, some of the above had settled somewhat, but I offered a construction of the recent developments as reflecting the difficulty of letting go of the old ways and uncertainties about moving on. We were able to touch on her previous expectation that life without her eating disorder would be perfect – she was beginning to realise that this would not be the case.

Session 14

Once again, prior to our meeting over two months down the line, I received another letter. During the past few months the relationship with Dean had consolidated. For a while, she had almost let him go as he teetered on the brink between her and his wife. But, somewhat at the eleventh hour, she told him (by letter) how much she loved him, what she regarded as the hardest, bravest and most important decision of her life. Since that time, they had been living together and for the first time she had taken the chance to trust and commit herself to a relationship. Since then, her eating had been much more settled, but a new development had now threatened to rock the boat.

She had discovered that her father had heart disease and this had brought her into closer contact with her parents. She felt in considerable conflict about this, given the unhappy experiences she had suffered with her parents. Sometimes she felt like it was all too late for her parents and she really had no control over the situation and should just let things run their course. Although somewhat guilty at feeling this, she felt she now had a real future and she had to put the past behind her. In her words 'I feel like life is just about to begin and am so excited'.

When we met a week or so later, she mainly confirmed these positive feelings and she felt quite happy to continue meeting infrequently. Our next appointment was not due for almost three months, but a few weeks later I received another letter and subsequently a phone call from her friend saying that Angela was in crisis and her friend feared for Angela's safety.

Session 15

I saw Angela as soon as possible because of this crisis situation. She told me that for the past few days she had been quite mixed up and disturbed, wondering if she was going mad. In fact, her thinking was most coherent and she gave me a very clear account of recent developments. The trigger for all of her distress seemed to have been an incident where her father came into the pub where she worked in a drunken state and brought to a head all the confused emotions that surrounded him and her parents in general. She felt that her father was going to die and that this had brought fears of death in her. Unfortunately, her new-found source of stability was absent as Dean was away on a work assignment. The confused feelings that had surrounded the family issues had brought her to the point of unreality.

My approach to this was to allow her plenty of time to express the various feelings and concerns, to help validate her construing of the situation and to reinforce the support that was available to her from her friend in particular. I suggested that for a while she needed to stand back from the family issues and not try to sort them all out at once – this would need time. I also suggested that she should concentrate on getting herself in a relaxed frame of mind to help her face her work, for which she was under pressure with essays. I agreed to write a letter of support to the tutor.

Sessions 16 and 17

These sessions had been arranged quite closely together and somewhat to my relief, Angela had managed to settle down again. She had focused on her immediate priorities and was trying not to think so much about the broader problems. Within a few weeks she was much brighter and back to her old self. She had successfully completed the essays, which had helped to overcome her doubts about her ability. She had also been in reassuring correspondence with Dean, as well as getting closer to several people, including her younger sister, whom previously she assumed was not interested in her. The main theme for Angela now was of having learned to trust people.

Session 18

Progress was maintained, she was feeling very positive about her course and her future. She was also getting on better with her mother and seeing a lot of her sisters. She felt confident to leave meeting for three months.

Session 19

Although she had some ups and downs, she was generally functioning well and she felt she had got over the eating problem. She felt I had helped her

	Always							Never
'Positive' constructs								
Concerned about learning	O/X	–	–	–	–	–	–	–
Show emotions	O/X	–	–	–	–	–	–	–
Care about hurting others	O/X	–	–	–	–	–	–	–
Tell the truth	O/X	–	–	–	–	–	–	–
Understanding	O/X	–	–	–	–	–	–	–
Caring	O/X	–	–	–	–	–	–	–
Listen to others	O	X	–	–	–	–	–	–
Sense of humour	O	X	–	–	–	–	–	–
Friendly	O	X	–	–	–	–	–	–
Can be themselves	O	X	–	–	–	–	–	–
Accept others	–	O	X	–	–	–	–	–
Intelligent	O	–	X	–	–	–	–	–
Interest in world affairs	O	–	–	X	–	–	–	–
'Negative' constructs								
Say what people want to hear	–	–	–	–	–	–	O/X	–
Concern about material things	–	–	–	–	–	O	X	–
Critical of others	–	–	–	–	–	X	O	–
Just switch off	–	–	–	–	–	–	X	O
Resent people doing better	–	–	–	–	–	–	X	O
Lack confidence	–	–	–	–	–	X	O	–
Difficulty with people	–	–	–	–	–	–	X	O
Use people to get what want	–	–	–	–	–	–	X	O
Negative about life	–	–	–	–	–	X	–	O
Try hard to seem confident	–	–	–	–	X	–	O	–
Fat	–	–	–	–	X	–	–	O
'Uncertain' constructs								
Sensitive	–	X	–	–	O	–	–	–

Key: O = Me ideally;   X = Me nowadays

Figure 9.3:   Self-construing summary from Angela's post-treatment grid

to do that and that now it was time for her to sort out for herself these problems of living. This was the last time I saw Angela and I received no further letters.

Post-treatment assessment

At the time we agreed to part ways the SELF-GRID was repeated, along with other forms of assessment. We can see from the self-esteem profile (Figure 9.3) that she had maintained the high level of proximity for her various 'positive' constructs. In terms of 'negative' constructs, however, she now shows no large discrepancies. In particular, she sees herself as far less lacking in confidence and is also less negative about life in general. There is a moderate discrepancy, however, for the 'uncertain' construct 'sensitive' which she is almost all the time and would like to be only sometimes. The overall effect of this is that the personal construct measure of self-esteem has reduced from the previous score of 1.5 to 1.0, a level that is well within the range typical of psychologically healthy people. I also examined change in terms of the conventional principal components analysis, which showed a very similar structure to pre-treatment, suggesting that fundamental reconstruction had not occurred.

In summary, Angela seemed to have been able to move on some way psychologically and presented a generally favourable view of herself, although her continuing sensitivity may have been the subject of some degree of dilemma and difficulty. Importantly, however, she was no longer bogged down and trying to deal with her vulnerabilities through weight control. The process of treatment was very much a 'bumpy ride' and I suspected that this would be the pattern of Angela's life, at least in the near future, until she could establish greater stability in her relationships with others. But Angela seemed to have the potential to learn and explore psychologically and I felt hopeful that she would find ways of coping with the ups and downs of her life. Her efforts in seeking me out were perhaps an example of what she was capable of. Her approach to her studies was also full of energy and enquiry and it seemed that she had quite a lot of potential to channelise her energies creatively.

Follow-up

It was just over three years later when I contacted Angela in connection with this book. In many respects she had moved on in life and indeed had achieved a lot. She had obtained an upper second honours degree, had completed a course of training in social work and had a job in the child welfare field. There had also been a lot of positive experience of love and affection and making many new friends. But in spite of all this achievement, Angela said that 'I never seem to fully accept that I have been as successful as I should be'. There was a strong sense of wanting to prove something to her parents, but however much she achieved it seemed to mean nothing to them. Although Angela realised she was very different from her family, she wanted to belong and be loved by them, but doubted whether she ever would be. She felt that only when she felt loved by them would she feel worthy of being loved by someone else (I think she meant a man).

So what has happened about the eating disorder? During her social work training she had thoroughly enjoyed herself. Her career seemed like the most important thing and she did not care what she ate or looked like, put a lot of weight on, but did not care. But now she thought:

I've dealt with my professional life . . . and now I feel it's time to deal with my personal life. However, that frightens me. I am terrified of slipping back into the bulimia routine . . . Several times in the past month I have binged – not to the extent that I used to but I have made myself sick . . . I want to do something about the weight, because then I think I could successfully enter a relationship again, but I will not allow myself to get involved until I feel I look good, because unless I do, I feel worthless.

Thus it seemed that during a long period of successfully putting her energies into her education and career, Angela had let go of weight concerns. But now that she was facing the issue of a possible relationship with a man, many of the eating-disordered themes had re-emerged, albeit to a lesser degree. Her score on the Eating Attitudes Test, for example had gone down from 80 to 21. On the Eating Disorders Inventory, her scores on the bulimia, ineffectiveness, interpersonal distrust and interoceptive awareness scales were also now within normal limits. But she still had high scores on the drive for thinness and body dissatisfaction subscales. In terms of more general measures, her score on the SCL90R (global severity index = 1.20) reflects a moderate amount of psychological disturbance, but she shows moderately positive self-esteem on the Rosenberg Self-esteem Scale (score 2).

I invited Angela to write something about the help she had received and these are some excerpts from what she had to say:

At the time I came to you I felt I was the only person in the world to have ever suffered from this and I was so embarrassed and ashamed of myself . . . you were the only person that seemed to make me feel that I was not abnormal in doing what I did . . . I thought and I hoped that one day I would come to you and in one of the sessions you would give me an answer that would make everything clear to me and which would solve my problems for ever. Of course life isn't like that . . . I don't think we ever touched on something important, yet I don't know what that is. I wish I could just be normal and lead a normal life. But does anyone? Does everyone have thoughts, feelings, worries and doubts similar to mine, that they can't understand either? . . . After attending a sexism awareness course I did come away thinking that it's all to do with the stereotypical images of males and females that have existed for so long . . . I know that it is all to do with a sense of self-worth which I was and am struggling to find . . . I think that the only 'normal' relationship I've had was with someone who liked me for what I was. That ended because I tried to be all the things I thought a man wanted me to be . . .

On a positive note, I really do feel that I have progressed as a person and that I am much happier, balanced, stronger and more in control of my life than I was . . . The first step to improving myself and dealing with my problem was coming to see you and being able to discuss my problem with someone who understood . . . I do not worry so much about things now (reading books on stress management has also helped) and I find myself dealing quite well with situations that would have made me fall apart a few years ago . . . I seem to take life in its stride now – I'm in control of it and it's not in control of me. I would say that 75 % of my problem has been dealt with and that I still have a little way to go. I feel that I can see the end of the tunnel now.

Concluding comment

Angela vividly demonstrates how it is possible to move away somewhat from the bulimic pattern and move on in life. But she had still not resolved the difficulties in her family relationships and, perhaps linked to that, relationships with the opposite sex. Faced with these difficulties again, she seemed to be returning to some old constructions about appearance and self-worth. The task of reconstruction is thus not complete, but I hope that she can use her considerable personal resources to eventually grow in her closest of relationships.

10   Helen

Helen was 33 when she was referred to me. She had a long history of anorexia nervosa and had received help off a number of people over the years. Her existing therapist was leaving and I was asked to take over. Thus, an existing experience of treatment had already been established and we were not starting completely from scratch. In retrospect, I think this probably created difficulties for both of us. She had come to have certain expectations of what treatment would involve. My perspective would inevitably be somewhat different from what she had experienced.

Helen's involvement with helping services had already been interrupted. After originally being seen for help when she was 21, she re-referred herself to the psychiatric colleague where I worked some six months before seeing me. When re-presenting, she expressed a desire to talk and had increased recognition that she had a problem. It seemed that a major factor in her seeking help again was that she had been experiencing considerable stress in her job. This had led to a slide in her weight from its previous steady level of around 7 st. (98 lb) down to about 5 st. 4 lb (74 lb). It seemed that she had reached a kind of crisis point that had brought her once again for help.

Her history was of a rather disturbed background in which she had a particularly unhappy experience of her mother. Her experiencing of parenting had been extremely disrupted. It seemed that her mother had great difficulty managing her life and could not cope very well with her children. Helen spent a lot of her childhood with her grandparents, eventually staying with her grandmother. Whereas Helen had positive recollections of her father, her experience of her mother was generally negative. While she described her as being good to the children when little, she never showed affection, for example, she never hugged.

Moreover, things seem to have deteriorated during Helen's adolescence, particularly after her father died. She described days when her mother would not talk and would slam doors. Helen's sister, Kathy, would fight back at her and sometimes get beaten and have things thrown at her. Helen would also sometimes be hit. When looking back on this, she had commented that she did not despise her Mum, but felt that she, like Helen, could not show emotions. Helen's sister Kathy was a major figure in her life, being in many ways a complete contrast. Whereas Helen had been rather quiet and withdrawn, Kathy was a better mixer. Kathy had been in and out of trouble with the police and was a drug abuser. Unlike Helen, she had had many relationships with men, albeit of a rather unstable sort.

It is often difficult to piece together the details of the onset of a disorder, particularly when many years have since passed. Her weight had previously been around 9 st. 7 lb to 10 st. (133–140 lb), which at a height of 5'3" sounds as if she had been somewhat plump. Around the age of 20, however, she went on holiday with some friends and felt the need to get her weight down before going so that she could wear a bikini. Over the next few years, the pattern of anorexia nervosa had set in. Apart from a brief course of psychotherapy from a child psychiatrist when she was 13 for 'nervous tension', it was not until she was 21 that she sought help for the eating disorder. Shortly after being assessed, a period of in-patient treatment was offered and accepted. Her stay in hospital involved fairly traditional treatment and she increased weight from 6 st. 4 lb (88 lb) to 7 st. 7 lb (105 lb) over a period of four months, but then discharged herself against medical advice, having shown very little change in attitude towards food and weight. She was seen a couple of times in the next few months, had predictably lost weight and remained entrenched in the old pattern and dropped out of touch.

In summary, Helen had a troubled past, led a rather withdrawn life without intimate relationships and for some 13 years had been stuck in the life style of anorexia nervosa. While she had received some help, her motivation to change seemed at best ambivalent.

Our first meeting was mainly concerned with discussing her feelings about a change of therapist. She had been apprehensive about meeting me, having anticipated that she would just 'clam up'. In fact, this was not the case and she talked quite freely and she said she felt comfortable with me. I stressed that I had no intention of leaping into any specific therapeutic initiative and that we would need time to get to know each other. After a couple of preliminary meetings, I felt it was time for more formal assessment and we proceeded to elicit her constructs about self and others using SELF-GRID.

Construct elicitation

Self and mother

She began by describing similarities, referring to both herself and her mother belittling themselves, lacking confidence, being insecure and needing someone to depend upon. On the other hand, her mother was very different from herself, using bad language, having a terrible temper, jealous, rowing a lot and violent. She also commented that she thought that her mother would not let her children grow up.

Self and father

She mainly saw similarities. Both she and her father were quiet, wanting an easy life, shutting self off and likeable. But she also saw her father as being different, in being approachable and a good listener. Thus, we see an immediate major contrast in the construing of her parents, with mother predominantly negative and father rather more positively construed.

Self and closest person (grandmother)

Helen chose her grandmother for this role. She began with similarities of being calm and understanding. She also repeated previous constructs of her grandmother also not liking rows. Helen commented that 'funnily enough' she did not see herself as like her grandmother. This is an example of where inviting people to consider similarities and differences can help to question polarisations of people. On the difference side, she saw her grandmother as always having to be right. This irritated Helen, because usually she *was* right!

Self and least liked person (colleague, Glenda)

Helen chose a colleague at work, Glenda. As is often the case with least liked figures, Helen saw all differences. Glenda was cocky, thought she knew everything, noisy, bubbly and two-faced. As if realising some of her dilemmas, Helen commented that she wondered if she would like to be like that herself.

Self and most liked person (colleague, Betty)

Another colleague, Betty, was chosen for this role. Helen saw several similarities: both of them being pleasant, do anything for anybody and interested in caring for people. She also repeated earlier constructs of being a good listener and likeable.

Additional Constructs

I asked Helen if there were any other important characteristics of people she could think of. She added that she liked people who were giving and loyal, just like Betty was. She also asserted about herself, almost as a question, that she was *not* hard, that she *could* feel female and be feminine.

	Always							Never
'Positive' constructs								
Loyal	O/X	–	–	–	–	–	–	–
Likeable	O/X	–	–	–	–	–	–	–
Understanding	X	0	–	–	–	–	–	–
Calm	X	–	0	–	–	–	–	–
Good listener	0	–	X	–	–	–	–	–
Do anything for anybody	X	–	0	–	–	–	–	–
Interest in caring for people	X	–	0	–	–	–	–	–
Giving	X	–	0	–	–	–	–	–
Bubbly	–	–	0	–	–	X	–	–
Pleasant	–	0	–	–	–	–	X	–
Can feel things	–	–	0	–	–	–	–	X
Feminine	–	–	0	–	–	–	–	X
'Negative' constructs								
Uses bad language	–	–	–	–	–	–	–	O/X
Jealous	–	–	–	–	–	–	–	O/X
Rows	–	–	–	–	–	–	–	O/X
Violent	–	–	–	–	–	–	–	O/X
Think they know everything	–	–	–	–	–	–	–	O/X
Two-faced	–	–	–	–	–	–	–	O/X
Cocky	–	–	–	–	–	–	0	X
Noisy	–	–	–	–	–	–	0	X
Terrible temper	–	–	–	–	–	0	X	–
Belittle self	–	–	–	–	X	0	–	–
Always in the right	–	–	–	–	–	0	–	X
Insecure	–	–	–	–	X	–	0	–
Hard	X	–	–	–	–	0	–	–
'Uncertain' constructs								
Need someone to depend on	–	–	–	–	0/X	–	–	–
Approachable	–	–	–	0	–	X	–	–
Want an easy life	–	X	–	–	0	–	–	–
Shut self off	–	X	–	–	0	–	–	–
Confident	–	–	–	–	0	–	–	X
Quiet	X	–	–	–	0	–	–	–

Key: 0 = Me ideally;   X = Me nowadays

Figure 10.1:   Self-construing summary from Helen's pre-treatment grid

Grid analysis

By examining Helen's self-esteem profile (Figure 10.1), we can see that her perceived strengths lie mainly in the absence of a number of negative characteristics, such as never using bad language, being jealous, rowing, being violent, etc. Thus her self-image is substantially defined in terms of what she is not. What she is not are particularly characteristics that she attributes to her mother. But she also shows a number of positive characteristics, such as being loyal, understanding, likeable and calm. Whereas there are quite a number of these strengths, there are also quite a few constructs on which she would like to be quite different. On the positive front, she would like to be more feminine, to feel things more and to be more pleasant and bubbly. Her most prominent 'negative' construct is being 'hard' (by which she meant not showing feelings), which she sees as always applying and she would like it to be only occasionally. The more uncertain or less clear-cut constructs include: needing someone, being approachable, wanting an easy life, shutting self off, being confident and being quiet. Although she would like to see quite a bit of change on some of these constructs, such as becoming less quiet, she clearly does not want to go too far. Overall, this portrays a rather mixed self-esteem, with a fair number of positive and negative features. The mean rating difference of 1.84 reflects this, as well as the fact that there are similar numbers of positive and negative constructs. This suggests to me that outside the predictable world of her eating control, her construction of herself is rather ambiguous.

We can also look at the more complex analysis provided by principal components analysis (Figure 10.2). In terms of the most meaningful first (vertical) component, we can see that virtually all the elements are contrasted with her mother. This includes all her selves and the other people, with the exception of Glenda, the least liked person. At her mother's end the most meaningful constructs are: noisy, use bad language, and violent. At the positive end, the most meaningful constructs are: loyal, understanding, and calm. Thus, on this major dimension, Helen is saying that she prefers to be where she is and that means well away from being like her mother.

On the second (horizontal) component, however, we can see that she is less satisfied, with ideal self being at opposite poles to her recent self. At the preferred end are constructs such as: confident, bubbly and feminine; whereas at the negative end the theme is: shutting self off, belittling self, hard, and insecure. It can be seen that the most extreme person at the positive end is the least-liked person, Glenda. This perhaps highlights a dilemma. If Helen goes too far, for example, in being confident, she risks taking on board the kind of undesirable characteristics she sees in Glenda.

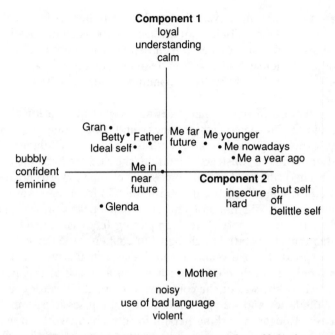

Figure 10.2:   Plot of elements in construct space from Helen's pre-treatment grid

For example, the correlation matrix showed that being confident was associated with being cocky, always in the right and two-faced. Thus, while at one level proclaiming the desire for change, there may be good reasons for not changing unless, of course, reconstruction occurs.

Treatment

Trying to develop a psychotherapeutic relationship with someone suffering from anorexia nervosa is no easy matter, particularly when the disorder is well-established, extending well over a decade in Helen's case. I knew it would not be easy and when one considers the grid results, clearly any kind of open relationship was going to be difficult. As mentioned earlier, I had made it clear to Helen that I had no intention of diving into a therapeutic agenda and we would take time together to work towards establishing a relationship. Our initial sessions were very much exploratory in nature and quite broad-ranging. Two major focuses were her work and her relationship with her grandmother, these being in effect the major elements of her life. At one point she commented that perhaps she uses work as a way of escaping – a routine. Moreover, she would isolate herself from colleagues and we explored the possibility that this lack of open communicating might be contributing to some of her difficulties at work. With regard to her grandmother, Helen would take her feelings out on her, again perhaps being indicative of her difficulty in communicating concerns in the work situation.

Another feature of our earlier meetings was of quite a lot of ups and downs in mood. On some occasions she would come along in a very 'bubbly' way, expressing considerable enthusiasm and excitement. For example, after doing the construct elicitation, she said she had enjoyed it and got quite excited when talking about possible change towards greater femininity. She proclaimed with great enthusiasm 'Go for it!'. As was often the case, however, this did not last and she soon became down again and returned to the status quo. After completing feedback on the grid, she commented that she wanted to change, but could not see herself changing. She also expressed anxiety about emotions, particularly that associated with her family. I gently confronted her with a choice at this point. She could stay where she was or she could explore possibilities for change. She opted for the latter and we agreed to an initial ten sessions, initially on a weekly basis. I began by asking her to do some homework, in which she was asked to write down the things she wanted to keep and that which she wanted to change, identifying the pros and cons.

When she returned, she mainly focused on her desire for change. She began by asserting 'I'm 34 years old – in six years time I'll be 40'. She felt she had done nothing with her life and did not want to remain lonely. Again, in optimistic mode, she added that 'life's too short – you've got to think positive'. She listed some of the implications of this – taking more care of appearance, needing more social outlets and being more open. I asked her where she saw eating as fitting in with all this. She replied that she gets insecure and eats (i.e. slightly breaks her normal rigid dietary control) and makes herself sick. This was a pattern she found difficult to change and she thought that if she could not put on weight herself, she thinks she would have to be in hospital (i.e. in-patient weight restoration). During the next couple of weeks or so, she showed evidence of some small changes, for example wearing earrings and generally improving her appearance. There was also a holiday abroad planned with some colleagues. But she was also grappling with some of the emotions associated with her volatile sister, who was getting into deep trouble with drugs. At the same time, there was increasing pressure at work. She cancelled a session and returned the following week extremely tearful. She told me that she had had what she called a 'spasm' at work, in which she became rigid and had difficulty breathing. This seemed to be related to a stressful situation with a colleague. Also, more generally, she said she was not getting anywhere and she felt she had been deceiving me by, for example, understating how often she was vomiting. This was why she had cancelled the previous week, because she could not face me. She had decided she had to go into hospital because she could not do it on her own. She added that she was pleased she had made the decision, part of the source of her frequent vomiting was anxiety about deciding. During the next few weeks, while she was waiting for a bed to become available, she talked about her anxieties. She felt it would be like losing a friend and it was going to be hard, but she could not go on like she was.

Regimes for the in-patient treatment of anorexia nervosa vary considerably in terms of detail, but tend to be similar in aiming for initial restoration of weight and normalisation of eating. The local service was no exception and Helen knew that she would be expected to eat regular meals at a quantity way beyond her normal experience. Moreover, there would be a marked element of supervision and monitoring of her behaviour and physical state, including her weight. This regime was a well-established one, which although gradually modified over the years, had quite firm expectations, which each patient was made well aware of. This aspect of her treatment was outside of my control, although I would continue to see her regularly while she was in hospital. All patients had such regular psychotherapy sessions during their in-patient stay. Thus, although the initial target of change was primarily on nutritional restoration, there was also considerable emphasis on a person's psychological reaction to it.

As is often the case with something new, Helen began full of good intention and, on the surface, presented as highly motivated. This was reflected at our psychotherapy sessions, where she would generally present an optimistic and cheerful face. Similarly, at group meetings held in the ward with other patients, she would talk a lot and in an apparently positive manner, as if things were going well. Below the surface, however, all was not well. After initial weight gain of about 6 lb during the first couple of weeks, this levelled out. The nursing staff confronted her with the fact that she showed evidence of self-induced vomiting. She began to acknowledge her immense fear of losing control of her weight and difficulty letting go of the vomiting. She was given a few days to think about whether she could comply with the regime. This time passed without change and she was invited to go home and think about it for a further three days. After this time elapsed, she contacted the ward to say she did not want to return. That, in effect, was the end of her in-patient stay, once again not staying the course.

The period following her discharge was a rather traumatic one. She had felt very pressurised, but being unsure about what she really wanted for herself. The nursing and medical staff had communicated to her that it was her choice if she wanted to stay chronically anorectic. At the same time, however, it was strongly pointed out to her that she ought to try to find a way of maintaining the status quo that did not involve the dangerous practice of vomiting and laxative abuse. She felt she needed to get away from her grandmother for a while and took up the offer of staying with an old friend and her husband in a nearby town. She had a very good relationship with them and was able to talk a lot about her feelings, particularly her childhood. This provided a stabilising effect on her and allowed her time to reflect on her situation.

It seemed that Helen's experiment with the idea of letting go of being anorectic had been prematurely terminated. During the next few months, she now fully acknowledged that she did not want to change. Although she still seemed to appreciate coming along to see me, her lack of motivation to change led to a spacing out of sessions from weekly to every two weeks. Although there was now no pretence of changing eating behaviour, there were other issues that she was comfortable with exploring. Initially, this focused on her need for a break from her grandmother and sister. Her friend and husband were very supportive and non-pressurising on her and for a while, she considered the possibility of living with or near them on a permanent basis. After a while, however, she began to feel homesick and realised that her roots were in her home city and that she wanted to return to her grandmother. She was also being increasingly confronted with the issue of giving up her job. Having stayed on sick leave for many months, she eventually accepted that she would have to terminate her job on medical grounds. This was a major loss for her and the process extended over many months before and after. Although at one level, she knew the job was not right for her, it was difficult letting go of the status she had once enjoyed from her position.

Although Helen would come along regularly for her sessions, it gradually began to feel that she was going nowhere in particular therapeutically. She commented at one of our meetings that she felt she was wasting my time. In the circumstances, we agreed to a further spacing out of sessions to once monthly. In essence, we moved to a more supportive kind of relationship. While such therapy is often scorned at in psychotherapy circles, I think there are sometimes good reasons for the use of support, as Kelly himself argued. There are times when major reconstruction may be too challenging and a period of support can help to hold things together until the person feels more able to change.

Having now been seeing Helen for about two years, I feel we have achieved a relationship where she can feel reasonably safe. One of the most striking features of our meetings is that she no longer presents a superficial smiling face. She seems to be able to be more natural and honest and she will share with me a range of feelings. I suspect that she needs to do a lot more of this kind of thing before she could even contemplate the prospect of letting go of anorexia nervosa. Although she has phases of feeling very low and stuck, she is gently beginning to explore change in her life, such as improving her education. She has also been doing relaxation classes, which she finds helpful in reducing tension and in feeling comfortable with the people she meets at the class.

Having reached this stage in therapy, it seemed appropriate to re-assess Helen's construing of herself. She readily agreed to once again sharing her constructs with me in a formalised manner. I decided to use the same procedure as previously, but to re-elicit constructs.

Follow-up grid

The process of construct elicitation followed a similar pattern to original assessment. Virtually the same number of constructs was elicited and about half of the constructs were repeated, typically emerging from comparisons with the same element. For example, she once again saw lack of confidence as a similarity between herself and her mother and quietness as a similarity between herself and her father. There were also some new constructs, such as the difficulty in expressing feelings, which was now the first construct to emerge in comparison with her mother. Interestingly, she also included some different elements for the role titles. For the least liked element, on this occasion she chose her sister, perhaps now reflecting her greater pre-paredness to acknowledge the issues surrounding her. Here, she began with similarities, such as that they both wanted to be loved, but that her sister could relate to the opposite sex better. Another important difference was that her sister got hurt easily whereas Helen would not allow people to get to her, by being 'hard', shutting herself off.

At the end of the elicitation I once again asked her if there were any additional important characteristics of people. She commented that when she did it last year, she was very quick, e.g with her mother, being very anti. She now realised that she did not hate her mother as she thought and regretted she never got to understand her. She thought her mother was very unhappy and regretted that they did not talk more. Helen continued that she tends to sit in silence, being always afraid to express herself in case she lost her temper, as her Mum did. Now she thinks she could control it, instead of spurting it all out. Before she thought she would just go mad.

After completing the grid Helen further elaborated upon such themes. I asked her what she made of it and she said she found it very interesting. She said it had made her realise that there was hope for herself to change. Before, she thought she had blamed herself and now knows it is not all her fault . . . 'it's growing up . . . becoming an adult'. She felt she had a lot more growing up to do and that she was no different from anybody else.

Grid analysis

The principal components analysis showed a very similar overall structure to the original grid, demonstrating that no fundamental reconstruing had taken place. In terms of the self-esteem profile (Figure 10.3) the main change is that there are now far fewer 'negative' constructs, but twice as many 'uncertain' constructs. From my research experience, the bias towards more 'positive' constructs is an encouraging sign associated with greater psychological well-being. This may be an early indication that she is moving towards a more positive stance rather than one in which she is

	Always							*Never*
'Positive' constructs								
Patient	–	–	0/X	–	–	–	–	–
Lovely personality	–	–	0/X	–	–	–	–	–
Take things in stride	–	X	0	–	–	–	–	–
Avoid upsets/quarrels	–	X	0	–	–	–	–	–
Understanding	–	–	0	X	–	–	–	–
Want to be loved	X	0	–	–	–	–	–	–
Likeable	–	–	0	–	X	–	–	–
Trusting	–	–	0	–	–	X	–	–
Full of enthusiasm	–	0	–	–	–	–	–	X
Bubbly/cheerful	0	–	–	–	–	–	–	X
Good listener	0	–	–	–	X	–	–	–
'Negative' constructs								
Copes with drink	–	–	–	–	–	–	–	0/X
Open about feelings	–	–	–	–	–	0	X	–
Bad temper	–	–	–	–	–	0	X	–
Swear and shout	–	–	–	–	–	–	0	X
Gets hurt easily	–	–	–	–	–	0	X	–
Hard	–	X	–	–	–	–	0	–
'Uncertain' constructs								
Quiet	–	X	–	0	–	–	–	–
Confident	–	–	–	0	–	X	–	–
Sit in silence	X	–	–	0	–	–	–	–
Difficulty expressing feelings	–	X	–	–	0	–	–	–
Lack confidence	–	X	–	–	0	–	–	–
Put self down	–	X	–	0	–	–	–	–
Confront disagreements	–	–	–	0	–	–	X	–
Likes talking	–	–	–	0	–	–	X	–
Like own privacy/quiet	–	X	–	0	–	–	–	–
Have to be right	–	–	–	–	0	–	X	–
Insecure	X	–	–	–	0	–	–	–
Lonely	X	–	–	–	0	–	–	–
Can relate to opposite sex	–	–	–	0	–	–	–	X

Key: 0 = Me ideally;   X = Me nowadays

Figure 10.3:   Self-construing summary from Helen's follow-up grid

primarily avoiding the negative (e.g. as symbolised by her mother). Perhaps in consequence, however, the self-esteem measure has worsened to 2.4 (versus 1.8 previously), maybe as she realises how far she has to go in realising her aspirations.

Concluding comment

Helen well exemplifies the entrenched position taken by many people who have become anorectic. I have not been able to help her to let go significantly of her rigid control on this area of her life. Whether she will ever be able to do so seems doubtful, but we seem to have forged a relationship of trust in which she feels able to explore and develop herself at her own pace.

11 Sonia

Quite a number of people who come my way present with marked problems associated with weight and eating, but they do not quite exhibit all the behaviours necessary for a strictly defined label of anorexia nervosa or bulimia nervosa. As has been discussed earlier, one way of describing such disorders is to use the term 'partial syndrome' eating disorder. Although their problems may seem less severe on the surface, they can be quite disabling and in my view are every bit as deserving of help. Intervention with such people can often be quite short term and successful and may well prevent the development of the more full-blown syndromes. Sonia is an example of such a person.

Sonia was 20 when she first came to see me. She had had problems with eating during the past couple of years. For a while she had more or less stopped eating and went from 9 st. (126 lb) down to 7 st. 7 lb (105 lb). Realising the effect of this, she began eating again, but then felt she had gained too much and dieted again. For a while, she managed to stay at about 8 st. (112 lb), which she was happy with. But about six months previously she had caught flu, became depressed and began binge-eating and making herself sick. The latter had not lasted long, however, and she had since put on about two stone (28 lb) in weight. She had become preoccupied about her weight, hated people seeing her and even hated seeing and the feel of herself, such as when washing. It had reached the point where she almost despised herself. She was extremely distressed that she could not diet and lose weight. Nor could she exercise because she hated to feel her body wobbling. Her whole world seemed to now revolve around eating and despising herself for it. She had also withdrawn from the social world and had not been out with friends for about five months.

From the standpoint of eating behaviour, the main clinical feature was binge-eating about three to four times a week, set in the context of a perception of failed dieting. There was very marked fear of weight gain, for example fearing getting like her sister who was very fat. Sonia also felt extreme guilt about eating and said that every day she felt like scratching her eyes out. Her level of concern about her size was marked, seeing herself like 'ten ton Tessy' and seeking to hide her body with loose clothes. Because Sonia had not been recently using any weight control mechanisms such as vomiting or laxatives, she could not be strictly called bulimia nervosa, hence the term 'partial syndrome'. Nevertheless, her scores on questionnaire measures of eating disorder confirmed that there was a marked problem. On the Eating Attitudes Test she scored 50, which is typical of eating disorders. Similarly, she had high scores on five of the subscales of the Eating Disorders Inventory (drive for thinness, bulimia, body dissatisfaction, ineffectiveness, interpersonal distrust and interoceptive awareness).

At a more general level, she said that she had always been a worrier and did not like herself. At age 15, she had taken an overdose and seen a child psychiatrist. She said at the time she felt she wanted attention and to feel needed. More recently and prior to seeing me, she had seen a psychiatrist and had been given antidepressants, but she had now more or less stopped the medication. Although the depression had eased, she was still showing a fair amount of general psychological disturbance. For example, on the SCL90R, her Global Severity Index of 1.56 is within the range typical of psychiatric out-patient populations.

Looking at her earlier life, she recalls having enjoyed junior school and done well, but hated secondary school and got involved with others who did not like school and did not really bother to work. It was around her time at secondary school (age 15–16) that she first went on a diet. After leaving school, she had not really settled to anything very well and had just given up a job she did not like.

Sonia's family life was disrupted when she was six by the divorce of her parents. Her mother was described as basically very loving, but she felt she did not understand her. She felt she could in many ways talk to her step-Dad more than her mother, he being seen as very understanding and wanting the best for her – 'he has always spoilt me rotten'. She also felt her natural father cares a lot, but she felt that he favoured her brother. She now got on well with both her siblings, seeing them as very caring. Looking at her family as a whole, she did not feel it was really happy, Mum not talking to Dad and sister not talking to step-Dad. She wondered why they could not be a normal happy family.

Outside of her family, Sonia had a few close friends, but basically had withdrawn from her wider social network. She had had a few boyfriends, but always worried about relationships with boys and she felt they often used to dump her. She said her last boyfriend could not stand her moods when she lost weight. In her relationships with other people in general, she was shy in getting to know people and always tried to please others and get on with everybody.

In discussing the future, Sonia wanted to get on in life and be happy with a family and nice job. Her main immediate aim, however, was to lose weight. Although I stressed that this would not be the main thrust of my help, she wanted to give it a go of trying to see if she could overcome her eating problems and find other ways of dealing with life. I was somewhat wary as to whether she could shift beyond a strictly weight focus, but I felt that we should be able to work together. I offered her an initial ten-session contract after which we would review things.

I had been struck on my first meeting with Sonia with how nervous and closed off she was. Her whole appearance was of someone who felt very bad about herself and wanted to hide herself from the world. But I sensed that underneath her wary exterior, there was a warm person who had the potential to open up. The elicitation of constructs and SELF-GRID proved to be a useful introduction to the person of Sonia.

Construct elicitation

Self and mother

The first construct was a difference. She felt, perhaps echoing what was said above, that her mother was not inclined to 'try to understand how people are thinking', whereas Sonia did. On the other hand, they both had in common in that they 'worry a lot' (she added that they both looked alike, but I did not enter this as a construct for the grid). Finally she said that she was more 'careful with money' than was her mother.

Self and father

She opened by saying there was not much similarity between them and began with the constructs 'racist' and 'outspoken', which applied to Dad but not Sonia. In spite of saying there was not much similarity, she went on to produce several similarities: they both 'like socialising/talking to people', 'love children'. In fact she said that all the family loved children. She also commented that she got on better with her father now, as opposed to feeling her brother was Dad's favourite.

Self and closest person (step-Dad)

Sonia produced a picture of all similarities with step-Dad. She said they thought alike. He picked things up if she was upset, knows what she wants, what she was thinking. She summarised the similarity as them both having a 'healthy mind'. They were also both seen as 'fun', 'loving', a 'good listener' and 'understands children'.

Self and least liked person (friend, Elaine)

Elaine was a friend and they both had in common that they 'want to go out and enjoy self'. But there were several differences, Elaine being 'inconsiderate', 'quick-tongued' and 'makes stories up'. She elaborated by telling me how Elaine seemed to be always competing with her and trying to make people like her.

Self and most liked person (friend, Theresa)

Theresa was a friend, but she said that she was more like a sister. She began by repeating a previous construct that marked a difference, Theresa being more outspoken. They had in common that they both 'like dancing/music' and were both very 'caring'. They would tell each other what they were thinking and both had 'an unsettled past'. Another difference was that Theresa 'has mood swings'.

Additional constructs

Having completed the above five comparisons I asked her if there were any additional important constructs, to which she replied that when thinking of herself compared with others, she 'worries about weight' and commented that it was as if she had shut out herself from the rest of people.

Comment

I asked Sonia what she made of the process and she said that it was interesting and made her think of things she had not done previously. She added that she had always wanted to look up to her brother and that when she was younger she was called 'porky' and thought that you had to be thin to be liked. From my point of view I was struck by the fact that Sonia seemed at ease with the task and did a fair amount of spontaneous elaboration of her construing and exemplification of what she meant. This further confirmed my feeling that she would be open to exploration.

	Always							Never
'Positive' constructs								
Love children	O/X	–	–	–	–	–	–	–
Loving	O/X	–	–	–	–	–	–	–
Caring	O/X	–	–	–	–	–	–	–
Try to listen/understand	0	X	–	–	–	–	–	–
Good listener	0	X	–	–	–	–	–	–
Understands children	0	X	–	–	–	–	–	–
Careful with money	–	–	0	X	–	–	–	–
Fun	0	–	X	–	–	–	–	–
Healthy mind	0	–	–	X	–	–	–	–
Sporty	–	–	0	–	–	–	X	–
Outspoken	–	–	0	–	–	–	X	–
Go out and enjoy self	–	–	0	–	–	–	X	–
Like dancing/music	–	–	0	–	–	–	X	–
Like socialising/talking	–	0	–	–	–	–	X	–
'Negative' constructs								
Racist	–	–	–	–	–	–	–	O/X
Quick-tongued	–	–	–	–	–	–	–	O/X
Make stories up	–	–	–	–	–	–	–	O/X
Inconsiderate	–	–	–	–	–	–	X	0
Has mood swings	–	–	–	–	–	–	X	0
Unsettled past	–	–	–	X	–	–	–	0
Worry about weight	X	–	–	–	–	–	–	0
'Uncertain' constructs								
Worry	–	X	–	0	–	–	–	

Key: 0 = Me ideally;   X = Me nowadays

Figure 11.1:   Self-construing summary from Sonia's pre-treatment grid

If we examine Sonia's self esteem profile (Figure 11.1), we can see that there is a predominance of 'positive' constructs. On quite a number of these she shows marked strengths. She values the fact that she is: loving, caring, loves children, good listener, understands children. There are also a number, however, where she feels very discrepant from her ideal. These particularly include her rarely nowadays: likes socialising/talking, wants to go out and enjoy self, sporty and outspoken. In terms of negative constructs, there are several constructs that show further strengths in not being: racist, quick-tongued, make stories up. She is, however, dissatisfied with being always worried about weight, which she would like never to do. The only 'uncertain' construct is 'worry', which she does almost always, but would like to do only often. Thus she sees worrying as something that has some value, but not all the time.

The overall picture from this profile is of a rather negative self-esteem, with a mean discrepancy of 2.05 – well within the range typical of psychological disorder. This is consistent with her high negative score on the

Rosenberg Self-esteem Scale (6, which is maximum on the original method of scoring). Her dissatisfaction seems mainly to centre on the social arena and it is perhaps not surprising that she has constricted her world to the narrow one of weight control. But at the same time, there are many perceived strengths and an overall positive emphasis to her construction, which could hopefully form the basis for future development.

Treatment

Sessions 1 and 2

The first couple of sessions were mainly taken up by the assessment, both of her construing and the eating diaries. I had given her some guidance as to trying to eat regular balanced meals and she was proving to respond quite well to this. There were only one or two 'binges' in the first couple of weeks and the quantities were not great. It had been helped by being at her sister's. This was a useful opportunity to examine the relevance of the social context she was in and how this could affect her eating.

Although her overall reaction to the grid had been positive, she had added, however, that it had made her realise how much she had changed. She came across as very tense, ill at ease and lacking in any spark during these first sessions. She clearly had quite a long way to go, but I tried to encourage her in the direction of making use of areas in which she felt comfortable to gradually build up her confidence again.

Session 3

There had been good progress with eating and she had not binged and was pleased that she had lost weight. She expressed a desire to stop the eating diaries, which I was happy to agree to. She was also noticeably brighter in mood and her physical appearance showed that she was making more of an effort in her presentation, for example by using makeup. Sonia was feeling wary about mixing with friends, whereas with her family she felt all right. As is often the case, people sometimes constrict their world to one with safe people, with whom there is perhaps less risk of invalidation. I therefore spent some time during the session exploring Sonia's construction of social situations with peers. It emerged that Sonia was very tuned into what people might think of her and was particularly aware of lads and girls going on about size. She was thus narrowing her focus to anticipating that social interactions would invariably be just concerned with evaluating her size, which she now construed as unacceptably large. As a therapist, I was faced with the difficult task of trying to illuminate a world beyond this limited social construction (even though it may have some social validity) and help to see that there were many other possible dimensions of relevance to such interactions. This was very much in the way of trying to encourage her to move beyond seeing people as objects and more as engaged in a social process in which a variety of constructions could be in operation. This is one of the most difficult issues to work on in this client group. It is quite a challenge to help young women move beyond the common construction that places so much attention to weight and appearance. It was a central issue for Sonia.

Session 4

Sonia's eating was still all right but she was not moving much on the social front. She was still playing pretty safe and told me of a very depressed day when she had been thinking negative thoughts about her former boyfriend. I find that people often look back to the past when they are unsure about moving ahead. It felt like she was still not ready to take a chance. But she was taking some small steps forward. For example, she had changed her hair style and she was less holding her head down, was looking up more.

Session 5

Perhaps her talk of her ex-boyfriend the previous week had been a fore-taste of a movement towards the opposite sex. We mainly focused during the session on her construing of men. She had come to see them as looking at women just in terms of their bodies. I pointed out that while this was likely to be a particularly important construct for a young man, it was likely that there were going to be other issues as well, such as being nervous and trying to impress. In my efforts to help her to widen her range of constructions of men, I suggested she start focusing more on men, to look at them more and talk to them more. In short she might discover something about how men construed the world.

At the end she commented that she realised she was hiding her body behind a pram a lot (with her sister's children) and construed having a dog to walk with in the same vein. Thus, she was still trying very hard to avoid other people being aware of her body.

Session 6

Sonia had managed to talk with a young man who had come to the house to do a job. She recognised him from before. Although initially nervous,

Sonia recognised that he was too and she managed to have an interesting conversation with him and it did not feel like he was just focusing on her body. She had also decided that she was going to write to an old friend.

As well as maintaining her stable eating behaviour, Sonia was now feeling more able to be more open about her problem. She had also taken some small steps towards breaking down her barriers, for example by talking to one or two people she had not spoken to for ages and had also had a go at driving, which she had not done for a long time.

Sonia was also looking ahead to the future and had obtained a place on a vocational course to start in a few months' time. She was looking forward to this.

Session 7

Further social progress had been made. She had been on a short holiday and trips out with her family. For the first time she said she was not focusing on her figure now – she had got lots of other things to occupy her. Sonia was also thinking that it was more important that people like her for what she is rather than weight. In contrast, she reflected back to when she was younger how she was conscious of being more advanced physically than other girls and wanting to be like them.

It seemed that reconstruction was now well in progress and the process of gradually 'dilating' her perceptual field, following massive 'constriction', was expanding. Sonia felt that she now needed to start going out with friends again and wearing old clothes she had been avoiding.

Session 8

Further small steps had been taken, having been to her old hairdresser and met up with her old friend. She had taken the step of planning to go back to the pub where she used to meet all her old friends. This really was a big step.

Session 9

She had been to the pub and met her old friends. It went well and she felt comfortable with them. She had now decided that she was going to have her 21st birthday party with almost a hundred guests. This was something a few months down the line, but she had previously considered that she could not possibly face it. Sonia was generally feeling positive about herself. She felt she had conquered the main hurdle. Now she had to face wearing dresses and skirts.

Session 10

Having reached the last of the planned sessions, she was doing really well. She had been socialising to a great degree and was really enjoying herself, letting herself go. She was eating OK and even had had some chips last night. She had also worn a dress and other clothes she had been avoiding.

She was about to start her course and although apprehensive about mixing with new people, she was hopeful from previous experience that she would soon make friends. She felt that she would be busy with this course and wanted to leave it for six weeks before meeting again to see how she had got on.

Follow-up

It turned out to be two months later when we met. Life was going well. She made a new friend on the course and was really enjoying it. In terms of eating, she did not tend to worry about it as she used to. For example, she would not see it as a major disaster to have crisps. Most of the time she had meals, but would often snack for convenience. She would eat most things and only rarely would feel guilty if she ate chocolate. She could now eat salads and enjoy them, rather than seeing them as dieting. Weight was not a major issue. She was now around about 9 st. (126 lb) and would like to be 8 st. (112 lb), but it was not the big issue it had been before. She was also having regular periods. Thus, although there was perhaps some mild anxiety and drive for thinness, it was by no means a central issue.

At a social level, she was going out a lot and had a boyfriend. Things had not been entirely straightforward, however, and she had got involved in some complicated situations with certain of her female associates. In one case, a boyfriend's ex-girlfriend had been threatening her and this had caused a lot of distress. It seemed to me that Sonia was not finding mixing with peers to be entirely straightforward and she had a lot to say about certain of her peers who did not seem to be behaving according to expectation. She felt, however, that she was handling these difficulties well and she seemed broadly optimistic and happy with herself. I did, however, do a bit of therapeutic work, pointing out to her that other people often have agendas quite different to our own and, hopefully, help her be more prepared for some of the complexities of human behaviour she could anticipate in the future.

	Always							Never
'Positive' constructs								
Love children	O/X	–	–	–	–	–	–	–
Like dancing/music	O/X	–	–	–	–	–	–	–
Caring	O/X	–	–	–	–	–	–	–
Try to listen/understand	–	O/X	–	–	–	–	–	–
Good listener	–	O/X	–	–	–	–	–	–
Fun	–	O/X	–	–	–	–	–	–
Outspoken	–	–	O/X	–	–	–	–	–
Like socialising/talking	–	–	O/X	–	–	–	–	–
Go out and enjoy self	–	–	O/X	–	–	–	–	–
Speak up for self	–	–	O/X	–	–	–	–	–
Loving	–	0	X	–	–	–	–	–
Understand children	–	0	X	–	–	–	–	–
Healthy mind	–	–	0	X	–	–	–	–
Careful with money	–	–	0	–	–	–	X	–
'Negative' constructs								
Racist	–	–	–	–	–	–	–	O/X
Quick-tongued	–	–	–	–	–	O/X	–	–
Make stories up	–	–	–	–	–	–	X	0
Has mood swings	–	–	–	–	–	X	0	–
Inconsiderate	–	–	–	–	X	–	0	–
Worry about weight	–	–	–	–	X	–	0	–
Unsettled past	–	–	–	X	–	–	0	–
'Uncertain' constructs								
Sporty	–	–	–	O/X	–	–	–	–
Worry	–	–	–	X	0	–	–	–

Key: 0 = Me ideally;   X = Me nowadays

Figure 11.2:   Self-construing summary from Sonia's post-treatment grid

On this occasion, I reassessed Sonia in terms of her self-construing. The results are summarised in Figure 11.2. As can be seen this reveals a much more favourable personal construction of self. On virtually all 'positive' constructs, she is broadly happy with herself. This includes the previous valued constructs of loving children, caring, etc. But she is also happy about herself in terms of socialising, going out, etc. In terms of 'negative' constructs, she has broadly maintained her previous self-construction, but with the important difference that she was now only sometimes worried about weight, having been always before treatment. On the 'uncertain' constructs, it is interesting that she is now content with her position on 'worry', which she now does often, previously having been almost always. I asked Sonia if there were any new constructs that were now important to her. She said that she now 'speaks up for herself' most of the time and says what she thinks. She had thus come a long way from the withdrawn young woman hiding behind food and her weight. The overall measure of self-esteem was

0.74 (versus 2.05 pre-treatment) which represents a high level of satisfac-
tion with self, well within the kind of range typical of healthy people.
Another change perhaps of note is that she had become less extreme about
her ideal. There were fewer 'always' and 'never' ratings, which perhaps
suggests she is becoming a bit more realistic about herself.

The change had taken place over a period of six months. Quite substantial change of this sort in this kind of time span is possible with some people
at the more partial syndrome end of the spectrum, particularly where the
person concerned has some positive constructions and a willingness to try
to understand himself or herself and other people. This certainly applied to
Sonia.

If I were to be sceptical, I could put her change down to her success in
getting her weight down substantially, but I found no indication during the
months of her recovery that Sonia was construing her successes in terms of
her lower weight. Let us hope that Sonia's construct system has evolved to
the point where she can learn to deal with the many facets of people, not all
pleasant, that she is likely to encounter and can build on her more positive
orientation to the world.

12   Kath

Although many of the clients I have worked with have presented to me during the throes of their illness, it is not uncommon to meet someone who seeks help some years after the worst of their plight. They may have had previous treatment elsewhere or perhaps had no previous help at all. They may thus have appeared to have partially recovered, but the underlying problem may not have changed. Their initial symptoms may have taken a new form, such as a switch from anorectic to more bulimic symptoms. Their earlier symptoms may have lain dormant, but perhaps a new challenge in their life has upset them again and thrown them back towards their old ways of coping.

Kath was an example of such a person. She approached me for help when she was 28. She told me that she had 'anorexia' at age 18, although she had been cutting down on food from age 16. Looking back, she felt that it was partly related to the pressure of A level exams, as she was rather a perfectionist in nature and also having been pushed very hard to do well by her parents. But she thought it was more than that, perhaps about not accepting herself and her body. Her weight went down to just over 5 st. (70 lb) and her periods stopped, with little doubt in my mind that she would have fulfilled criteria for anorexia nervosa at that time. She did not receive specialised treatment at that time, but was taken to her family doctor and given pills to increase her appetite. She did not take the pills and in fact seemed to have put on weight again of her own accord after successfully completing her A levels with good marks. On reflection, Kath recalled being very unhappy then, feeling podgy in her face and the suddenness of the change in her body felt like it was 'not me'. Although on the face of it she had moved away from a frankly anorectic picture, she soon began making herself sick in the context of some binge-eating. Over the years, her symptoms waxed and waned, but essentially she felt she had been hiding the problem, rather than facing it. She had thought it would get better with the years, but she could not seem to overcome it on her own. Having not received any substantive help over the years, she was now seeking help, it seemed, mainly because she wanted to have children and wanted to sort it out before having them.

Her present eating pattern she described as 'irregular'. On 'good' days, she would have a very strict diet, trying to eat 'sensibly' – mainly fish, vegetables and fruit. On bad days, she would try to have breakfast, but in the evening, if stressed and worried, she would eat sugary things like loads of biscuits and make herself sick afterwards. This would vary in frequency, but sometimes could occur as much as four times in a week. It seemed that this pattern usually occurred in the evenings. In the day at work, she was often busy and happy with 'no time', in fact on some days she missed lunch. In terms of other behaviours, she did not use laxatives or exercise excessively, although she had done this in the past. Her weight was 7 st. 1 lb (99 lb) at a height of 5'3", which was certainly thin, but not dangerously so. But she did want to be thinner. She found it very hard to put on weight, her maximum ever having been only 7 st. 5 lb (103 lb). In terms of menstrual status, she had been on the pill for seven years and had regular bleeding. Formal assessment confirmed the above clinical picture. On the Eating Attitudes Test, she had a very high score of 84. On the Eating Disorders Inventory, she had high scores on drive for thinness, bulimia, perfectionism and maturity fears subscales.

Looking beyond the eating problems, she described herself as: kind, liking children, enjoying her job. On the negative side, she saw herself as very nervous/anxious and emotional. She had difficulty relaxing and would sometimes have difficulty breathing or swallowing. She worried a lot, both for herself and others. Her husband, in contrast, was very easy-going, had lots of friends and did not worry. In this respect she felt he had helped and she did not worry quite as much as she used to. Kath felt that their relationship was good, except that her eating problem worried him, for example the problems about going out to dinner. Outside of work, Kath's life seemed to be mainly at home. Although there were couples they would see, she mainly preferred more solitary pursuits, such as reading.

Looking back to her family, her mother was described as very kind and loved children. They got on well now, but when she was overtly anorectic, Mum could not understand and felt it was a reaction against the family and an insult to her cooking. Father was very strict when she was little and created a great deal of pressure to do well. He seemed rather distant when she was young and did not play with her, seeming to prefer 'discussion'. But she said she loved both her parents and phoned them regularly. Kath had one sister, aged 26, who was very different from her, lacking in ambition.

She commented, perhaps in comparison, that 'they think I'm weird because of my eating'.

From our first meeting, it was thus clear that Kath had a long-standing eating disorder, set against a background of being a worrying, anxious and sensitive person, who perhaps in childhood had learned to conform to the wishes of others. This came over in her manner, being very pleasant and smiling most of the time. We agreed to meet again a week later to complete assessment and firm up on the possibility of help.

Construct elicitation

At our second meeting, I introduced the SELF-GRID as part of getting to know her better. She took to this fairly easily and a total of 23 unipolar constructs were elicited.

Self and mother

She saw all similarities here. They were both considerate and generous, but they also shared a tendency to being anxious and worrying.

Self and father

She first mentioned a similarity, namely that they both liked to discuss things. It seems, therefore, that in spite of what she had earlier said about her father, that she also as an adult shared this with her father. The comparison with father, however, revealed rather more in the way of differences. Kath saw herself as more emotional and able to take jokes. She also saw herself as more worrying about weight. On the other hand her father was more tight with money.

Self and closest person (husband)

Reflecting some of the things she had said earlier, the first constructs here were that her husband was less anxious. He was more inclined to see a good side, whereas she was more pessimistic. Her husband was also more impulsive. The only specific construct on which they were similar was both having a childish sense of humour. In spite of a lack of identifiable similarity constructs, she added that they agreed on most things, so that there was presumably some commonality of construing.

Self and least liked person (mother-in-law)

As is often the case in this comparison, the only constructs to emerge were differences. She commented that her mother-in-law did not help, being selfish and not caring. Perhaps, as a matter of qualification, Kath added that she did not hate her for it, but she did find it hard to handle and could cope with her only for a few hours at a time.

Self and most liked person (friend, Liz)

Kath began by stating that she felt comfortable with Liz. The similarities were that they were both vegetarian and also sympathetic, kind and generous, thus repeating some of the kinds of themes that emerged with her mother. There were also differences, Kath having more difficulty disciplining and being less confident.

Additional constructs

As usual, I asked if there were any further constructs and Kath came up with several. On the negative side, Kath said that she did not like people who were selfish, rude and intolerant and tended to pretend/hide things. An important positive construct was being proud. She liked to think she could cope with things on her own and added that coming here to see me was difficult in that respect.

I felt encouraged by Kath's response to the elicitation of constructs. She had shown herself to be open to exploring her constructions of people and I was hopeful that we would be able to work together. We went on to complete the SELF-GRID and a summary of her self-esteem profile is displayed in Figure 12.1. It can be seen from this profile that there is a reasonably even mix of 'positive' and 'negative' constructs. In terms of the positive constructs, there are a large number of 'strengths'. In particular, she seems to like being considerate, generous and caring. Other obvious strengths include liking to discuss things, being vegetarian and strong-willed. Interestingly, she also seems to prefer to be emotional. The main deficit in terms of positive constructs is her only sometimes being able to see the good side of life.

From the point of view of negative constructs, she likes the fact that she is not tight with money, selfish, rude, intolerant and impulsive. The largest discrepancy here is worrying about weight, but she would also like to be less inclined to pretend/hide things and less anxious. The only 'uncertain' construct is having a childish sense of humour, which she seems broadly

	Always							Never
'Positive' constructs								
Considerate	0	X	–	–	–	–	–	–
Generous	0	X	–	–	–	–	–	–
Like to discuss things	–	0/X	–	–	–	–	–	–
Emotional	X	0	–	–	–	–	–	–
Can take jokes	0	X	–	–	–	–	–	–
Caring	0	X	–	–	–	–	–	–
Vegetarian	0	X	–	–	–	–	–	–
Strong-willed	0	X	–	–	–	–	–	–
Sympathetic	0	–	X	–	–	–	–	–
Can cope on own	–	0	X	–	–	–	–	–
Confident	–	0	–	X	–	–	–	–
See good side of life	0	–	–	–	X	–	–	–
'Negative' constructs								
Tight with money	–	–	–	–	–	–	–	0/X
Selfish	–	–	–	–	–	–	X	0
Rude	–	–	–	–	–	–	X	0
Intolerant	–	–	–	–	–	–	X	0
Impulsive	–	–	–	–	X	0	–	–
Pessimistic	–	–	–	–	X	0	–	–
Difficulty disciplining	–	–	–	X	–	0	–	–
Anxious/worrying	–	–	X	–	–	0	–	–
Pretend/hide things	–	–	–	X	–	–	–	0
Worry about weight	X	–	–	–	–	0	–	–
'Uncertain' constructs								
Childish sense humour	–	–	–	X	0	–	–	–

Key: 0 = Me ideally;   X = Me nowadays

Figure 12.1:   Self-construing summary from Kath's pre-treatment grid

satisfied with. Overall, Kath shows a rather mixed self-evaluation. On my self-esteem measure, she scores 1.57, which reflects a moderate degree of dissatisfaction. Broadly speaking, however, there is a sound foundation of perceived strengths from which to build.

After completing the grid, we went on to discuss her attitude towards help. She indicated that she wanted to eat normally – three meals a day without craving, to relax without turning to food and not to feel different. She also referred to some of the mixed feelings she had about herself. She quite liked herself, but did not like the 'dark side' of herself, feeling she had a tendency to violent feelings towards others. Moreover, she wanted to reduce her mood swings and improve her relationship both with her husband and her family. I offered her a ten-session contract which she accepted, although expressing reservations about having time off work, perhaps indicative again of her conscientious, perfectionist approach.

Treatment

Session 1

We began by perusing her eating diary. She commented that it was good for the first week and indeed there was a pattern of regular, fairly reasonable-sized meals. As is often the case, she said she felt good after seeing me and this had clearly had a good effect initially. During the second week, however, she had been on holiday to her parents' home and there had been a few incidents of vomiting there. The main precipitant of these, seemed to have been negative mood states and this especially related to her family. For example, she had an argument with her sister and there was also a general issue of trying to please her parents and not upset them. These incidents highlighted an area in which her construing of social situations directly became translated into disturbed eating behaviour. I pointed this out to her and on the assumption that one cannot always avoid upsets with family, we explored some of the possible alternative ways of coping with such situations. I particularly pointed to the need to develop communicative strategies, such as talking to people about how she was feeling or even writing it down.

She was also anticipating returning to work after holidays and the issue of how she would deal with eating arose in this context. Previously, she had been isolating herself from colleagues by not eating with them. But she now realised that she needed to eat with them at lunchtime. It seemed likely that this would potentially open up benefits both in terms of strength of relationship and in terms of avoiding the gaps in eating likely to set off later binge-eating.

Session 2

There had been a few bad moments during the previous week. She partly related this to having a period, but she also felt she had not dealt with situations in a more direct manner, e.g there had been an argument with her husband, but she had turned to food rather than dealing with it face on. Her negative feelings about these events brought out the broader issue of her expectations of herself. As had emerged in the elicitation of constructs, she was expressing concern about the theme that she should be able to cope, she should not need people. In an effort to loosen up her construing in this area, I set her some homework of trying to enquire of how other people cope when faced with difficulties.

Session 3

She had done her homework and discovered that other people sometimes turn to food as she did. This seemed to help her get a somewhat less negative perspective on her particular response to difficult times. Overall she felt she was making good progress. She was now eating regularly with colleagues at work. There had been some stressful days at work, where she had got very upset. Although on a few occasions during the past fortnight, she had turned to food, she had managed to avoid carrying over such eating by talking about how she was feeling with her husband and sticking to having a meal even if she had binged.

Session 4

Since the last session, the first week had gone well, but the last week had seen one or two bad days. It seemed that the critical time was early evening after coming home from work, when her husband was not around. I suggested that she needed to try to plan for her needs at such times. It seemed that often when she was turning to food, it was in the context of angry feelings, which had perhaps emerged at work. Anger was not something she tended to express directly, however, and I suggested that this was something she could try to experiment with.

Session 5

Kath had been unwell and had been off her food, with some weight loss. This seemed to have set off an old pattern of illness setting off the desire to lose weight. The old anorectic thinking seemed hard to completely let go of and I discussed with her the idea that we often turn to old ways of coping when we are faced with difficulties. She was feeling critical of this aspect of herself. My approach, however, was to invite her to reconstrue this as reflecting the strength of meaning associated with the idea of weight loss. I suggested that it may be difficult to shake off this completely, but that in time she could work at developing meaning in other directions. This, I argued, would require a lot of practice.

Session 6

Generally Kath felt she was progressing well, but there were still times in the evening when she was turning to food. She was, however, gradually developing alternatives, such as going swimming, which she enjoyed. Generally, Kath was seeing the need to become more social and I suggested possibly ringing people up or writing. I am not sure in what context it had emerged, but my notes refer to an intriguing philosophical construction, which Kath had spontaneously come up with. She quoted Descartes as having said, 'I think, therefore I am. I doubt therefore I am.' This seemed like a useful construction, not without relevance to a constructivist position, which gave some indication that Kath was by no means a passive participant in the therapeutic process.

Session 7

There were continuing pressures at work, which were affecting both her sleep and her eating and she was feeling less supported because her husband was busy. We looked at the need to diversify her dependence, so that she had other outlets and less time to brood on her own. Most of the session was taken up with her anticipations about a forthcoming trip to her parents. Following the last trip she was apprehensive about expectations surrounding meals by her parents. They apparently did not know she still had an eating problem and she did not want to upset them. We spent some time examining the whole issue of whether one needed to conform to other people's constructions and also whether we could necessarily rely on our own expectations of those constructions. I put it to her that her parents may not necessarily be construing the situation exactly as she feared. Moreover, that her needs and view of the situation was also important. Maybe there were ways of being with them in which both parties' constructions could be considered and responded to.

Session 8

In the event, the trip to her parents went well. She was relaxed and able to do all kinds of things that she enjoyed without feeling under due pressure. Neither did this seem to have any adverse consequences as far as her family were concerned.

Once again we turned to the familiar territory of difficulties at work. It seemed that there were still times when food seemed preferable to normally attractive options like gardening, swimming or music. Once again there were negative feelings around, which seemed to lead very easily into turning to food. I suggested that she might try writing down feelings or talking into a tape recorder when she was upset.

Session 9

It seemed that some of the anticipatory preparation concerning work had been useful. Things had been going well at work and also she had had a pleasant weekend with her in-laws, having normally not felt comfortable with her mother-in-law. She was feeling relaxed, which felt like a new feeling for her. There were no worries about food currently. I reminded her that next week we would be reviewing our sessions.

Session 10

Kath felt that she had gained a lot from our sessions and was generally dealing better at work, with her visits to her parents and in her social life. But she was currently feeling very unsettled about a clash of interests between her husband and herself. Her husband was exploring quite dramatic changes in life style associated with his work. She was worried about the financial implications of this. She was very much feeling she wanted a child, but this seemed financially difficult and she was also unhappy in her rented flat, wanting to buy their own home.

It seemed that in this context, she felt somewhat powerless and I emphasised the need to communicate with her husband exactly what she felt and thus have power to influence the situation. She seemed very unsure, however, about what she wanted and I suggested she perhaps needed to sit down and work out what her priorities were right now.

We had thus come to the end of our initial contract, but we agreed to have a few more sessions, something that was somewhat compromised by the fact that I was about to move on to a new job.

Session 11

Kath and her husband had talked through their feelings about their overall situation and had managed to sort things out. They had decided to indeed buy their own home and she felt a lot better through now knowing where she was going. She had not really had time to think about eating and she had been able to cope well with times on her own, which previously had been difficult. We agreed to follow-up and likely discharge in a month's time.

Session 12

Kath had enjoyed her summer, had been very relaxed and had not bothered thinking about food. She did not feel the need to turn to food, but was

eating regular meals and her weight was stable and not really a major issue. .
Although Kath was wary about coping with future work pressures, she
generally felt more confident and felt she had a wider range of resources
for dealing with future difficulties. This especially included people and
there is no doubt that she had learned to spread her dependency needs on
people in a much wider way than previously where her husband was virtually the only person. Because of my job move we had to part ways, but it
seemed likely that she would now have the potential to draw on other
people should she get into further difficulty.

Overview

In the relatively short period while we had worked together, I felt we had
developed a constructive and comfortable relationship where Kath had
been open to exploring alternative ways of dealing with problems. I expected that she would continue to be vulnerable to turning to food at times
where she felt under pressure. A few months is but a short time to change a
life-long pattern of responding. It had been clear from sharing together the
way she dealt with the various ups and downs, that she had the potential to
make use of sharing with others. On her own, she could get very bogged
down with the pressures she could create for herself when tuned in to the
coping/perfectionist kinds of construction.

In terms of formal assessment, Kath showed remarkable improvement
on eating behaviour measures. On the Eating Attitudes Test her score was
now down to 16. On the Eating Disorders Inventory, all the previously high
scores were now within normal limits. She was eating regular meals, having
most foods and only very occasionally bingeing/vomiting. She said it was
not even an attractive option any more.

From the personal construct point of view, I also repeated the SELF-
GRID and, as can be seen from Figure 12.2, this also revealed improvement. The overall measure of self-esteem was now down to 1.0, which is
quite typical of healthy controls. The most dramatic change was for the
construct 'worry about weight', which now only applied sometimes as opposed to always previously. There were also improvements on other constructs, such as confidence and seeing the good side of life. There was also
no loss in terms of her important constructs such as being considerate and
generous. Thus on all fronts there was improvement.

Postscript

In deciding to include Kath as a case study, I followed her up and

	Always							Never
'Positive' constructs								
Considerate	0	X	–	–	–	–	–	–
Generous	0	X	–	–	–	–	–	–
Like to discuss things	–	0/X	–	–	–	–	–	–
Can take jokes	–	–	0/X	–	–	–	–	–
Caring	0	X	–	–	–	–	–	–
Vegetarian	0	X	–	–	–	–	–	–
Strong-willed	–	0	–	–	X	–	–	–
Sympathetic	0	X	–	–	–	–	–	–
Can cope on own	–	0	X	–	–	–	–	–
Confident	–	0	X	–	–	–	–	–
See good side of life	–	–	0	X	–	–	–	–
'Negative' constructs								
Tight with money	–	–	–	–	–	–	X	0
Selfish	–	–	–	–	–	–	0/X	–
Rude	–	–	–	–	–	–	X	0
Intolerant	–	–	–	–	–	–	–	0/X
Impulsive	–	–	–	–	X	0	–	–
Pessimistic	–	–	–	–	X	0	–	–
Difficulty disciplining	–	–	–	–	X	–	0	–
Anxious/worrying	–	–	–	–	X	0	–	–
Pretend/hide things	–	–	–	–	–	X	–	0
Worry about weight	–	–	–	–	X	0	–	–
'Uncertain' constructs								
Childish sense humour	–	–	–	0/X	–	–	–	–
Emotional	–	–	X	–	0	–	–	–

Key: 0 = Me ideally;   X = Me nowadays

Figure 12.2:   Self-construing summary from Kath's post-treatment grid

discovered that just over a year after I last saw her she had sought psychiatric help again. Her doctor commented that the improvement in her seemed to have led to increasing strain on her marriage. This in turn had led to some relapse in her eating behaviour, with loss of appetite and some weight loss, although not great. Unfortunately, as I was no longer available she had to see a general psychiatrist. This proved to be only a one-off contact. By the time she had been seen and with the help of marital counselling things had improved in the marriage and she had also engaged in some group work concerning eating disorders, which she was finding helpful. She was offered a follow-up appointment by the psychiatrist, but in the meantime there had been a most intriguing development. With the continuing improvement in her relationship with her husband she had become pregnant. Her appetite was returning to normal and it was not felt necessary for her to continue with psychiatric help at that time.

This post-therapy development confirmed my expectation that she would continue to be vulnerable and in ideal circumstances I would have offered her further 'booster' sessions to help her consolidate her improvement and deal with some of the ramifications. Nevertheless, Kath had shown that she was able to make use of further help to build on her progress. So how would Kath deal with the challenge of motherhood?

Kath wrote to me some three years after our first meeting and told me of the developments during the past couple of years. These are some excerpts from what she had to say:

> After I stopped coming to see you things were fine for a while even though I was still bingeing from time to time ... However last year our marriage hit a low point. We had to face the fact that we were not happy with each other although we still loved each other a lot. We had different goals and had grown apart over the last few years without realising it ... We decided to go to Relate [marriage guidance counselling] and I decided to go to a group for eating disorders as by then I was not eating at all (apart from a couple of biscuits a day!). Although I was not ready for group therapy when I saw you, it proved to be tremendous help last year. I had to admit not only to myself but to others that I had an eating problem due to emotional problems without my relationship with my husband. And that I could not solve one without acknowledging the other and doing something about it. It was not an easy time: I felt emotionally empty and even had a few days feeling suicidal. I was prescribed antidepressants, which helped. We went to Relate for two months and worked very hard at each session – we did not always enjoy things that we were saying but at least we were communicating and telling each other how we *really* felt and what we wanted from our relationship. Out of this came the fact that we still loved each other and were ready to do our best to save our marriage. My husband also agreed to have a few sessions of counselling on his own.
>
> During that time I gained a lot of confidence and self-esteem. Since the therapy we seem to always have a lot to say to each other and we are not afraid to say how we feel any more. Life is definitely happy and we are more relaxed in each other's company.
>
> During the therapy I found out I was pregnant and after the initial shock (for my husband) and surprise (for me) we got used to the idea. My husband had two days when he was fiercely against the idea, thinking that we needed to sort out our relationship first and being worried about my being able to eat properly and sensibly throughout my pregnancy. By then I was over the moon, I wanted to keep my baby and was ready to try very hard to eat properly. Anyway, from then on things went from good to better ... Emma is our pride and joy and she has given me a tremendous boost to my confidence. I felt that I have been able to control my eating habits and have created this beautiful baby. I have so much to look forward to and my days are so busy that eating is not a 'big deal' any more. Life is full of promises and tomorrow is not a threat anymore, not a battle like when I used to dread the next day because I knew that I would be bingeing and getting into that uncontrollable circle again. People at work have commented on my attitude. I think that I am more calm and collected now ... I am trying to set up my own business ... so as you can see my life is full and I am enjoying every minute of it! My

weight has stabilised at 7 st. 1 lb (99 lb) which is not enormous but I am eating properly. I do not have time for snacks but I make sure I eat three meals a day. I am not obsessed by my weight any more. I would not like to gain too many kilos as my clothes would not fit any more! But it seems that by eating sensibly and regularly my body is quite content and I have enough energy to do all the tasks I want to during the day.

It can be seen that following the earlier set-back, Kath and her husband had made good use of further help and were flourishing in their new role as parents. Kath continues to need to control her weight, but in other respects she is functioning very well. Questionnaire measures of eating behaviour, self-esteem and well-being all showed healthy scores, although she had a high score on the perfectionism scale of the Eating Disorders Inventory. Doubtless she will face further challenges in the coming years, but her life seems to have taken off and she has a purpose and direction over and above the defensive posture of weight control.

13 Sally

Sally is a married lady who was 28 when she was first referred for help. When we first met she presented herself as having three main problems:

- *Just food.* She complained that once she started eating she could not stop. Even when she was full, she would carry on eating until she ran out of food.
- *Being sick.* Before expecting her child a few years ago she had been sick after every meal. She stopped for a while because she did not want to lose her baby, but she still did it occasionally.
- *Just knowing I should lose weight.* Weight had always been a problem. She was a lifetime member of Weight Watchers (an organisation that helps people with slimming), but said that she had only been to 'goal' twice in the past ten years. She would lose weight well for about a month, then eat and eat.

The history of her weight problem dated from childhood and she was regularly teased and given nicknames over her size. For a while as a child she used to go to evening classes for overweight children, where she was taught about eating proper foods, etc. Although she did not like being overweight, she was not worried about it all the time as she was now. She had assumed she would be big, like her Dad. By her late teens she was up to 15 st. 7 lb (217 lb) and was taken to Weight Watchers by her Mum. The regime was very strict and there was pressure to reach 'goal'. She was told she had to lose 4 st. (56 lb) and said she did ever so well till reaching 12 st. (168 lb). For a while she felt 'wonderful', but gradually it crept up again and at assessment she weighed 17 st. 2 lb (240 lb) at a height of 5'10".

Her eating pattern would start fairly normally in the early part of the day, although she might sometimes eat as much as two packets of biscuits with her morning coffee. Typically, however, by late afternoon, she would have embarked on an almost continuous spell of eating. She would eat while she was preparing her family's dinner. She would always cook too much and end up finishing off her son's meal and anything else left. At night, if there was anything around she would eat it. To her, it felt like there was binge-eating every day and she felt out of control and unable to stop. Sometimes after dinner she would nip upstairs and be sick. Although she had rules stuck on her fridge about what she should have, she would often break the rules and end up feeling guilty. She felt preoccupied with food and spent a lot of her time looking at cookery books and making food. But there was no enjoyment in it and she hated herself and was frightened of getting bigger and bigger.

Having heard what Sally saw as the problem, I asked her about more general aspects of herself. When asked how she would describe herself to someone who had never met her she replied, 'I'd tell them my height first, then my age and name . . .'. I asked her if she liked herself and she burst into tears and said she did not like the way she looked, her size. If she was shorter, she thought that nobody would have noticed her. But when she was thin she did not care if the whole world looked at her.

I asked her about her family and she described her mother as a worrier, but a good mother who was always there and you could turn to for everything. But she had not felt able to confide in her about her eating problems, feeling this would add to her mother's own problems. Her father was described as a very big man, but she did not see him as fat, just 'impressive'. But he was under pressure to lose weight from his doctors. She said he was 'terrific' and would do anything for you. But he was very 'black and white' and could 'hit the ceiling' in anger. He also did not know about her eating problem, but he had put pressure on her to lose weight, fearing she would end up having his health problems. Sally had a younger brother, Paul, who had considerable nervous problems, involving worry about his health. He was a 'gentle giant', but had been tiny and thin as a child. She got on reasonably well with him, in contrast to her elder brother, Bob, who she described as very self-centred. Bob always had to be the odd one out and was inclined to temper tantrums. He was fiery like her Dad, as well as being quite overweight. Sally's relationship with Bob was presented as a matter of putting up with him.

At our first interview Sally had requested that her husband Ken sat in with her, an indication I think of her nervousness and lack of confidence. In the circumstances, it may have been difficult for her to be entirely open about their marriage. She said that their relationship was more settled and calm now and that they were getting to know each other better and family life was good at present. His contribution to the interview was to say that Sally was a different person now. She used to be cheerful and buoyant but had become rather depressed and inclined to hide away. He said that he would like her to be happy and not bothered about her weight. She added that she did not feel attractive and wondered whether he felt the same, but he did not reply. My impression was that Ken did not have much understanding of her eating/weight problems.

One of the most positive features of Sally's life was her five-year-old son. But here again her weight worries had had their effect. She said she used to underfeed him (from the breast) for fear of him ending up like herself. But this seemed to have passed and she said that she no longer worried over this, seeing her son as able to eat anything, just like Ken.

It was clear that Sally was very distressed about the effect all this was having on her life. As well as feeling unhappy about her behaviour, she was wary about mixing with new people, feeling that they would be looking at her badly in terms of her size. It had been a big step for her to seek help, having only recently confided to anybody about it. She burst into tears again at the end saying she had been living for this day and was afraid I would say no to the possibility of help.

I asked her to complete assessment questionnaires and an eating diary and to return in two weeks. When she returned we discussed the questionnaires and her diary. These were consistent with what she had already told me. She had high scores on most subscales of the Eating Disorders Inventory: drive for thinness (14), bulimia (18), body dissatisfaction (27), ineffectiveness (11), interpersonal distrust (7) and interoceptive awareness (11). She also had very low self-esteem as measured by the Rosenberg Self-esteem Scale (score 6) and a moderate degree of general psychological disturbance (score 15) on both the 30-item General Health Questionnaire (Goldberg, 1972) and the SCL90R (global severity index 1.21). Moreover, her eating diaries revealed an average of about two binges per day and vomiting once a week. There was, of course, no doubt that she fulfilled psychiatric criteria for the label bulimia nervosa.

I explained the kind of philosophy and approach I took to eating disorders and she responded very positively. We therefore agreed to an initial ten sessions. The first session was mainly focused on discussing her eating diary. This helped to identify some of the factors that were associated with variations in her eating behaviour. As is often the case, one of her worse times was when she had nothing to do. She also found it particularly difficult on the day she went to her Mum's. This was a weekly ritual and Mum was inclined routinely to offer her cakes, etc. To her, of course, this was a forbidden fruit and we did some early exploration, gently questioning whether it has to be the case that an overweight person cannot eat cakes. In my experience, there is nothing more compellingly attractive than a forbidden food. The difficulty with Mum proved to be an indication of a recurrent theme of not asserting herself, so that she easily could find herself in situations where unnecessary pressures were placed upon her.

Not entirely unexpectedly, in the first two sessions she presented a much more positive air, feeling happier in herself, making more of an effort with her appearance and being busy in a creative way. She was also beginning to question her assumptions and thus showing a positive response to my approach. Our second session was mainly taken up with completing the SELF-GRID.

Construct elicitation

Sally was asked to compare herself with five people and the following constructs emerged from these comparisons.

Self and mother

She commented that she and her mother were very alike, both being: easy going, putting family first, worry, and like to plan/organise. They differed in one respect, which was that mother was 'small', unlike Sally.

Self and father

The first thing she mentioned was a difference, in that she was 'calm' whereas her father 'gets irate'. But they were similar in several respects being: big, will do anything for anybody, and get on with everybody.

Self and closest person (husband, Ken)

She began by saying that Ken differed in being 'confident'. He also 'spends for today', whereas she 'saved for tomorrow'. She was 'cautious', whereas Ken 'jumped in with two feet'. They also differed in that Ken 'only ate when hungry', whereas she would 'eat regardless of hunger'. She also repeated some constructs, saying that they were both easy going and would do anything for anybody. Ken was also more calm than Sally.

Self and least liked person (Aunt Fay)

She began by saying that most people got on with her aunt but that she irritated Sally. She saw several differences. Aunt Fay was very 'house-proud', very 'fussy about clothes' and 'liked to keep up with the Joneses'.

	Always							Never
'Positive' constructs								
Put family first	–	0/X	–	–	–	–	–	–
Tall	X	0	–	–	–	–	–	–
Like to plan/organise	0	–	X	–	–	–	–	–
Do anything for anybody	0	–	X	–	–	–	–	–
Get on with everybody	0	–	X	–	–	–	–	–
Easy going	0	–	–	X	–	–	–	–
Save for tomorrow	–	0	–	–	X	–	–	–
Calm	0	–	–	–	X	–	–	–
Confident	0	–	–	–	–	X	–	–
Fussy about clothes	0	–	–	–	–	X	–	–
Spend for today	0	–	–	–	–	–	X	–
Small	0	–	–	–	–	–	X	–
Only eat when hungry	0	–	–	–	–	–	X	–
'Negative' constructs								
Keep up with Jones's	–	–	–	–	–	–	0/X	–
Gets irate	–	–	–	–	X	–	–	0
Jump in with two feet	–	–	X	–	–	0	–	–
Worries	–	X	–	–	–	–	–	0
Big	X	–	–	–	–	–	–	0
'Uncertain' constructs								
Cautious	–	–	–	–	0/X	–	–	–
Eat regardless of hunger	X	–	–	–	0	–	–	–

Key: 0 = Me ideally;   X = Me nowadays

Figure 13.1:   Self-construing summary from Sally's pre-treatment grid

Self and most liked person (her friend, Viv)

They both 'liked to help anybody', were both 'tall', were 'easy going' and generally liked similar things.

Comments

Sally seemed to quite enjoy this exercise, saying it made her think, which was to be typical of her subsequent approach to our sessions. She came across as keen to explore and was open to new ways of looking at her situation. As far as her overall self-image goes, this is graphically illustrated in Figure 13.1. The discrepancies between self and ideal self are mainly quite large and the biggest discrepancies are concerned with her size and eating behaviour. But she is also clearly concerned about other characteristics such as lack of confidence and worrying. The overall mean discrepancy of 3.2 is very high, reflecting a generally poor self-esteem. Nevertheless, she is also able to identify several strengths, such as putting her family first, being tall, planning/organising and doing anything for anybody. In fact, another notable feature is the preponderance of positively labelled constructs, which I have found to be more typical of a psychologically healthier person. Thus, while she was not generally construing herself in a very positive light, she did have available a number of positive constructs.

Treatment

The following is a summary of the main themes of each session.

Session 3

Following her initial success, I was not at all surprised when Sally returned saying she had slipped back in terms of bingeing, although she had not been vomiting. A number of situational factors were identified as apparently relevant to this eating pattern. These included getting upset, for example about her son, but also importantly with the pressure of her mother not knowing about her eating behaviour. This created situations where she would feel obliged to eat food to avoid displeasing her mother. We discussed the possibility that her mother might behave differently if she was aware of Sally's difficulties. There were also several factors concerned with the availability of food that seemed to prime her towards thinking in terms of eating. She was quite positive about taking the initiative in dealing with these kind of issues, such as telling her mother. A long-term issue seemed to be her difficulty in asserting herself.

Session 4

She reported a good week, somewhat to her surprise because she had anticipated a bad week. She had told her mother about her eating disorder, but her mother thought she should lose weight. She became tearful in the session, feeling as if everybody was thinking she should be thin and not liking her. It seemed that this piece of evidence from her mother quite easily fed into her construction that people were thinking of her primarily in terms of her weight, rather than seeing this as perhaps a reflection of parental anxiety. I explored the idea with her that weight may be but one way of looking at a person and that there may be many other ways. I suggested she try looking at herself in different ways. She was very responsive to this kind of idea and mentioned the possibility of going swimming with her son.

Session 5

Once again Sally was down and was tearful and distressed during the session. The weight construct was again being brought in to make sense of various events. She had confronted Ken about his lack of affection to her and he said it was her weight and that he wanted her to lose weight. Moreover, the nurse at her doctors had found high cholesterol in a check-up. She was feeling that everybody wants her to lose weight, but she knew she would still have a problem if she lost weight. Once again, we explored possible non-food ways of dealing with her current difficulties, while at the same time recognising that it was difficult for her to let go of the weight construing.

Session 6

Sally felt much more positive, having talked it all through with Ken. She made it clear to him that she has to be the way she is, rather than being pressurised. Although initially negative in response, he eventually came round and agreed to give her space. She felt a lot happier and closer. She had been binge-free for four to five days and there were many examples where she dealt with difficult situations without turning to food.

Session 7

This week was not quite as good, but the binges were much smaller in quantity. Sally had also been working on other ways of dealing with difficulties, such as going to bed with a book rather than eating.

Session 8

She had had some difficulties to face, but she had not gone overboard with food as she had previously. She had confronted things more, whereas previously she would have not faced speaking up. She had, however, been tempted to vomit, but realised it was to get at her husband and held back because she would have suffered more than him.

Session 9

Sally felt she had really taken off in terms of attitude change and had had no problems this week. She felt like she was growing up. This was noticeable in her speech and manner. Earlier it had been much more girl-like, but she was coming over much more confidently. She talked virtually non-stop, perhaps indicative of the fact that there was a fair amount of psychological movement going on.

Session 10

Once again there was a set-back – she felt back to square one with her family. As so often in the past, she felt that her size had been focused upon and she had retreated into dieting behaviour. My response was to explore alternative constructions of the events that had triggered this and I pointed out to her that she tended to focus on size at times of uncertainty.

Session 11

Clearly there had been a lot of ups and downs during the ten sessions and our prearranged review offered an opportunity to take stock of her overall progress. Sally said she had learnt a lot from our sessions, particularly to accept herself as she is. She now realised that she mattered and had opinions of her own. She added that she used to blame food/size before rather than recognising that she was unhappy. She still saw food as a big part of her life, enjoying cooking etc., and realised that this is what makes her think of food a lot. At the same time, she could see the need to develop other avenues, e.g she had started amateur dramatics.

She said that she enjoyed coming and wanted to carry on working on things. But she did not want to become too dependent and thought she should come less frequently.

Further sessions

Having been meeting Sally weekly we began to space sessions out to about monthly. During this time Sally had continued to have ups and downs, but the general direction felt like progress. There had been many occasions when she had been confronted with challenging events, where she had introduced the issue of her size as a potential barrier. For example, she got very worked up about appearing in a play. She had feared that all eyes would be on her. In the event, it had been a great success and her fears had not been realised. One of the interesting things had been her gradual move away from food and more on issues/situations that she had found difficult. Repeatedly, however, she had learned to overcome difficulties and had proved to be a very resourceful person, with many interests and friends.

Our sessions became increasingly spaced out, with our last meeting occurring almost two years – 22 sessions – after initial assessment. This meeting had been planned as probably her last. Sally told me that she knew when she was coming it was going to be the last time, she was ready for it, had wanted to stop and felt she had achieved something. She now felt she had got a 'line', there were not the extremes with food and mood
and she was 'plodding along', which was the way she liked it. Sally now mostly liked herself and did not think she was going to change anymore than she had done – 'I think this is me now'.

We had another more formal look at this *me* through the eyes of the SELF-GRID. In view of the long time lag since first assessment, I decided to re-elicit constructs. For reasons of space, I will not give the full details, but a few comments seem appropriate. In terms of constructs, only four constructs were repeated and none of the constructs to do with size, appearance and eating emerged. She did refer to she and her father being the same size, but said that it was not important anymore. Thus the themes that Sally was focusing on were quite different and there were several new constructs, such as 'can see the funny side of things' (Sally and her mother) and 'accept people for what they are' (Sally and her friend Viv).

Turning to the self-esteem profile (Figure 13.2), we can see that her overall self-evaluation is broadly positive, reflected in a much lower score on the self-esteem score (1.4 as opposed to 3.2 initially). There are many strengths, such as 'see the funny side', 'home-bird', 'show appreciation', etc. This is also reflected in a relative absence of negative qualities, such as using people. On the 'weakness' front, the largest discrepancy is for being 'able to say no, without feeling guilty', something she only rarely does. Perhaps, in similar vein, on the 'uncertain' construct 'do things on the spur of the moment (without thinking what others are thinking)' there is some dissatisfaction. Sally was thus still very aware of what others think of her, often putting her desire to be liked before her natural inclinations.

We discussed the grid afterwards and Sally remarked that she had found it easier to work things out this time. She found it easier to understand people and could see bits she liked and did not like now. For example, with her Dad, she accepted him, but could now see through him and saw him as he was rather than just the image of him. She also commented on the fact that she had now chosen her elder brother, Bob, as her least liked person, something she could not have admitted before. Although she did not like him, she still loved him and accepted him as he was – 'you can't change

	Always						Never
'Positive' constructs							
Can see the funny side	–	0/X	–	–	–	–	–	–
Home-bird	–	0/X	–	–	–	–	–	–
Show appreciation to others	–	0/X	–	–	–	–	–	–
Generous	–	–	0/X	–	–	–	–	–
Family is important	–	–	0/X	–	–	–	–	–
A listener	0	X	–	–	–	–	–	–
Heart of gold	0	X	–	–	–	–	–	–
Accepts people	0	X	–	–	–	–	–	–
Can make friends	0	–	X	–	–	–	–	–
Self-confident	–	0	–	–	X	–	–	–
Can express self in writing	0	–	–	–	–	X	–	–
Able to say no without guilt	–	0	–	–	–	–	X	–
'Negative' constructs							
Use people	–	–	–	–	–	–	–	0/X
Need reason to do something	–	–	–	–	–	–	X	0
Selfish	–	–	–	–	–	–	X	0
Put work first	–	–	–	–	–	X	0	–
Self-centred	–	–	–	–	–	0	X	–
Worrier	–	–	X	–	–	0	–	–
'Uncertain' constructs							
Silly sense of humour	–	–	–	–	0/X	–	–	–
Have to be right	–	–	–	–	0	X	–	–
Have to have their say	–	–	–	–	0	X	–	–
Get put on	–	–	X	–	0	–	–	–
Call a spade a spade	–	–	–	0	–	X	–	–
Do on spur of moment	–	–	–	–	0	–	–	X

Key: 0 = Me ideally;   X = Me nowadays

Figure 13.2: Self-construing summary from Sally's post-treatment grid

others, not the person'. With regard to herself, she commented that if you can accept others as they are, you have to accept yourself. From my point of view I was struck by the whole manner of Sally's approach to this task. She appeared calm and to be enjoying standing back and looking at herself. She seemed to have a pretty clear idea of how she saw herself and others, but gave it careful thought and consideration. In short, she came over as having a balanced view of herself and those she was close to.

The broadly favourable view of herself in terms of personal constructs is also reflected in formal assessments using questionnaire measures. She scored only five on the Eating Attitudes Test, zero on the General Health Questionnaire and on all scales of the Eating Disorders Inventory, except the 'body dissatisfaction' scale, she scored in the normal range. Even on the latter scale, however, her score was much reduced. Her score on the Rosenberg Self-esteem scale was also much improved, consistent with the personal construct measure of self-evaluation.

A while before our last meeting I asked Sally if she would be interested in writing something to express her view of how things had changed for her. Sally found it difficult to express herself in writing, but her friend Viv helped her put her thoughts on paper and this is what she had to say:

> I am overweight and have been for most of my life, but for the first time I am beginning to like myself as me, not what the media say I should be.
>
> I ate when I was sad, happy, worried – the more I ate the more I hated myself so I would diet. I would feel better for a while until the next problems when I would fail again. My whole life revolved around food – I thought of nothing else. After a while you do not enjoy life because you are too wrapped up in food and how you look and feel. It's a vicious circle. Even when I was at an 'ideal weight' I was still watching everything I ate in case I put on weight and I can now see that being an 'ideal weight' was not the answer – it did not solve anything!
>
> I finally sought help and found there was more to life than food. I began to recognise the reasons why I ate and how I could deal with them. What really helps is having someone to talk to who understands and is unshockable. I have started to live again – acting, keep fit – I do not put off things now until I am thin because I may never get there and what a waste of life.
>
> I matter to myself not to the rest of the world. The media can be wrong – I can be liked/loved for me even if my size is all wrong. If you accept yourself you will find that other people will accept you. I still have bad days but they are fewer and I can see a way out.

Summary

Sally's life had been dominated by food and weight issues and her self-image mainly focused around seeing herself as unacceptably big. Although she has not completely lost the negative construction of her size, this is no longer the central issue. She has been able to move on quite a bit as a person who can like herself and know that she can be liked without having to be a particular weight. She now seems to be *living*. People like Sally must find it very difficult to escape from the negative media image of fatness in women. But she has found that she *does* have other avenues to pursue and does not need to be constricted by the strait-jacket of societal construction.

14   Christine

I have chosen Christine for two main reasons. First, I think she exemplifies a kind of presentation of an eating disorder in which there are multiple problems, rather than simply problems with eating. Secondly, therapeutic work is still very much actively in progress. The story is by no means complete and as she said to me – 'we don't know how it's going to end up'. I suspect that including such a client will bring alive the therapeutic process in a way that is difficult to achieve with those individuals viewed either partly or mainly in retrospect. At the same time, however, this is not without risk. It is all too obvious to me that my therapeutic constructions are at risk of invalidation by the unfolding events during the coming months and years. This is also the case, however, for Christine, who was a willing participant in this enterprise, as in all aspects of the therapeutic process.

The background

Christine was 37 when I first met her. I was asked to see her initially for assessment during a spell of in-patient treatment, which had been precipitated by a crisis in her life involving disordered eating, heavy drinking and a general breakdown in her ability to function. Christine had a long history of contact with psychiatric services extending back to her teens. Just in the past few years, she had been admitted to hospital on several occasions and she had received a fair amount of therapeutic input. Referral to me seemed to reflect a feeling of being stuck by the psychiatric team. My initial brief was to give an opinion, but as we will see, this turned into a commitment to offering a therapeutic input.

I decided to begin by exploring Christine's construing of her self and significant others, using SELF-GRID:

Construct elicitation

Self and mother

Christine described all difference between them. Her mother was a 'coper' (in a practical way), she 'organises people' and is 'controlling'. Interestingly and perhaps surprisingly in view of what was to follow, Christine spontaneously added that they were not faults in her mother – just things about her.

Self and father

She began with similarities, she and her father both having a 'tendency to get down in mood' (for no particular reason) and 'tend to allow self to be controlled' (I think, by implication, this mainly meant by mother). She then moved to a couple of differences, first repeating the construct about coping practically, which also applied more to her father. She also saw her father as 'dependable', which she was not. Christine then returned to similarities at the physical level, saying they were both 'dark-skinned' and 'small'. She commented that he and others had remarked upon their physical and temperamental similarity, but she did not agree with this, saying that she thought she was a bit like her mother. Finally, she added a difference, in that her father (in fact, both parents) was 'aggressive'.

Self and closest person (friend, Maurice)

Christine had great difficulty initially in providing a person to fit this role and wondered what I meant. Perhaps reflecting doubt about the status of the relationship, she decided on Maurice . . . 'I suppose'. Maurice was a former college tutor, whom she had befriended some years ago. She began with several similarities, seeing them both as 'quietish' ('but I'm more willing to share myself'), 'closed', 'shy' and being 'left-wing'. They were also 'gentle' and 'physical', but Maurice was more 'calm', 'clever' and 'self-contained'.

Self and least liked person (colleague, Olivia)

Once again, Christine found this difficult, but she eventually came up with Olivia, a colleague she had worked with. She had no difficulty, however, in identifying the constructs here, with differences on several fronts. Olivia was 'noisy', 'manipulative', 'narrow-minded' and 'organised in herself'.

Self and most liked person (brother, Jack)

She chose one of her brothers, Jack. Christine began with a difference by repeating the above construct of 'coping with practical things', which also applied to Jack. But a number of similarities applied. She repeated the constructs about being 'physical' and 'quiet' and added that they were both 'rash in doing things', 'secretive' and 'can be detached'. Finally, she referred to differences of Jack being more 'likeable' and repeated the above construct of him being more 'clever'.

Additional constructs

Christine added several constructs. She said that she liked people like Maurice, who were 'trustworthy' and 'warm', but disliked people who were 'judging' or 'aggressive'. We had thus elicited 30 constructs, which is quite a large number, and it seemed that Christine had quite a rich range of ways of construing people. She seemed to find the task interesting and I was struck by the way she spontaneously elaborated on her constructions.

Initial SELF-GRID

Let us begin by examining the self-esteem profile in Figure 14.1. The first thing I would like to comment upon is the fact that there is a fairly even mix of 'positive' and 'negative' constructs and quite a few 'uncertain' constructs. This suggested to me that there was likely to be a fair amount of self-uncertainty. We can see that there are a few clear-cut strengths, notably being 'left wing', 'physical' and 'trustworthy', but on most of the positive constructs there is some degree of discrepancy. The greatest of these is never being 'organised in herself' and only rarely being 'good at coping with sad events'. In terms of negative constructs, she seems to have a pretty clear idea of what she is not. Consistent with her ideal, Christine rarely or never sees herself as: controlling, aggressive, noisy, manipulative, narrow-minded, or judging. On several constructs again, however, there are quite large discrepancies, being: dark, allow self to be controlled, rash in doing things, and get down in mood. Finally, on the 'uncertain' constructs, several of them seem to relate to the social context, where Christine seemed to want some change, but not to go too far, such as becoming more 'likeable' and less 'secretive'. Looking at this in global terms, the overall self-esteem measure of 2.6 represents a high degree of self-dissatisfaction, not atypical of someone with a long psychiatric history.

Looking at the principal components analysis, we can examine Christine's construing of others (Figure 14.2). On the first (vertical) component,

	Always							Never
'Positive' constructs								
Left wing	X	0	–	–	–	–	–	–
Physical	0	X	–	–	–	–	–	–
Trustworthy	0	X	–	–	–	–	–	–
Small	X	–	0	–	–	–	–	–
Gentle	0	–	X	–	–	–	–	–
Closed	–	–	0	–	X	–	–	–
Calm	–	0	–	–	X	–	–	–
A coper	–	–	0	–	–	–	X	–
Dependable	–	–	0	–	–	–	X	–
Warm	0	–	–	–	X	–	–	–
Self-contained	0	–	–	–	–	X	–	–
Copes well with sad events	–	0	–	–	–	–	X	–
Organised in self	–	0	–	–	–	–	–	X
'Negative' constructs								
Controlling	–	–	–	–	–	–	–	0/X
Noisy	–	–	–	–	–	–	0/X	–
Aggressive	–	–	–	–	–	–	X	0
Manipulative	–	–	–	–	–	–	X	0
Narrow-minded	–	–	–	–	–	–	X	0
Judging	–	–	–	–	–	–	X	0
Shy	–	–	–	–	X	0	–	–
Get down in mood	–	–	X	–	–	–	0	–
Rash in doing things	–	X	–	–	–	–	0	–
Allow self to be controlled	–	X	–	–	–	–	–	0
Dark	X	–	–	–	–	–	–	0
'Uncertain' constructs								
Quiet	–	–	–	X	0	–	–	–
Can be detached	–	–	–	X	0	–	–	–
Organising	–	–	–	0	–	X	–	–
Clever	–	–	–	0	–	X	–	–
Secretive	–	–	X	–	0	–	–	–
Likeable	–	–	–	0	–	–	X	–

Key: 0 = Me ideally;   X = Me nowadays

Figure 14.1:   Self-construing summary from Christine's pre-treatment grid

there was a very large polarisation between mother and Olivia on the one hand and her self/ideal self and most other elements in contrast. Christine was thus most centrally saying that she was not like her mother (and Olivia) and did not want to be. The most salient constructs here was about being 'controlling', 'manipulative' and 'organising'. The second main strand to her construing (component 2 – horizontal) was of a major contrast between her ideal self and all her selves, except the far future. Symbolising the ideal self here was Maurice and to a certain extent her brother Jack. The main constructs defining this ideal were of being 'warm', 'calm' and 'self-contained'.

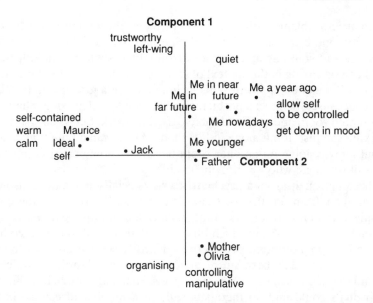

Figure 14.2: Plot of elements in construct space from Christine's pre-treatment grid

A couple of days later, we had a feedback session, where I showed Christine the kind of picture that had emerged. The main thing she picked up on was her constructs about her physical appearance, with particular reference to her size. She said she got irritated with how people comment on it, that it ought not to matter. But she felt that people treated small people as lacking influence, childish and helpless, when she thought that one could be just as powerful, if not dangerous. She also commented on the construct of 'likeable', to which I referred above. She said it was 'loveable' that she wanted to be. In her view, for people who were likeable, it could be superficial only.

We also talked about her experience and expectations of a psychological approach to help. She recalled having a previous therapist with whom she had got on well, but who had left. With this therapist, Christine had felt on an equal level, in contrast to some doctors whom she felt had power over her.

I also asked her whether she would want to change. The main things she wanted to change were wanting more power over her life, to stop feeling guilty/bad/dirty and to change the way she felt about her body.

Setting up a psychotherapeutic relationship

At the time I first met Christine, she was in the midst of a pretty massive breakdown in her ability to function. Although she had long-term psychiatric problems dating back to her teens, during the past year or so she had gone increasingly downhill. She had been drinking very heavily, bingeing and vomiting and overdosing on tablets such as pain-killers. This had been occurring in the context of various changes in her life that she was having difficulty coping with. This included losing a job, having to sell her house because of financial problems and having to sell her dog. She moved to a rented room and obtained some part-time work, but when she was not working she just drank alone in her room. At the same time bingeing and vomiting was going on and her room became a 'complete tip', full of the signs of someone who was proving unable to look after herself.

She sought help from a psychiatrist who specialised in eating disorders, rather than from an alcohol treatment service. There is a subgroup of people with eating disorders, sometimes called 'multi-impulsive' (see, for example, Lacey, 1985), in which bulimia and alcohol abuse often go hand-in-hand. From a different perspective Orford (1985) has also drawn attention to the parallels between a range of 'appetite disorders', which can extend to include such things as excessive sexual and work behaviour. Such individuals could end up therapeutically in a number of camps. Indeed, Christine had contacted an alcohol advice centre, but her previous good relationship with my eating disorders specialist colleague seemed to be the main influence on where she gravitated.

From Christine's point of view, she saw four main problem areas: loneliness, alcohol abuse, bulimia, and feeling sad and depressed. She was also faced with practical issues of finding somewhere to live and getting a job. In the midst of this sea of negatives, I enquired of what she considered as strengths or positive resources. She felt as though she no longer had any personal strengths, although she looked back to past achievements, such as looking after her siblings and the intellectual discipline of completing a degree and postgraduate qualification. Outside of herself, she got a lot of support from Maurice, who she saw from time to time and was in letter and telephone contact. Christine was single and I asked her about her family. She commented that the most difficult thing was in being honest to others about how she felt towards her family. Looking back now, this seems surprising to me in view of the amount of focus there has been on her family, but it is consistent with the above comment she had made about the constructs applying to her mother not being 'faults'. It seems that she probably felt a fair amount of guilt about her feelings towards her family.

Following these initial interviews, Christine's psychiatrist asked me whether I would feel able to work with Christine. Hospitalisation was playing a role of containment, stabilisation and giving help with finding alternative accommodation, but the general view was that she would need a longer-term psychotherapeutic relationship. I recall feeling unsure as to what I could hope to achieve in the face of so much adversity and multiple, chronic problems. At that time I was due to soon go away on a lengthy vacation and it would not have been appropriate to start work at that point. It was therefore decided to reappraise the situation on my return.

During my absence, there had been an incident where Christine had broken a rule about drinking and had been asked to leave, but had returned a week later. This had created a lot of immediate bad feelings and issues about her relationship to people in authority positions, but essentially the underlying problems were unchanged. She was keen to try working on these problems and I found her to be open to a psychological approach and comfortable with me. Although I anticipated that she would need long-term help, I felt it would be helpful to have the structure of an initially limited fixed-term contract. I suggested that we experiment with a different approach over 12 sessions and then review how useful it had been. Christine agreed.

The first phase of treatment

At the beginning of this first phase of treatment, Christine was still an in-patient and thus part of a containing and medically orientated environment. She was thus being supervised and treated for various aspects of her difficulties. It was recognised by both Christine and those involved in her treatment, however, that this was only temporary and that she needed to move on fairly soon. The main obstacle to change was her lack of suitable accommodation and this took a couple of months to sort out. The prospect of moving from hospital seemed to be eagerly sought after, but also full of apprehension. My initial work with Christine was coloured quite strongly by this anticipated move, but also by the need for her to bring some control, order and direction back into her recently disordered, if not shattered life.

We began by focusing quite closely on day-to-day behaviour and experience, looking at various aspects of her problems partly through the medium of diary keeping. At first, Christine found this difficult and did not produce it in a very complete form. On exploration, this turned out to reflect concerns about privacy. We talked this through and once she was able to see that she had control over what she entered and what she shared, she seemed comfortable to carry on with it. Diary-keeping highlighted the variations in her behaviour, which opened up the possibility for seeing the ability to anticipate and have some control over events. It was very striking, for example, how often she was filled by negative feelings, often focused on feeling empty/alone and linked with reflecting on the past and losses. Somewhat hidden away underneath the predominantly negative themes, however, was a certain amount of positive experience, such as interactions with certain staff and patients, in which she had felt good. Although she had been receiving antidepressant medication, I was presenting her with a model in which her mood could be understood, anticipated and by implication controlled by examining the way she viewed herself and her interactions with others. In fact, her medication was eventually stopped, without any obvious effect on her mood and behaviour.

Out of such observations, we were able to see how Christine's constructions of events (past, present and anticipated) helped to make sense of her emotions and behaviour. The latter clearly particularly included drinking and eating behaviour. Although there was still a fair amount of problem behaviour, she was able to see that there were other possibilities. For example, she was finding mornings more manageable, there being various kinds of routines and activities that helped to fill the time, e.g. washing, reading papers, writing letters. But other times of day were more difficult, such as afternoon, when she could feel flat, agitated and inclined to go into a low mood. We thus spent time looking at possible ways of structuring and planning the more difficult times of the day.

In this kind of way, there was a gradual shift from the position where drink and binge-eating had dominated Christine's life, but particularly in terms of the latter behaviour, the issues of weight control and a reluctance to give up old ways of dealing with food and eating were still very prominent. Although Christine had gone some way towards stabilising her eating, she was very concerned about the risks of getting fat and needing to control her weight by eating and/or vomiting. Quite a recurrent issue was of eating with other people, which Christine was generally rather reluctant to do. My approach to this was not to try to push her into doing it, but of exploring the whole context. There seemed to be an issue of privacy that was very important and broadly speaking, Christine preferred to eat in private. But I also tried to help her elaborate on the social side of eating, by encouraging her to try working on eating with people she felt more comfortable with and also to try to focus more on the non-eating aspect of the situation. Maybe eating together could be an opportunity, for example, to get to know someone better, rather than just a context in which people could see her as greedy.

During this time, Christine was offered the option of going to live in a hostel for a while. After several preliminary meetings with staff there, she tentatively agreed to go there, but this proved to be a gradual process. Christine found the change from the ward environment to be quite considerable. There was far less structure – for example, people could more or less come and go as they pleased, whereas she had become used to having to seek permission to leave the ward. The approach to eating in the hostel was also quite different, with a very unstructured approach. In her parent's home, however, meals were very formal occasions and there were many rules about how you did it, such as placings of cutlery, waiting for permission to begin etc. In the context of all this change, Christine was feeling some regrets about the loss of security provided by such structures and powerful figures like doctors and nurses. There was also, of course, the change of environment and leaving behind familiar things and people. The management of this change was an important example of how to cope with change in general. Gradually she was able to let go of the ward and eventually made the break with the ward. Her sessions with me, however, provided an important link and continuity. It was made very clear that our work was ongoing.

At the end of our 12 sessions we reviewed the work we had done together. In terms of presenting problems, Christine felt she had improved in some areas, but not in others. For example, she did not see her drinking as a big issue now, she could drink socially, but she recognised it could become a problem in the future if eating went out of control, but she thought it would not be to the same extent. Her mood was now not persistently low and swung in response to events, rather than seeing it as 'in me'. She anticipated she would always get such moods, but that would be all right as long as she was not overwhelmed by it. She still found being alone to be a problem when it occurred, but it was happening less because she was in more contact with others. She now had a home, but was looking towards alternative, less institutionalised accommodation. In terms of eating behaviour, she was eating with others more, although she still hated it. Binge-eating was far less frequent and she was making more and more decisions not to binge. Vomiting was persisting, but not on a daily basis. Her concerns about her size were somewhat greater, she felt, because she had allowed her weight to go up somewhat.

Looking at the therapy as a whole, Christine said that she had found it useful, particularly in terms of feeling more in control and having choices. She reflected on how she had expected me to be more like a doctor and at times had perhaps wanted that. For my part, I felt that Christine had worked hard at the therapeutic process, she seemed comfortable working with me and seemed open to the kind of approach I was taking. It seemed to me, therefore, that our experiment had shown that we could work together to good effect and that she could make changes in her life through a psychological medium. Christine was keen to continue working together on help, but she felt there could now be a narrower focus, particularly on control issues, relationships and her eating/weight focus. I felt that she had started moving out of the stuck position she had got into, but clearly had a long way to go. She did not seem ready to let go of help and indeed it seemed likely that long-term psychotherapy was merited. The structure of having a set number of sessions followed by a review seemed to suit Christine and we agreed to a further 12. In fact, we have now had near to 50 sessions and we continue to review progress every 12 sessions.

Going beyond food and weight

After the first stage of psychotherapy, Christine's life was moving again and it was not long after moving into the hostel that she displayed evidence of itchy feet. Although it had provided her with a base, she soon expressed a desire to move on. She was seeking greater freedom and independence and wanted greater privacy in her life than was possible there. Christine was also looking for work, so that she seemed to be generally in the business of *dilating* her perceptual field. But in terms of food and weight issues, she was still wedded to her old ways, albeit in a less pervasive way than had been the case before we met. During the course of the year leading up to the time of writing, we seem to have been centrally dealing with the issue of going beyond food and weight. This still largely remains at the anticipatory level and I would now like to consider and try to make sense of some of the ways in which Christine needs to hang on to it.

Christine often goes back to earlier times in her life and often gets very bogged down in her view of her family, and her parents in particular. Her experience of her parents seems to be of feeling controlled, particularly by her mother. At times she seems to blame her parents for her problems and can get very angry about it. In fact, at times this is presented in a very negative way, as if evidence of this somehow has condemned her. It has been my impression (a construction I have shared with her) that Christine is particularly likely to turn to this kind of construing when she is faced with something difficult, possibly even change itself. Much of Christine's construing of the world seems to have rested on a theory that others have treated her badly – a theory that at times includes people who have been involved in her treatment. The approach I have taken with her about this is not to question the rights or wrongs of her view. Indeed, it often seems very understandable that she should feel how she does. But my aim is to try to help her make sense out of other people's behaviour. For example, in the case of her parents, listening to the examples she gives, it seems that they both show evidence of considerable psychological vulnerability. I have tried to help her place the behaviour they exhibit towards her in terms of their own attempts to achieve some degree of predictability and control over their lives. Although Christine may wish that they were different, it may be difficult for them to change. Often this is expressed as disappointment at a lack of validation or support for her. It seems likely that Christine's personal agenda is often unlikely to meet with parent's approval – I try to help her anticipate this and move beyond needing external validation for where she is going. This seems, however, to be a very hard lesson to learn – maybe after many years of feeling defined by others it is hard to switch to a perspective that raises the possibility of *making oneself*. Moreover, such reconstruction may be particularly hard in well-established relationships, such as that with parents. Much of the reconstruing is therefore focused on other people in Christine's life.

One such person is Maurice. In contrast to her parents, Christine has generally felt very comfortable and safe with Maurice. The general theme with Maurice is of being accepted and cared about. But at times, Christine seems to get bogged down here too. One of the themes in her relationship with him is of wanting to be small, protected and almost childlike. It seemed that Maurice may well have been comfortable with this kind of relationship, so that they validated each other's construing. At times, however, it has seemed that this has blocked progress. For example, Christine has become aware of her advancing years and has sometimes felt that Maurice does not like the physical changes in her. Clearly, if she sees Maurice as the sole source of validation, then this could be a block to her giving up the quest for being thin. I have tried, instead, to introduce Christine to a conceptualisation of relationship *development* in which the relationship can move on as the construing of each partner changes. Not only did it seem likely that Christine was changing, but so was Maurice and maybe he had changing needs in relation to her. Christine was also seeing the possibility of developing relationships with other men and was aware of her need for greater intimacy and possibly a sexual relationship, something that she had never been able to achieve. She had, for example, recently befriended another older man, Jim, and she felt very comfortable with him. Although this was in the early stages of development, this relationship does not seem to have been born out of her size, nor was it apparently characterised by seeking approval and acting like a child. Instead it seems to have developed out of common interests and a mutual interest in each other.

In this and other ways, Christine acknowledges that she is diversifying her relationship with others and relating to people differently. Kelly's theme of needing to spread our dependencies on other people is one I have frequently offered to Christine and she seems readily able to make sense out of it. It is noticeable how when she was in hospital and soon afterwards, her relationships centred very much on the therapeutic milieu. As well as people such as doctors, nurses and myself, other patients, particularly those with eating disorders, were very important. This makes a lot of sense if one considers the significance of 'commonality of construing' in relationship formation. It seemed that shared concerns about weight and food were very prominent in these relationships. But as time has gone by, Christine seems to have increasingly let go of such relationships. Similarly, for a while she was frequently homesick and was often going home to her parents. Although she still visits them, she generally seems much more integrated within her community and is involved with several groups of people and organisations representing vocational and cultural interests. Christine still does not have paid employment, but she is striving to broaden her education to increase her chances of success in this field. She also seems to benefit from learning in its own right and this is a direction I have actively encouraged her to experiment with. Recently she has been attending a course concerned with women in society, which she seems to be enjoying considerably and seems to be helping her to move away from being preoccupied with her individual psychopathology towards a more socially shared view of issues such as body image.

In many ways, Christine seems to have moved on. She has since made further moves on in terms of accommodation, having moved into her own flat, a major move towards independence. She is involved in various organisations, has a number of interests, a broadening range of social contacts and is trying to build a career. She has also moved some way from her 'illness'. She has in fact sometimes commented how she had lived her life as a sick person, but she is not that person any more and does not want it. Christine also acknowledges that our relationship is not permanent. She told me at one of our meetings, however, that when she had help in the past that she had opted out of treatment prematurely. She felt in retrospect that she had possibly held back from completely losing her problems, almost as an insurance to being able to come back again. Although, we have moved our sessions from once a week to once every other week, and will probably soon move to further spacing out, it seems important to bear in mind her likely continuing need to relate to me as a kind of anchor. I have made it very clear to her that contact with me is not dependent on her having an eating problem. I hope that in time, however, Christine will have developed sufficient resources within herself and her social context to be able to let go. It remains to be seen whether Christine can do the same with weight control. To let go of the central theme of over 20 years of life is a tall order. I would anticipate, however, that if she continues to develop her ability to grow and relate to people without getting bogged down by control/approval issues that there is every possibility that it can be relegated to the realms of history.

So what does Christine make of it all? I recently invited her to put on paper her views.

I think the first step towards recovering from bulimia is really wanting to be free of it without reservations. Then it is a case of learning to live with your body as it is, even if it means being a bit heavier and fatter than before. It's not easy and it takes a lot of time and help and hard work and I still have a long way to go.

Bulimia is very destructive physically and emotionally and the financial toll can be dreadful. It leads to deceitful behaviour, lies and secrecy, which in turn lead to shame and guilt and depression. The worst part of it is the loneliness that comes from never allowing anyone to get really close because it makes you feel that nobody could really like you if they knew how disgusting and devious you were. What people see of you is the façade you allow them to see and you become more and more lonely until in the end you realise that the few relationships and social outlets you have don't mean anything to you because it's not you they are relating to. I have tried to stop bingeing and vomiting many times and have not succeeded because the fear of gaining weight held me back. In the brief periods when I did manage to stop I became very depressed and bulimia then became a way of coping with depression.

I have had food problems throughout my adult life. Bulimia began when I was 17 but I had problems with my weight and eating before then. As a young teenager I gained a lot of weight and was very unhappy about it especially when a teacher at school made fun of me about my size. My GP prescribed amphetamines to help me diet and over the next 18 months I lost 4 st. 7lb (63 lb) but I had become very depressed and anxious at times and during that year I had started cutting myself with knives and bits of broken glass and took an overdose. I started overeating when I came off the appetite suppressants and began to use alcohol as a way of getting through the episodes of anxiety I went through. I was also aware that I wasn't really in a state to go back to school any more and take A levels and that also upset me. I began a cycle of bingeing, vomiting, starving, drinking and cutting myself that has lasted for nearly 20 years. Fatness represented unhappiness and loneliness and thinness made me acceptable, somehow I thought I would find love if I were thin, and if I didn't, well at least it disguised the grossness of the feelings I felt so ashamed and guilty about. I don't know why loneliness is such a difficult thing to own up to but I think a lot of people find it hard to admit it and I am one of them. I always kept it to myself in the same way that I kept my chaotic eating patterns a secret. When I was a student I was regarded as quite happy and successful and fairly confident, as I was in my last three jobs. Having other people's approval is very important to me and that has sometimes been a drawback in treatment because there have been times when things have been very difficult and I've been bingeing badly but not said anything to the person helping me. I wanted to stay in control of what I ate and so control my weight but in fact I wasn't in control, I was being controlled by food and fear. I wanted to change but I wasn't able to let go of my eating pattern and its chaos nor able to trust the people who were trying to help me and this ambivalence stopped some of the treatment I had from working.

Bulimia is still not a thing of the past but I am recovering. It's hard to say exactly how and why I've been able to let go because it has happened slowly, but two things in particular seem important. Through the hospital treatment I've had over the last 18 months I've been helped to see a very positive side of my nature, that of a good person with a lot to give. We did this by moving away from the image of me as a sick and powerless person, as I had seen myself and my parents and family had seen me, to seeing me as someone able to make decisions about my life and carry them through. I have been given time to talk about myself and my ideas and feelings and develop a real trust in the person helping me. We explored present and future possibilities and my sense of confidence increased so that I began to believe in myself more and believe that I could change and be happy. I've been able to get involved in local activities and in my church without feeling it is all a façade and I have begun to make real relationships with people I feel communicate with the whole of me and not just some small superficial part. The second thing is that in hospital I learnt how to change my eating pattern in very practical ways, like eating three meals a day and not craving for food. It was as if I was being given permission to enjoy food without guilt and without feeling I had to get rid of it straightaway. In some ways I think I had always felt that I did not deserve to be fed and that feeling is beginning to leave me.

Concluding comment

For a client such as Christine, the process of change is likely to be slow and protracted. Personal construct therapy offers no 'quick fix' of well-being to replace many years of emotional pain. But with patience, persistence and support, the person can be enabled to discover positive aspects of themselves, which open up the potential for a more meaningful and rewarding life.

Part IV

ISSUES AND FUTURE DIRECTIONS

15 Issues and future directions

I hope that I have succeeded in communicating something of the flavour of a personal construct approach to the understanding of people with eating disorders. We have seen how the conceptual framework advanced by George Kelly in the 1950s can be applied to a clinical problem that was not common in Kelly's days. I'm sure, however, that had he been alive today he would have had some valuable insights to offer into the struggle with which so many young people engage in these days to try to put things right through their weight and size. Although I would be surprised if his ideas on the subject would not have been rich and penetrating in a way I could not hope to emulate, I suspect his approach to such understanding would not be dissimilar to my own. Ultimately, this is about exploring the individual's construal of his or her very personal world. At the same time, however, I am conscious of the fact that I have sometimes strayed some distance away from this principle in my efforts to make generalisations about people with eating disorders. In a sense, this is as unsatisfactory as making generalisations about any group, such as the elderly, AIDS sufferers or women. But, we should not be surprised to find some commonalities in construing among a group who seem to share some behavioural similarities. I hope I have struck a reasonable balance between these contrasting aspects of my enquiry.

I would like to turn now to a consideration of some of the main issues that I think emerge from a personal construct approach to eating disorders. In so doing, I shall be pointing towards possible future developments. The issues I have chosen to focus on are: making sense of eating disorders; the prospect for change; therapeutic issues; gender issues; relationship with other applications of personal construct psychology. Lastly, I shall indulge in some personal reflections and anticipations.

Making sense of eating disorders

I have argued strongly throughout this book that a personal construct approach can help to make sense of people with eating disorders. Although I do not claim to understand all the complexities of such people's relationships with food, I do find that I can generally make some kind of sense of what they are aiming at if I work at it. The framework of personal construct theory offers me a way of conceptualising the problem, which I do not assume is right, but I find it helps me chart possible directions for change. This conceptualisation does have a general form, namely that *being eating disordered helps a person to anticipate events*. As such, it helps to make life reasonably predictable, controllable and understandable, even though the person concerned may not like many aspects of his or her eating-disordered existence. Although this general hypothesis is one that guides me in my approach to clients presenting with eating disorders, it still needs to be translated into the specifics of a particular client.

My hunch on meeting such clients is thus that their behaviour has helped them to anticipate events, but I do not know what events, nor do I know the particular form or content of their anticipations. That is a matter for exploration with the client and I have outlined some of the procedures that can be used to explore a person's construing. I have made extensive use of repertory grids in such exploration, but I am all too aware of their limitations and they will certainly not be to everybody's liking. They do have the attraction of being structured and offering the possibility of measurement, but they can easily deceive unless viewed with a strong dose of scepticism. Moreover, grids do not always succeed in tapping into the more crucial constructions, which may explain the resistance to change. They may offer a starting point, but there is surely scope for innovative experimentation in the use of other methods of exploration, such as self-characterisation, drawings, music or poetry. In addition to broadening the range of techniques, I think there is a good case for broadening the context of such enquiry. Up to now, personal construct exploration of people with eating disorders has mainly centred on the construing of people or eating situations. Based on my clinical experience, I think there is a good case for more exploration of the construing of relationships in eating disorders. I am increasingly beginning to doubt the value of focusing on person construing without reference to person-to-person construing. In all the case studies in this book, for example, the clients' constructions of themselves were heavily influenced by their construction of certain key relationships that were problematic. Ryle and Lunghi's (1970) method of dyad grids, in which the elements are relationships (self–mother, self–father etc.) would seem to have promise, but there is no reason why non-grid methods could not also be used to study relationships.

I have been making a case for the maximum potential of a personal construct approach being in the understanding of the individual. If there is one message I would want to leave, it is that people with eating disorders do not all construe in the same way. Although they show similarities of some of their behaviour and attitudes, their view of the world is highly personal and crucial to any attempt to extricate them from the preoccupation with food and size issues. I would thus caution against the tendency to make grand generalisations concerning the aetiology of eating disorders. But this does not rule out the possibility of there being similar themes and some commonality of construing.

Personal construct research does produce one pretty consistent theme, which is of the negativity of self-construing which characterises people with eating disorders. This would not be true of all who follow this particular track, but it is mostly the case. In this respect, people with eating disorders are no different from people presenting with other kinds of psychological disorder. This is consistent with my argument (e.g. Button, 1985b) that eating disorders emerge within a context of general vulnerability in psychological processes. Thus the starting point for an eating disorder may not be dissimilar from the starting point for a phobic, depressive or substance abuse disorder. It may be that social (e.g. peer behaviour) and biological (e.g. a propensity towards obesity) factors point a person towards weight and food control, rather than, say, towards experimenting in drugs or avoiding going out.

Once the person embarks on the food/weight control path, there is the possibility that the behaviour will become so meaningful as to become a way of life. This way of life can be construed as unhealthy and damaging in many ways, just as can apply to something like heavy drinking or drug abuse. But, just as is the case with drug/alcohol abuse, the behaviour persists because the person at the centre of it is looking at it from a perspective different from relatives', health professionals' and society's at large. From their point of view, at least for a while, it has some meaning. It seems possible that construing processes may play a part in determining how far along this track people will go.

One such possibility is the existence of a rather limited, less multidimensional construct system, particularly for construing people. Quite strong evidence has emerged from my research to support this theory as far as anorexia nervosa goes. It seems quite likely, therefore, that a lack of flexibility and less multidimensionality of construing is implicated in the aetiology of anorexia nervosa, perhaps in keeping with Bruch's (1962) emphasis on conceptual rigidity. I would like to stress, however, that this does not seem to apply to all anorectics and I have come across quite a few who seem to have a wide repertoire of constructs, which they apply in a quite flexible way. In the case of bulimics, I find no evidence of any particular structural style of construing. This suggests to me that bulimic disorder may reflect more a disorder of *content* rather than of process/structure. This is perhaps borne out by my significant finding that bulimics are much more likely to produce constructs concerned with eating, weight or appearance than are anorectics. It may, of course, be that the anorectics are in some way concealing such constructs from me, but it also seems possible that the finding reflects a different kind of agenda for the two groups. Perhaps for the anorectics, their whole sense of self is at risk (as perhaps expressed by a client who said she 'didn't exist'), whereas for bulimics it is more a case of not liking the particular construction of self (e.g. being fat).

A further piece of evidence from my research also points in this kind of direction. It will be recalled that anorectics had a more favourable construction of self when younger than bulimics, but this difference was not evident for self 'nowadays'. This is consistent with Weinreich, Doherty and Harris's (1985) concept of anorectics having a 'plummeting identity crisis'. My tentative hypothesis to explain this finding is that this plummeting may reflect the kind of structural deficit of construing implicated above. A more black and white form of construing may work within a highly contained and controlled family setting, perhaps validated by family members who share similar construing. But it is in danger of being invalidated when the person is faced with a wider interpersonal field, as is likely in adolescence and early adulthood. Such a person is likely to encounter many more ways of construing, both in others and possibly themselves. It would be surprising if such *dilation* of the perceptual field did not seriously undermine the person's ability to anticipate events and in turn lower self-esteem. *Constriction* to the world of weight control would probably be consistent in structural terms to their existing construing and hence they could continue to function.

In the background of the disordered eating, we have seen that wider psychological disturbance, particularly affecting self-image, relationships and mood are commonplace. It has become quite popular recently to conceptualise such dysfunction as secondary to the eating disorder or what has become known as 'eating restraint' (e.g. Herman and Polivy, 1984). For example Garner et al (1990) have described research which suggests that such deficits in bulimics are secondary to chronic dietary chaos. While this may be a partial explanation of such dysfunction, I am not personally convinced that it is a sufficient explanation. There is no doubt in my mind that eating disorders produce all kinds of negative effects in their wake, but I would suggest that some explanation needs to be found for the excessive dietary restraint in the first place. For example, I am currently carrying out a study in which a large cohort of 11–12 year old girls are being followed up at age 15–16 (Button, 1990a). The aim of this study is to investigate whether self-esteem at age 11–12 is predictive of the development of disordered eating in later adolescence. Such longitudinal studies focused on a potentially vulnerable cohort, should help to throw some light on whether eating disorders are a consequence of some broader vulnerability or just the outcome of excessive dieting. Both may of course be true for some individuals.

Given that eating disorders generally develop in young people, I think there is a case for more research on the processes of development during these years. It may be, for example, that a better understanding of eating disorders may arise from taking a closer look at the process of identity formation, during the transition to adulthood. Erik Erikson (1959, 1968) has pointed to the importance of the task of constructing a clear sense of identity during adolescence. To operationalise Eriksonian identity, most researchers in this field have used Marcia's (1966) 'identity status model'. Of the four statuses, both 'achievers' and 'moratoriums' are active in self-exploration, but the former group have resolved a crisis and are committed, whereas the latter group are attempting to resolve a crisis. Neither 'fore-closures' nor 'diffusions', however, engage in self-exploration, the latter group being uncommitted, whereas the former group have firm self-definition acquired automatically from significant others, especially parents. Berzonsky (1989) has presented differences in identity status and 'identity crises' as reflecting different styles of self-theorising and personal construct structure. For example, the most differentiated construing was found among the 'moratorium' group. In considering these concepts, I am struck by the parallels between the contrasting styles of the anorectic (fore-closure, perhaps?) and bulimic (moratorium/diffusion, perhaps?). There seems to be considerable scope for examining weight/eating construing within the context of the overall process of identity development, perhaps using such concepts. Such investigation might help to clarify how people come to use weight/eating construing within their overall attempt to construct their self-theory.

As alluded to when considering assessment procedures, there seems also to be a need for more research on the role of the construing of relationships in eating disorders. There is no doubt that as a group, people with eating disorders do not enjoy particularly good relationships with others and it seems likely that this plays a role in the development of these disorders. Parent construing seems particularly important, but I would like to see this research extended to also examine parental construing of the eating-disordered person. Perhaps of particular interest would be the extent to which there is evidence of 'sociality' between eating-disordered people and their parents. That such research might be illuminating is perhaps suggested by Hall and Brown's (1983) semantic differential comparison of the attitudes of a sample of anorectics and their mothers versus control females and their mothers. Interestingly, both groups showed evidence of good awareness of each other's construing between mothers and daughters. But the anorectic daughters and mothers differed from the controls in rating sickness, arguments and tension more favourably than the control group. Such research on parent–child construing could also be extended to examining the whole family construct system along the lines described by Procter (1985) and Feixas (1992). Moreover, such relationship construing could be investigated in other areas, such as with the opposite sex, which often seem to be problematic for people with eating disorders.

In closing this section, I would like to reiterate that although bulimics and anorectics seem to show some differences in construing as a group, there is considerable overlap and too much generalisation seems unwarranted. The similarities are perhaps greater than the differences and I would not wish to encourage a compartmentalised approach to further enquiry in this area. We should also not forget that the two disorders are not mutually exclusive and they thus need to be looked at as a whole. Whatever point on the spectrum is being examined, however, I suggest it is the meaning of the behaviour which is of more relevance than the behaviour per se.

The prospect for change

One of my aims in presenting the case examples was to illustrate the kind of change that can occur in people with eating disorders. We have seen several examples of people whose lives seem to have changed dramatically. These examples do not constitute scientific evidence for any particular theory, but they are based upon real people who did change their construction of themselves in such a way as to allow the process of living without an eating disorder to occur. It was a real privilege and pleasure to glimpse this process and to see people enjoying life again.

Although some people seem to be able to move on from eating disorders, they do not necessarily completely lose their eating disordered constructions. Consistent with Hsu's (1990) overview of outcome, it seems that a person can be eating normally, be at a normal weight, not using vomiting/ laxatives etc., but to still be somewhat concerned about the need to control weight and eating. Moreover, at times of difficulty, such constructions seem more likely to come into play. In the same way as adults are sometimes capable of construing and behaving like a child (e.g. on going home to Mum or when ill), there seems to be no reason why a formerly eating-disordered person cannot go back to worrying about weight and cutting back. I would contend, however, that such 'regressions' do not have to be permanent and can be seen to be transitional or situational in nature. I am often asked this kind of question by clients at the end of therapy. Quite naturally, they wonder whether the change will last. I obviously cannot answer the question with any certainty, but I tell people that I would expect ups and downs, but that I would also expect them to feel more confident about this as they build on what they have learned during treatment.

A personal example seems relevant here. About 20 years ago, I went through an episode of quite marked depression, which I managed to get through without treatment. I was wary for some time as to whether it would return, but for some years now it has not held such fear. Out of what I have learned about myself and people in general over the past 20 years, I feel quite optimistic that I can handle things without going down that particular track. I may be proved wrong, of course! But I will deal with that issue if and when it arises. I think the eating-disordered client similarly needs a lot of experience of life outside eating disorder before he or she can feel confident about letting it go.

Even where a person manages to more or less completely leave behind eating-disordered constructions, he or she may still be subject to a fair amount of problems and disturbance. Life beyond an eating disorder is no easy ride – there is no obvious counterpart to Bruch's (1978) *The Golden Cage*. In fact, in many ways it could end up being a much more difficult proposition. The title of Mel Brooks' film *Life Stinks* taps into a sentiment that may be familiar to many of us in our darker hours. It seems to me that life can stink, but it can also be fun, boring and many other things besides. One thing about it though, is that it does not stay the same. There is enough to test the most flexible of construers. It may well be that people who have been eating-disordered are still left with a quite high level of psychological vulnerability, perhaps from both biological and experiential factors. This may particularly manifest itself as mood disturbance as suggested in Hsu's (1990) review. But it is possible to make sense of and manage that disturbance without dealing with it through weight control. In the same way as we can develop constructs for anticipating people, we can have constructs for anticipating and making sense of mood. From such anticipation naturally comes a measure of control.

Not everyone manages to change and there are many people, such as Helen, who cannot seem to let go of the world they have created. I find this sad and sometimes feel very frustrated and inadequate at my inability to help them move on. Maybe another person with a different approach could achieve more, but all too often with such people other therapists have tried before to no avail. Why some people can make use of help and others cannot is still something of a mystery to me, although our earlier review of outcome would suggest that those with more disturbed personality and relationships with others are likely to be most resistant. From my doctoral study of in-patient anorectics (Button, 1980) there were a number of quite strong personal construct prognostic indicators. The most notable of these was greater unidimensionality and more extreme self-construing. This needs further investigation within the somewhat different context of a mixed group of anorectics and bulimics receiving psychotherapeutic treatment at out-patient level. It may well be that further exploration of differences in response to treatment may throw light on what psychological factors are most relevant to resistance to change.

Therapeutic issues

I have presented one particular approach to helping people to move on from the world of an eating disorder. I am personally somewhat uncomfortable with terms such as 'therapy' and 'treatment', which seem to carry the flavour of a medical model, but convention leads to the perpetuation of such language. Franz Epting (1984) also addresses this issue in his fine book *Personal Construct Counselling and Psychotherapy*. Epting also makes the point that the term 'therapy' conjures up the image of treatment being 'actively administered to a rather passive recipient called the patient' (p. 3). As he points out, this bears no resemblance to the kind of relationship envisaged by Kelly and to which I and others aspire. I see my clients as co-collaborators and the aim is not to cure them of an illness, but to work together with that person in the hope that they can come to 'deal more effectively and creatively with life' (Epting, 1984, p. 4). Thus, what I am calling personal construct psychotherapy is a rather ill-defined and unique set of relationships between people. Personal construct theory offers a framework for those involved in helping relationships, but it is not a set of techniques and cannot be prescribed or packaged. I am aware of the fact that this frustrates many people, such as colleagues who repeatedly ask me 'What do you actually *do*?' In practice, what I do may often not look too different from what others are doing, but there is an underlying language and framework that guides me. That framework helps me to know where I am going in my role as *therapist*, in the same way that the framework of our *personal construct system* guides us in a more personal sense. I cannot disguise my hope that others will be tempted to try out this kind of approach with people with eating disorders (and more generally). But there is no neat recipe. Neither do I make claims that my approach is generally superior to that of others, whether they be feminist, psychoanalytic, cognitive-behavioural or eclectic. To me this would be like saying that speaking in German is better for people than speaking in Japanese. I speak neither of these languages, but I imagine that they offer quite different possibilities. I also would envisage that there are very contrasting relationships within both societies, some pretty good and some rather awful.

My stance on the nature of a personal construct approach does not thus lend itself too amenable to the world of efficacy research. My approach to researching my work has been mainly restricted to a critical and systematic monitoring of individual case work, including seeking regular feedback from clients. It would, of course, be perfectly possible to enter a personal construct approach into a sophisticated psychotherapy research design, say comparing it with a cognitive-behavioural approach and indeed there may be a good case for it. But I am personally rather more interested in the question of what kinds of relationships help what kinds of people, than what therapy works best. I have been rather more impressed by the evidence that the nature of the relationship, as perceived by clients, has more bearing on the success of psychotherapy than any technical features. (e.g. Sloane et al, 1975). One very relevant question is whether some clients may be more suited to a personal construct approach than others. Previous research (e.g. Caine, Wijesinghe and Winter, 1981; Winter, 1985) would lead one to anticipate that this may well be the case. From my point of view, I would look towards such characteristics as a preparedness to explore, rather than the seeking of a 'prescriptive' approach.

Assessing the value of a personal construct approach is but one therapeutic issue. I think there is a broader question, as to whether therapy in general is of value for people with eating disorders. Although individual therapeutic relationships may be very helpful, some can be positively harmful and perhaps best avoided. My overall stance on this issue is 'not proven', particularly with regard to anorexia nervosa. In the case of bulimia nervosa, the question is rather more open. More longer-term studies seem necessary. I would like to propose that the key to recovery from eating disorders is the nature of the person's relationships with others.

Broadly speaking, I would argue that when a person is comfortable with themselves and in relationship to others then they are less likely to need to be eating-disordered. I have been struck by seeing how change in people's relationships seems to go hand in hand with change in their eating behaviour. I see psychotherapy as being part of that process. Psychotherapy is offering a new kind of relationship, which may hold the key to a new world. But I would expect that not all psychotherapeutic relationships will work. Some may not fit for a particular client and they may not occur at the right point in time.

For example, I am currently working with someone who I shall call Mary-Anne who presented with severe bulimic symptoms. Some 18 months ago she was referred to me for help and we engaged in very sporadic contact. She proved to be a very irregular attender and she eventually dropped out of contact. She found the sessions very difficult and, for example, on one occasion ran out of the session. But, about a year later, she contacted me again seeking further help. I must admit to having been very doubtful about her ability to stay the course, but I was struck by her having apparently moved on somewhat as a person, being more prepared to face the issues. During the past few months I have been seeing Mary-Anne regularly on a weekly basis. Although she finds the sessions very painful, she is managing to hang in and it feels like we are beginning to work together on the complex and deep-seated issues that lead her to turn to food to deal with her emotions. In the same way as one needs to be ready for the commitment of marriage, maybe one has to be ready for psychotherapy. Moreover, we do not have to view psychotherapy as all about one relationship at one point in time solving all life's problems. Like relationships in general, maybe we can see different therapeutic relationships as having their own distinctive contribution. Quite often clients will have previous therapy before coming my way. Even though they are currently struggling, earlier help may have played an important role at the time. Similarly, my personal construct intervention may help free up the person sufficiently to embark on the process of change. But the person may well need to move on to further help. For example, I might be able to help a person reconstrue life so that he or she did not have to pursue weight and eating control. But that person may well feel that he or she needs to work on relationships with other people. Taking up some form of group therapy may well be the next step.

A good example of this kind of thing was Tina. Tina had got bogged down with concern about being fat and was in a vicious circle, with eating to comfort herself only exacerbating her concerns. Over a period of several months, Tina was able to make sense of the way she was using food and gain some perspective about herself as a person beyond her size. She had effectively put food and weight in perspective. But this work had identified the important underlying issue of sexual abuse. I did some further work with her trying to help her make sense of her bad experiences with men and move some way towards a reconstruction of such relationships. On follow-up, Tina felt that her work with me had been very valuable and she was generally coping with life much better and was much more confident. But she still felt there were aspects of herself with which she felt dissatisfied and felt there was still something that was not quite right that needed to come out – she wondered for example about something like hypnosis. I made it clear to her, however, that this was not within my expertise. I also felt there was an element of needing to let go of what had become a rather dependent relationship on me. Tina agreed with this and we decided it was time to part ways and were able to come to a comfortable ending. I think we both felt that our relationship had been good and constructive, but maybe it had gone as far as was possible. We shared the metaphor of her having completed her 'O levels'. Maybe she would later choose to move on to her 'A levels'.

I would also like to suggest that therapeutic relationships do not have to be confined to professional psychotherapy. The experience of a good relationship with someone, such as a new partner, can bring about considerable reconstruction in the same way that professional psychotherapy can. For example, Quinton and Rutter (1985) have shown how the intergenerational transmission of psychological disorder can be ameliorated by the effect of a good relationship. But while someone is totally immersed in the world of food they may keep such therapeutic influences out of reach. It may require the model of an initial therapeutic relationship to unlock the door to such potential relationships. I believe we have seen this process with several of the case examples, such as Anna. Most fresh in my mind, however, is Joanne, who initially was a very closed off person, very wary of letting anybody into her world. As she has grown to feel safe to be herself with me, she has opened up herself to others and she is developing relationships with others that are beginning to play an important and valued part in her life. There is no reason why we have to see therapeutic qualities as the exclusive province of the professional. Indeed, the client may come to develop such therapeutic qualities in himself or herself. The setting of a self-help group can be an important arena where such qualities can be expressed to mutual benefit.

All the work I have described has been one-to-one psychotherapy, perhaps being typical of the whole field of personal construct psychotherapy, where individual work has predominated. Kelly noted seven reasons why group therapy may have advantages over individual therapy:

- as a base for experimenting with people
- to learn about discrimination between different people
- to challenge 'pre-emptive construing' (use of 'nothing but' constructs)
- to confront 'constellatory construing' (use of stereotypic constructs)
- to provide a variety of validational evidence
- to encourage dispersion of dependency
- to be economically viable.

He also presented a series of stages of development of therapy groups. Although personal construct group psychotherapy has not been since extensively elaborated, there have been a number of examples of its use (e.g. Dunnett and Llewelyn, 1988) and Winter (1992) sees considerable potential for further development. I have conducted my own experiment with a group form of personal construct psychotherapy with a mixed group of people with eating disorders (Button, 1987). The group was modelled on Landfield and Rivers' (1975) interpersonal transaction group, originally described in treating a group of alcoholics. The focus of the group was on the clients' construing of each other, on the assumption that deficits in person construing underlay their eating disorder. The group embraced the spirit of the 'sociality corollary' by inviting members to aim at working towards understanding each other without making judgements. A lot of the activity was done in pairs, with group members carrying out short exercises where they were required to enquire about each other's construing in some area, e.g. talk about situations where you feel in control. There was no direct emphasis on eating behaviour in the group, although clients often brought out issues such as weight. The group ran for 20 sessions and clients were assessed at various stages using grids.

The most dramatic change in construing of group members was of a reduction in extremity of construing. This change was evident by mid-group, suggesting that the group may have provided moderating feedback about themselves quite early on. The focus of the group on trying to understand each others' construing perhaps had the effect of reducing the more extreme constructions of themselves and others. Perhaps as a consequence of less polarisation, there was also an overall improvement in self-esteem and self-isolation. But there were quite marked differences between group members in terms of the extent of change. Some people changed a lot whereas others seemed to dig their heels in and a few dropped out. Where change occurred, emotional disturbance understandably followed. Rachel, for example, an overweight group member, discovered that the type of person you were did not depend on weight and recalled feeling that 'the idea upon which I based my entire thinking life . . . the only reason I had for living had been stolen from me' (Button, 1987, p. 241). Fortunately, Rachel was eventually able to get through this loss and move on – 'to think in a more constructive way . . . to move into a life of many more choices'.

Looking back on this group, I felt that the experiment of mixing anorectics, bulimics and overweight people together in the group was perhaps a mistake. The anorectic members seemed generally ill-equipped to handle the group format and may have been better suited to individual therapy. I think another problem was that a number of group members were more interested in focusing on weight and eating than exploring each other as people. I do not know if this can be avoided with such a relatively homogeneous population, although Batty and Hall (1986), describing a personal construct approach to self-help groups for eating disorders, showed that such groups do not need to be dominated by such concerns. It may be, however, that a person-oriented group should be delayed until some preliminary eating-focused therapy has been completed. Alternatively, perhaps the eating work could run in parallel to the person-oriented group. Although the ultimate goal of therapy may be an improvement in ability to deal with people, it may well be that some initial reconstruction of food and eating may be necessary, just as was outlined for individual therapy. I see the potential of a group for experimenting with people to be considerable, but I suspect that selection and timing may need more careful consideration.

One final therapeutic issue I would like to draw attention to is the relationship between personal construct psychotherapy and other forms of psychotherapy. Perhaps the most obvious sister of personal construct psychotherapy is cognitive-behavioural therapy, which as we have seen has been highly influential in the treatment of bulimia nervosa. Within the personal construct field there is currently a major debate between those who favour cross-fertilisation (e.g. Neimeyer, 1988) and those such as Larry Leitner (1989) who argue for highlighting the uniqueness of the personal construct approach.

Doubtless, there will be readers of this book who will see my work as cognitive-behavioural dressed up in a different language. I would not wish to deny that possible interpretation, but I take the view that the approaches differ in several respects. The most important of these is that personal construct therapy is not concerned with correcting 'cognitive errors' so much as trying to facilitate the evolution of the person as a whole. There does, however, seem to be signs of some convergence, as reflected by Mahoney (1988) in his tracing of the development of the 'family of theories' he terms 'constructivism'. Such theories all recognise that cognitive structures help to protect and perpetuate the integrity of the person.

It also seems likely that psychotherapists of other persuasions (e.g. psychoanalytic) may see some similarities of emphasis, particularly perhaps in my emphasis on relationships. Indeed a number of authors, such as Soldz (1988), have seen the potential for cross-fertilisation between psychoanalytical and personal construct approaches. Moreover Ryle's (1990) 'cognitive analytic therapy' draws heavily on personal construct theory. Similarly, authors such as Procter (e.g. 1985) and Feixas (1992) have been developing a systemic approach based on personal construct theory. I welcome cross-fertilisation between personal construct and these and other approaches, but like Leitner (1989) I am still of the persuasion that the personal construct perspective has a distinctive contribution to make. This is certainly the case in the field of eating disorders, which seems to cry out for an approach which seeks to *understand*, rather than to impose meaning and change.

Gender issues

It may seem odd that a book about disorders that primarily continue to affect females should be written by a man. This, perhaps, reflects a general trend in society and I will not attempt to speculate on the complex sociological factors involved in this process. But I think it is a legitimate question to ask whether a man can hope to understand these problems. Indeed, I am often asked it by clients, colleagues and others. I would like to try to answer this question by taking a personal construct perspective to the issue.

It will be recalled that Kelly had something to say about the social aspect of human experience. Taking his *commonality corollary* first, Kelly was addressing the likelihood that where people were employing similar *constructions of experience* their psychological processes are similar. Thus, two women may share similar constructions and consequently may behave similarly. But it does not automatically follow that all women construe similarly. It is not the experience per se that can make for commonality, but the *construction* of that experience that matters. Possibly for both biological and social reasons, women end up sharing many similar constructions, as do men. But it is equally possible for men and women to share similar constructions. For example, in a profession such as psychology, men and women exist in similar numbers and I would see myself as being about as likely to share similar constructions with a female colleague as with a male colleague. Although the distance between men and women's typical construing of bodies may still be quite large, I do not see that as a fundamental obstacle to men either developing eating disorders or playing a therapeutic role in relation to women with eating disorders. I think the latter question requires an understanding of Kelly's *sociality corollary*.

Although there is evidence that commonality of construing facilitates relationship formation (e.g. Duck and Spencer, 1972), at least as much emphasis needs to be placed on *sociality* of construing. It will be recalled that sociality involved the extent to which a person *construes the construction processes of another*. The latter is necessary if one is to *play a role in a social process involving the other person*. Being a therapist is one such role and much has been written on the significance of such *role relationships* by Leitner (1988). Although being a woman may make it more likely that a female therapist will share similar constructions with a female client, it does not follow that she will necessarily have the ability to construe her client's constructions. The question is whether the therapist (male or female) can transcend his or her own constructions and attempt to look at the world through the client's eyes. If therapists were to be limited to their own area of construing, then we would have to have elderly therapists for elderly clients, right-wing therapists for right-wing clients and drug-abusing therapists for drug-abusing clients! Although Kelly advocated a wide range of experience as being one of the qualities of a psychotherapist, we are inevitably limited in our constructions. I do not therefore regard the above possibility as either realistic or desirable.

What seems to matter is the way the client and therapist relate to each other. If they construe and relate to each other just in terms of their gender then their relationship may be predictable, but not necessarily fruitful. This applies whatever the construct. I recall one client who shared nationality with me – both of us being Welsh. I was aware of how easy it was to get sucked into construing each other as Welsh – very validating to both of us, but not necessarily conducive to change. It was only when I was able to construe him in other terms (and vice versa) that we were able to move forward.

Although I am making a case for the potential acceptability of male therapists with female eating-disorder clients, I do not in any way deny the possibility that gender construction may be an important therapeutic issue. Clients should also have the right to seek out a particular gender therapist. Whether or not the client has expressed a preference for a male or female therapist, we need to be vigilant to the possibility that client and/or therapist are construing each other in primarily gender or sexual terms. I have, for example, had a number of female clients who have been sexually abused by men and where the ability to experiment with relating to a man in terms other than sexuality has provided an important avenue to reconstruction.

As well as the question of therapist–client relationship, relationships with the opposite sex may well be an important therapeutic issue in eating disorders. This can be as much an issue for the male with an eating disorder as for the female. For both the men I have recently worked with, there have been difficulties with women and we have needed to work on their construing of women, which in both cases was rather limited. My aim is to help such clients work on trying to understand how people of the opposite sex may construe the world. For example, we can come to construe someone of the opposite sex in exclusively threatening terms. As understandable as this might be, it will blind us to any understanding of the opposite sex, e.g. that men may have anxieties and uncertainties about women. My hope is that clients can learn how to interact with a *person*, to be able to move beyond more fixed expectations of someone just because they happen to be a man, woman, fat or thin.

Relationship with other applications of personal construct psychology

If, as I believe, it is the underlying process of personal construction that is at the root of eating disorders (and other psychological disorders; see Button, 1983b) then there should be a lot to be gained by looking at the above work alongside other applications of the personal construct approach. I was struck, for example, by an article by Fay Fransella (1987) on her work with stuttering. She described herself as trying to build a 'causeway' along which her clients could travel from the world of stuttering to that of fluency. I was reminded of the roots of this work in my own on eating disorders and of the close parallels between her conceptualisation and my own. I too am trying to help a person cross a causeway.

It is in the area of psychological disorder (or what elsewhere may be called psychiatric illness) that I wish mainly to concentrate on here, particularly since we know that people with eating disorders share much in common with other such disorders. Personal construct theory has been highly fertile in generating research and therapeutic innovations with a wide range of disorders. Structural research has been particularly heavily focused on the excessive use of *tight* or *loose* construing. The most widely researched area must be schizophrenia, beginning with Bannister's extensive research on thought disorder (Bannister, 1960, 1962) and his 'serial invalidation hypothesis' (Bannister, 1963).

Bannister proposed that repeated invalidation of social anticipations could lead to a loosening of construing that would eventually lead to thought disorder. As with the field of schizophrenia research in general, however, this research area is full of inconsistencies (for a review see Pierce, Sewell and Cromwell, 1992). One other area associated with loose construing that perhaps deserves mention is suicide. Landfield (1976) has found that people who make serious suicide attempts are characterised by relatively disorganised personal construct systems. We should be mindful of this possibility when the eating disordered client finally loosens construing about weight, as perhaps illustrated by Rachel above.

It is with the area of *tight* construing, however, that closest parallels can be drawn. Tight construing has been commonly found in studies of neurotic clients, particularly in the area of construing self and symptoms (see Winter, 1992). Perhaps of most compelling comparability to the anorectic is the obsessional client. Although there is no evidence that the obsessional client is any more tight in construing than neurotics in general, Fransella (1974) has suggested that the obsessional's construing of his or her obsessional concerns may represent an area of tightness amidst the 'vagueness and confusion' of a personal construct system with generally loose organisation.

While the major emphasis of such research has been on structural characteristics of construing, quite a number of studies have examined the *content* of construing and how it relates to psychological disorder. For example, negative self-construing has consistently been found in depressive and neurotic subjects, who also tend to construe self in polarised terms and very dissimilar to others (see Winter, 1992). Moreover, less of an emphasis on 'positive' constructs has also been shown to be a feature of non-psychotic psychological disorder in general (Button, 1990b). Another area of content research is in the construing of the client's complaint. There have been many examples where the construing of a complaint by a client or client group seems to carry some 'payoffs'. Rowe (1971), for example, described a depressed woman who construed people as either 'good, "poorly" people' or 'bad, "well" people'. The client did not respond to therapy, presumably because she preferred to see herself as 'poorly' (and

good). Rowe (1983) went on to elaborate her view that one of the propositions that enclose depressed clients is 'I'd rather be good than happy'. I
would be hesitant to substitute an analagous generalised proposition for
eating-disordered clients, but I suspect we could often substitute 'fat' for
happy. Although such positive constructions of complaints have often been
reported, there have also been a number of examples of clients viewing
their complaint very negatively and life outside of it very positively. For
example, Winter and Gournay (1987), studying agoraphobics, found that
clients and partners imagined that after treatment they would be more
ideal than they were even before the onset of their symptoms. The more
marked was this tendency, the more severe were their symptoms and the
authors suggest they were resistant to testing out the validity of their
idealistic assumptions. The loss of such an idealised view of the world may
risk the need for massive revision of core constructs. Here again, we have
seen similar themes with many eating-disordered clients. It may well be
safer to continue the fantasy of the unobtainable.

A further area of enquiry has been the relationship between construing
and the process of therapy. For example, 'tight' construing (as with my
anorectics, Button, 1980) has been found to be associated with a poorer
response to psychotherapy in several studies (e.g. Orford (1974) in alcoholics; Sperlinger (1976) in depressives and Winter and Gournay (1987) in
agoraphobics). Evidence of structural changes during therapy, however,
are less consistent, possibly as Winter (1992) argues, because such changes
in construing are likely to be cyclical in nature and harder to identify. Much
more consistent evidence, however, has been obtained of changes in the
content of construing, similar to that in eating disorders described above.
Typically, therapeutic improvement has tended to be accompanied by
more positive self-construing, greater perceived similarity with others and
a resolution of dilemmas. Support for an emphasis on positive construction,
for example, comes from Schwartz and Michelson (1987). The authors
found that agoraphobics receiving treatment moved from an excess of
negative to positive self statements of a degree approximating the Golden
Section ratio (62% negative, 38% positive) as described by Benjafield and
Adams-Webber (1976) to the converse (70% positive) at follow up. In
keeping with such findings, I have argued (Button, 1990b) that perhaps
psychological treatment should focus less on problems and more on the
enhancement of 'positive' constructs from the client's standpoint.

Personal reflections and anticipations

It is now about 20 years since I first entered the field of eating disorders. I
recall a colleague asking me just before I went to the Royal Free Hospital

to work with Fay Fransella, 'What do *you* know about eating disorders?' I believe my reply went something like, 'Not a lot . . . but I'm prepared to learn'. Well, I like to think I am still learning, but I think that at the time I had no idea about what I was getting myself into. This is something I suspect that I have in common with my clients. As Anna also recalled, she had no idea when she started her grapefruit diet that it would lead her into anorexia nervosa and all that entailed.

So what did and does eating disorders mean to me? At first, it was very much tied in with trying to develop myself in an academic sense. Having been a rather lazy and consequently academically unsuccessful under-graduate, I wanted to somehow rectify this and the possibility of doing research and aiming for a doctorate in psychology seemed like an exciting prospect. So like the grapefruit diet for Anna, studying eating disorders was, for me, linked with the anticipation of some personal development in myself. Perhaps going for a PhD in a clinical psychologist is no more surprising than going for a diet in a young woman? To my knowledge, the medical world has not yet invented a disease called 'doctoratism' or 'doc-torholic'. But it strikes me that the path towards a doctorate can become as much of a single-minded preoccupation (see e.g. Salmon, 1992) as the path of dieting and anorexia nervosa. I carried on with the PhD because it became of central significance in defining my personal direction and iden-tity. Although many people (not everyone, I can assure you!) can make sense of the sacrifices that a PhD involves, I guess this is less so with an eating disorder. It is perhaps harder to understand, but not necessarily fundamentally different in principle.

After some seven years I gained my doctorate, thus achieving my initial goal, but that was not the end of the story and I have proved unable to let go of this particular part of me. The construction of myself as something of an expert on eating disorders is something I seem reluctant to let go of. I figure that it has become very meaningful for me and it has become a central part of my professional (and by implication) personal identity. This construction is, of course, not just held by me. It is widely shared by people around me, many of whom love to talk and sometimes joke about it. Similarly, for people like Anna, it seems to me that the construction of themselves as having an eating disorder is something that becomes very central to their view of themselves. So from starting out with the experi-ment of a diet (or some related piece of behaviour), the person eventually seems to create a construction of themselves, which may also come to be shared by others. We may find it easier to be an *anorectic,* a *bulimic,* or a professional *eating disorders specialist* rather than risk the less predictable world of straying into less familiar waters. So for me, as for my clients, eating disorders mean an awful lot.

Looking back on my work with eating disorders, I am struck by the memory of many very intimate personal relationships. Those relationships have been richly varied. Often, I have felt touched by how close I have become to a person's world, at other times I have felt distinctly uneasy by the distance and barriers that have been put up. There have been times of great excitement and anticipation, as doors have been opened into a new world, but also there have been times of gloom and despair. I can also recall those mixed moments of saying goodbye, tinged with both pleasure at a completion and with the sadness of letting go, I suspect for both of us. What I remember least is the eating, to me that is a side issue to the main drama. Others I know would see it as different, but for me the central task is with a *person*, each one very different, even though superficially similar. It is when that person's unique perspective can run free that I feel that we are getting somewhere.

In the spirit of personal construct psychology, it is perhaps fitting to end on an anticipatory note. Well, I anticipate that eating disorders are here to stay in the foreseeable future. I can see no indication of food and body control going out of fashion; if anything, the contrary might be the case. Although I have heard clients and others say that they are sick to death with the whole media emphasis on these matters, I cannot see much sign that too many people are listening. If, as Hsu (1990) suggests, the prevalence of eating disorders is directly proportional to the prevalence of dieting behaviour in the population, it seems likely that people like ourselves will continue to receive requests for help from large numbers of people presenting with an eating disorder. Crisp (1988) has outlined possible approaches to the primary prevention of eating disorders, but the task of trying to change global societal attitudes is considerable and beyond the more personal focus in this book.

I am anticipating, hopefully, that I will have succeeded in helping to throw some further light on the kinds of personal issues involved for these people. Rather more ambitiously, I hope that a few more people can be helped to find some meaning in their lives, whether with or without their eating disorder.

References

Agras, W.S., Rossiter, E.M., Arnow, B. et al (1992). Pharmacologic and cognitive-behavioural treatment for bulimia nervosa: a controlled comparison. *American Journal of Psychiatry*, **149**, 82–7.

American Psychiatric Association (1980). *Diagnostic and Statistical Manual of Mental Disorders, 3rd edition (DSMIII)*. Washington DC: American Psychiatric Association.

American Psychiatric Association (1987). *Diagnostic and Statistical Manual of Mental Disorders, 3rd edition revised (DSMIIIR)*. Washington, DC: American Psychiatric Association.

Andersen, A.E. (1990). *Males with Eating Disorders*. New York: Brunner/Mazel.

Andrews, G. (1981) A prospective study of life events and psychological symptoms. *Psychological Medicine*, **11**, 67–78.

Baillie-Grohman, R. (1975). The use of a modified form of repertory grid technique to investigate the extent to which deaf school leavers tend to use stereotypes. Unpublished MSc dissertation. University of London.

Bannister, D. (1960). Conceptual structure in thought disordered schizophrenics. *Journal of Mental Science*, **106**, 1230–49.

Bannister, D. (1962). The nature and measurement of schizophrenic thought disorder. *Journal of Mental Science*, **108**, 825–42.

Bannister, D. (1963). The genesis of schizophrenic thought disorder: a serial invalidation hypothesis. *British Journal of Psychiatry*, **109**, 680–6.

Bannister, D. (1977). The logic of passion. In D. Bannister (Ed.) *New Perspectives in Personal Construct Theory* (pp. 21–37). London: Academic Press.

Bannister, D. and Agnew, J. (1977). The child's construing of self. In J.K. Cole and A.W. Landfield (Eds) *Nebraska Symposium on Motivation 1976: Personal Construct Psychology* (pp. 99–125). Lincoln, NE: University of Nebraska Press.

Bannister, D. and Fransella, F. (1971). *Inquiring Man: The Psychology of Personal Constructs*. Harmondsworth: Penguin.

Batty, C. and Hall, E. (1986). Personal constructs of students with eating disorders: implications for counselling. *British Journal of Guidance and Counselling*, **14**, 306–13.

Beail, N. (Ed.) (1985). *Repertory Grid Technique and Personal Constructs: Applications in Clinical and Educational Settings*. London: Croom Helm.

Beck, A.T. (1976). *Cognitive Therapy and the Emotional Disorders.* New York: International Universities Press.

Beck, A.T., Rush, A.J., Shaw, B.F. and Emery, G. (1979). *Cognitive Therapy of Depression.* New York: Guildford.

Bee, H.L. and Mitchell, S.K. (1984). *The Developing Person: A Life Span Approach.* New York: Harper & Row.

Bell, R.C. (1990). Analytic issues in the use of repertory grid technique. In R.A. Neimeyer and G.J. Neimeyer (Eds) *Advances in Personal Construct Psychology* (vol. 1) (pp. 25–48). Greenwich, CT: JAI Press.

Bell, M., Billington, R. and Becker, B. (1986). A scale of the assessment of object relations: reliability, validity and factorial invariance. *Journal of Clinical Psychology,* **42**, 733–41.

Benjafield, J. and Adams-Webber, J. (1976). The golden section hypothesis. *British Journal of Psychology,* **67**, 11–16.

Berzonsky, M.D. (1989). The self as a theorist: individual differences in identity formation. *International Journal of Personal Construct Psychology,* **2**, 363–76.

Bieri, J. (1955). Cognitive complexity-simplicity and predictive behaviour. *Journal of Abnormal and Social Psychology,* **51**, 263–8.

Boskind-Lodahl, M. and White, W.C. Jr (1978). The definition and treatment of bulimarexia in college women: a pilot study. *Journal of the American College Health Association,* **27**, 84–6.

Bringmann, M.W. (1992). Computer-based methods for the analysis and interpretation of personal construct systems. In R.A. Neimeyer and G.J. Neimeyer (Eds) *Advances in Personal Construct Psychology* (vol. 2) (pp. 57–90). Greenwich, CT: JAI Press.

Bruch, H. (1962). Perceptual and conceptual disturbances in anorexia nervosa. *Psychosomatic Medicine,* **24**, 187–94.

Bruch, H. (1973). *Eating Disorders: Obesity, Anorexia Nervosa and the Person Within.* New York: Basic Books.

Bruch, H. (1978). *The Golden Cage: The Enigma of Anorexia Nervosa.* London: Routledge & Kegan Paul.

Button, E.J. (1980). Construing and clinical outcome in anorexia nervosa. Unpublished PhD thesis, University of London.

Button, E.J. (1983a). Construing the anorexic. In J. Adams-Webber and J. Mancuso (Eds) *Applications of Personal Construct Theory* (pp. 305–16). Toronto: Academic Press.

Button, E.J. (1983b). Personal construct theory and psychological well-being. *British Journal of Medical Psychology,* **56**, 313–21.

Button, E.J. (1985a). *Personal Construct Theory and Mental Health: Theory, Research and Practice.* London: Croom Helm.

Button, E.J. (1985b). Eating disorders: a quest for control? In E. Button (Ed.) *Personal Construct Theory and Mental Health* (pp. 153–68). London: Croom Helm.

Button, E.J. (1985c). Women with weight on their minds. In N. Beail (Ed.) *Repertory Grid Technique and Personal Constructs: Clinical and Educational Applications* (pp. 61–74). Croom Helm: London.

Button, E.J. (1987). Construing people or weight? An eating disorders group. In R.A. Neimeyer and G.J. Neimeyer (Eds) *Personal Construct Therapy Casebook* (pp. 230–44). New York: Springer.

Button, E.J. (1988a). SELF-GRID: A Systematic Methodology for Personal Construct Exploration of Self-Image. Unpublished Manuscript, Department of Psychiatry, University of Southampton, UK.

Button, E.J. (1988b). Music and personal constructs. In F. Fransella and L.Thomas (Eds) *Experimenting with Personal Construct Psychology* (pp. 531–8). London: Routledge & Kegan Paul.

Button, E.J. (1990a). Self-esteem in girls aged 11–12: Baseline findings from a planned prospective study of vulnerability to eating disorders. *Journal of Adolescence*, **13**, 407–13.

Button, E.J. (1990b). Rigidity of construing of self and significant others and psychological disorder. *British Journal of Medical Psychology*, **63**, 345–54.

Button, E.J. (1992). Eating disorders and personal constructs. In R.A. Neimeyer and G.J. Neimeyer (Eds.) *Advances in Personal Construct Psychology* (vol. 2) (pp. 185–213). Greenwich, CT: JAI Press.

Button, E.J. (1993). Personal construct measurement of self-esteem. *International Journal of Personal Construct Psychology* (in press).

Button, E.J. and Whitehouse, A. (1981). Subclinical anorexia nervosa. *Psychological Medicine*, **11**, 509–16.

Caine, T.M., Wijesinghe, O.B.A. and Winter, D.A. (1981). *Personal Styles in Neurosis: Implications for Small Group Psychotherapy and Behaviour Therapy*. London: Routledge & Kegan Paul.

Ciliska, D. (1990). *Beyond Dieting: Psychoeducational Interventions for Chronically Obese Women: A Non-Dieting Approach*. New York: Brunner/Mazel.

Coish, B.J. (1990). A Personal Construct Theory of Bulimia. Unpublished PhD Thesis, La Trobe University, Australia.

Cooper, P.J. and Fairburn, C.G. (1986). The depressive symptoms of bulimia nervosa. *British Journal of Psychiatry* **148**, 268–74.

Cooper, P.J., Charnock, D.J. and Taylor, M.J. (1987). The prevalence of bulimia nervosa: a replication study. *British Journal of Psychiatry*, **151**, 684–86.

Crisp, A.H. (1967). Anorexia nervosa. *British Journal of Hospital Medicine*, **1**, 713–18.

Crisp, A.H. (1980). *Anorexia Nervosa: Let Me Be*. London: Academic Press.

Crisp, A.H. (1988). Some possible approaches to prevention of eating and body weight/shape disorders, with particular reference to anorexia nervosa. *International Journal of Eating Disorders*, **7**, 1–17.

Crisp, A.H. and Fransella, F. (1972). Conceptual changes during recovery from anorexia nervosa. *British Journal of Medical Psychology*, **45**, 395–405.

Crisp, A.H., Norton, K., Gowers, S. et al (1991). A controlled study of the effect of therapies aimed at adolescent and family psychopathology in anorexia nervosa. *British Journal of Psychiatry*, **159**, 325–33.

Dally, P.J. and Sargant, W. (1960). A new treatment of anorexia nervosa. *British Medical Journal*, **i**, 1770–4.

Derogatis, L.R. (1977). *Administration Scoring and Procedures for the SCL90R*. Baltimore: Clinical Psychometric Research.

Duck, S.W. and Spencer, C. (1972). Personal constructs and friendship formation. *Journal of Personality and Social Psychology*, **23**, 40–5.

Dunnett, G. (Ed.) (1988). *Working with People: Clinical Uses of Personal Construct Psychology*. London: Routledge & Kegan Paul.

Dunnett, G. and Llewelyn, S. (1988). Elaborating personal construct theory in a group setting. In G. Dunnett (Ed.) *Working with People*. (pp. 186–201). London: Routledge & Kegan Paul.

Eckert, E.D., Goldberg, S.C., Halmi, K.A. et al (1979). Behaviour therapy in anorexia nervosa. *British Journal of Psychiatry*, **134**, 55–9.

Epting, F.R. (1984). *Personal Construct Counselling and Psychotherapy*. New York: Wiley.

Epting, F.R. and Nazario, A. Jnr (1987). Designing a fixed role therapy: issues, techniques and modifications. In R.A. Neimeyer and G.J. Neimeyer (Eds) *Personal Construct Therapy Casebook* (pp. 277–89). New York: Springer.

Erikson, E.H. (1959). Identity and the life cycle. *Psychological Issues Monograph Series* (No.1). New York: International Universities Press.

Erikson, E.H. (1968). *Identity, Youth and Crisis*. New York: Norton.

Fairburn, C.G. (1981). A cognitive-behavioural approach to the management of bulimia. *Psychological Medicine*, **11**, 707–11.

Fairburn, C.G. (1991). The heterogeneity of bulimia nervosa and its implications for treatment. *Journal of Psychosomatic Research*, **35**, 3–9.

Fairburn, C.G., Jones, R., Peveler, R.C. et al (1991). Three psychological treatments for bulimia nervosa. *Archives of General Psychiatry*, **48**, 463–9.

Feixas, G. (1992). Personal construct approaches to family therapy. In R.A. Neimeyer and G.J. Neimeyer (Eds) *Advances in Personal Construct Psychology* (vol. 2) (pp. 215–55). Greenwich, CT: JAI Press.

Fransella, F. (1972). *Personal Change and Reconstruction*. London: Academic Press.

Fransella, F. (1974). Thinking in the obsessional. In H. R. Beech (Ed.) *Obsessional States*. London: Methuen.

Fransella, F. (1985). Individual psychotherapy. In E. Button (Ed.) *Personal Construct Theory and Mental Health: Theory, Research and Practice* (pp. 277–301). London: Croom Helm.

Fransella, F. (1987). Stuttering to fluency via reconstruing. In R.A. Neimeyer and G.J. Neimeyer (Eds) *Personal Construct Therapy Casebook* (pp. 290–308). New York: Springer.

Fransella, F. and Bannister, D. (1977). *A Manual for Repertory Grid Technique*. London: Academic Press.

Fransella, F. and Crisp, A.H. (1970). Conceptual organisation and weight change. *Psychosomatics and Psychotherapy*, **18**, 176–85.

Fransella, F. and Crisp, A.H. (1979). Comparisons of weight concepts in groups of (a) neurotics (b) normal and (c) anorexic females. *British Journal of Psychiatry*, **134**, 79–86.

Fransella, F. and Dalton, P. (1990). *Personal Construct Counselling in Action*. London: Sage.

Furnham, A. and Alibhai, N. (1983). Cross-cultural differences in the perception of female body shapes. *Psychological Medicine*, **13**, 829–37.

Garfinkel, P.E. and Garner, D.M. (1982). *Anorexia Nervosa: A Multidimensional Perspective*. New York: Brunner/Mazel.

Garner, D.M. (1992). Psychotherapy for eating disorders. *Current Opinion in Psychiatry*, **5**, 391–5.

Garner, D.M. and Bemis, K. (1982). A cognitive-behavioural approach to anorexia nervosa. *Cognitive Therapy and Research*, **6**, 1–27.

Garner, D.M. and Garfinkel, P.E. (1980a). Sociocultural factors in the development of anorexia nervosa. *Psychological Medicine*, **9**, 273–9.

Garner, D.M. and Garfinkel, P.E. (1980b). The eating attitudes test: an index of the symptoms of anorexia nervosa. *Psychological Medicine*, **9**, 273–9.

Garner, D.M., Olmsted, M.P. and Polivy, J. (1983). Development and validation of a multidimensional eating disorders inventory for anorexia nervosa and bulimia. *International Journal of Eating Disorders*, **2**, 15–34.

Garner, D.M., Garfinkel, P.E., Schwartz, D. and Thompson, M. (1980). Cultural expectations of thinness in women. *Psychological Reports*, **47**, 483–91.

Garner, D.M., Olmsted, M.P., Polivy, J. and Garfinkel, P.E. (1984). Comparison between weight-preoccupied women and anorexia nervosa. *Psychosomatic Medicine*, **46**, 255–66.

Garner, D.M., Olmsted, M.P., Davis R. et al (1990). The association between bulimic symptoms and reported psychopathology. *International Journal of Eating Disorders*, **9**, 1–15.

Garner, D.M., Rockert, W., Olmsted, M.P. et al (1985). Psychoeducational principles in the treatment of bulimia and anorexia nervosa. In D.M. Garner and P.E. Garfinkel (Eds) *Handbook of Psychotherapy for Anorexia Nervosa and Bulimia* (pp. 513–72). New York: Guildford.

Goldberg, D. (1972). *The Detection of Psychiatric Illness by Questionnaire*. London: Oxford University Press.

Goodsitt, A. (1985). Self-psychology and the treatment of anorexia nervosa. In D.M. Garner and P.E. Garfinkel (Eds) *Handbook of Psychotherapy for Anorexia Nervosa and Bulimia* (pp. 55–82). New York: Guildford Press.

Gull, W.W. (1874). Anorexia nervosa (apepsia hysterica, anorexia hysterica). *Transactions of the Clinical Society of London*, **7**, 22–8.

Hall, A. (1985). Group psychotherapy for anorexia nervosa. In D.M. Garner and P.E. Garfinkel (Eds) *Handbook of Psychotherapy for Anorexia Nervosa and Bulimia.* (pp. 213–39). New York: Guildford Press.

Hall, A. and Brown, L.B. (1983). A comparison of the attitudes of young anorexia nervosa patients and non-patients with those of their mothers. *British Journal of Medical Psychology*, **56**, 39–48.

Heesacker, R.S. and Neimeyer, G.J. (1990). Assessing object relations and social cognitive correlates of eating disorder. *Journal of Counselling Psychology*, **37**, 419–26.

Herman, C.P. and Polivy, J. (1984). A boundary model for the regulation of eating. In A.J. Stunkard and E. Stellar. *Eating and Its Disorders* (pp. 141–56). New York: Raven Press.

Herzog, T., Hartmann, A., Sandholz, A. and Stammer, H. (1991). Prognostic factors in outpatient psychotherapy of bulimia. *Psychotherapy and Psychosomatics*, **56**, 48–55.

Hinkle, D. (1965). The change of personal constructs from the viewpoint of a theory of construct implications. Unpublished PhD thesis, Ohio State University.

Holland, A.J., Hall, A., Murray, R. et al (1984). Anorexia nervosa: a study of 34 twin pairs and one set of triplets. *British Journal of Psychiatry*, **145**, 414–18.

Hsu, L.K.G. (1980). Outcome of anorexia nervosa: a review of the literature (1954–1978). *Archives of General Psychiatry*, **37**, 1041–6.

Hsu, L.K.G. (1990). *Eating Disorders.* New York: Guildford Press.

Kelly, G.A. (1955). *The Psychology of Personal Constructs*. New York: Norton.

Kelly, G.A. (1969). The psychotherapeutic relationship. In B. Maher (Ed.) *Clinical Psychology and Personality: The Selected Papers of George Kelly* (pp. 216–23). New York: Wiley.

Kelly, G.A. (1973). Fixed role therapy. In R.M. Jerjevich (Ed.) *Direct Psychotherapy: 28 American Originals* (pp. 394–422). Coral Gables, Florida: University of Miami Press.

Keys, A., Brozek, J., Henschel, A. et al (1950). *The Biology of Human Starvation.* Minneapolis, MN: University of Minnesota Press.

Klerman, G.L, Weissman, M.M., Rounsaville, B.J. and Chevron, E.S. (1984). *Interpersonal Psychotherapy of Depression.* New York: Basic Books.

Koch, H.C.H. (1985). Group psychotherapy. In E. Button (Ed.) *Personal Construct Theory and Mental Health: Theory, Research and Practice* (pp. 302–26). London: Croom Helm.

Kohut, H. (1971). *The Analysis of the Self.* New York: International Universities Press.

Lacey, J.H. (1985). Time-limited individual and group treatment for bulimia. In D.M. Garner and P.E. Garfinkel (Eds) *Handbook of Psychotherapy for Anorexia Nervosa and Bulimia* (pp. 431–57). New York: Guildford Press.

Landfield, A.W. (1971). *Personal Construct Systems in Psychotherapy.* Chicago: Rand McNally.

Landfield, A.W. (1976). A personal construct approach to suicidal behaviour. In P. Slater (Ed.) *The Measurement of Intrapersonal Space by Grid Technique (vol. 1): Explorations of Intrapersonal Space.* London: Wiley.

Landfield, A.W. and Rivers, P.C. (1975). An introduction to interpersonal transaction and rotating dyads. *Psychotherapy: Theory, Research and Practice,* **12**, 366–74.

Lasègue, E.C. (1873). On hysterical anorexia. *Medical Times Gazette,* **2**, 265–6.

Leitner, L.M. (1988). Terror, risk and reverence: experiential personal construct psychotherapy. *International Journal of Personal Construct Psychology,* **1**, 251–61.

Leitner, L.M. (1989). Me Too Iguana: on the relationship between PCP and psychology. Paper presented at 8th International Congress on Personal Construct Psychology, Assisi.

Mahoney, M.J. (1988). Constructive metatheory: II. Implications for psychotherapy. *International Journal of Personal Construct Psychology,* **1**, 299–315.

Mair, J.M.M. (1977). The community of self. In D. Bannister (Ed.) *New Perspectives in Personal Construct Theory.* London: Academic Press.

Mancuso, J.C. and Jaccard, J. (1988). Parent role repertory grid and self role repertory grid: a manual for the collection and analysis of matrix-form data. Unpublished manuscript. Albany, NY: University of Albany.

Marcia, J.E. (1966). Development and validation of ego identity status. *Journal of Personality and Social Psychology,* **3**, 551–8.

Marshall, P. (1988). The description and measurement of specific abnormal cognitions in anorexia nervosa: a controlled study. Unpublished MPhil thesis. University of Leicester, UK.

Minuchin, S., Rosman, B.L. and Baker, L. (1978). *Psychosomatic Families: Anorexia Nervosa in Context.* Cambridge, MA: Harvard University Press.

Morgan, H.C. and Russell, G.F.M. (1975). Value of family background and clinical features as predictors of long-term outcome in anorexia nervosa: 4-year follow-up of 41 patients. *Psychological Medicine,* **5**, 355–71.

Morton, R. (1694). *Phthisiologia: Or a Treatise on Consumptions.* London: S. Smith and B. Walford.

Mottram, M.A. (1985). Personal constructs in anorexia nervosa. *Journal of Psychiatric Research,* **19**, 291–5.

Munden, A. (1982). Eating problems amongst women in a university population. Unpublished manuscript, Department of Psychiatry, University of Southampton, UK.

Nasser, M. (1986). Comparative study of the prevalence of abnormal eating attitudes among Arab female students of both London and Cairo Universities.
Psychological Medicine, **16**, 621–5.

Neimeyer, G.J. and Khouzam, N. (1985). A repertory grid study of restrained
eaters. *British Journal of Medical Psychology*, **58**, 365–8.

Neimeyer, R.A. (1985). *The Development of Personal Construct Psychology*. Lincoln, NE: University of Nebraska Press.

Neimeyer, R.A. (1987). An orientation to personal construct therapy. In R.A.
Neimeyer and G.J. Neimeyer (Eds) *Personal Construct Therapy Casebook* (pp.
3–19). New York: Springer.

Neimeyer, R.A. (1988). Integrative directions in personal construct therapy. *International Journal of Personal Construct Psychology*, **1**, 283–97.

Neimeyer, R.A. and Neimeyer, G.J. (Eds) (1987). *A Personal Construct Therapy
Casebook*. New York: Springer.

Nylander, I. (1971). The feeling of being fat and dieting in a school population. *Acta
Sociomedica Scandinavica*, **3**, 17–26.

Olmsted, M.P., Davis, R., Garner, D.M. et al (1991). Efficacy of a brief group
psychoeducational intervention for bulimia nervosa. *Behaviour Research and
Therapy*, **29**, 71–83.

Orbach, S. (1985). Accepting the symptom: a feminist psychoanalytic treatment of
anorexia nervosa. In D.M. Garner and P.E. Garfinkel (Eds) *Handbook of Psychotherapy for Anorexia Nervosa and Bulimia* (pp. 83–104). New York:
Guildford Press.

Orford, J. (1974). Simplistic thinking about other people as a predictor of early
drop-out at an alcoholism halfway house. *British Journal of Medical Psychology*,
47, 53–62.

Orford, J. (1985). *Excessive Appetites: A Psychological View of Addictions*. Chichester: Wiley.

Palazzoli, M.S. (1978). *Self-Starvation: From the Intrapsychic to the Transpersonal
Approach to Anorexia Nervosa*. New York: Aronson.

Palmer, R.L. (1979). The dietary chaos syndrome: a useful new term? *British Journal of Medical Psychology*, **52**, 187–90.

Palmer, R., Christie, M., Cordle, C. et al (1987). The Clinical Eating Disorder
Rating Instrument (CEDRI): a preliminary description. *International Journal of
Eating Disorders*, **6**, 9–16.

Patton, G.C. (1988). Mortality in eating disorders. *Psychological Medicine*, **18**, 947–
52.

Paykel, E.S. (1978). Contribution of life events to causation of psychiatric illness.
Psychological Medicine, **8**, 245–53.

Pierce, D.L., Sewell, K.W. and Cromwell, R.L. (1992). Schizophrenia and depression: construing and constructing empirical research. In R.A. Neimeyer and G.J.
Neimeyer (Eds) *Advances in Personal Construct Psychology* (vol. 2) (pp. 151–
84). Greenwich, CT: JAI Press.

Piran, N. and Kaplan, A.S. (1990). *A Day Hospital Group Treatment Program for
Anorexia Nervosa and Bulimia Nervosa*. New York: Brunner/Mazel.

Polivy, J. and Herman, C.P. (1987). Diagnosis and treatment of normal eating .
Journal of Consulting and Clinical Psychology, **55**, 635–44.

Procter, H. (1985). A construct approach to family therapy and systems intervention. In E. Button (Ed.) *Personal Construct Theory and Mental Health: Theory,
Research and Practice* (pp. 327–60). London: Croom Helm.

Pumareiga, A.J. (1986). Acculturation and eating attitudes in adolescent girls: a comparative and correctional study. *Journal of the American Academy of Child Psychiatry*, **25**, 276–9.

Quinton, D. and Rutter, M. (1985). Parenting behaviour of mothers raised in care. In A.R. Nichol (Ed.) *Longitudinal Studies in Child Psychology and Psychiatry*. Chichester: Wiley.

Rosenberg, M. (1965). *Society and the Adolescent Self-Image*. Princeton, NJ: Princeton University Press.

Rossner, S. (1984). Ideal body weight – for whom? *Acta Medica Scandinavica*, **216**, 241–2.

Rowe, D. (1971). Poor prognosis in a case of depression as predicted by the repertory grid. *British Journal of Psychiatry*, **118**, 297–300.

Rowe, D. (1983). *Depression: The Way out of the Prison*. London: Routledge & Kegan Paul.

Russell, G.F.M. (1970). Anorexia nervosa – its identity as an illness and its treatment. In J.H. Price (Ed) *Modern Trends in Psychological Medicine* (vol. 2). London: Butterworths.

Russell, G.F.M. (1979). Bulimia nervosa: an ominous variant of anorexia nervosa. *Psychological Medicine*, **9**, 429–48.

Russell, G.F.M., Szmukler, G.I., Dare, C. and Eisler, I. (1987). An evaluation of family therapy in anorexia nervosa and bulimia nervosa. *Archives of General Psychiatry*, **44**, 1047–56.

Rutter, M. (1979). Protective factors in children's response to stress and disadvantage. In M.W. Kent and J.E. Rolfe (Eds) *Primary Prevention of Psychopathology: Social Competence in Children*. Vol. 3. Armidale, AL: Hanover Press, University of New England.

Ryle, A. (1990). *Cognitive-Analytic Therapy: Active Participation in Change: A New Integration in Brief Therapy*. Chichester: Wiley.

Ryle, A. and Evans, C.D.H. (1991). Some meanings of body and self in eating-disordered and comparison subjects. *British Journal of Medical Psychology*, **64**, 273–83.

Ryle, A. and Lunghi, M. (1970). The dyad grid – a modification of repertory grid technique. *British Journal of Psychiatry*, **117**, 323–7.

Salmon, P. (1992). *Achieving a PhD: Ten Students' Experience*. Stoke-on-Trent: Trentham Books.

Schwartz, R.M. and Michelson, L. (1987). States of mind model: cognitive balance in the treatment of agoraphobia. *Journal of Consulting and Clinical Psychology*, **55**, 557–65.

Slater, P. (1977). *The Measurement of Intrapersonal Space by Grid Technique: Volume 2. Explorations of Intrapersonal Space*. London: Wiley.

Sloane, R.B., Staples, F.R., Cristoll, A.H. et al (1975). *Psychotherapy versus Behaviour Therapy*. Cambridge, MA: Harvard University Press.

Soldz, S. (1988). Constructivist tendencies in recent psychoanalysis. *International Journal of Personal Construct Psychology*, **1**, 329–47.

Smith, M.C. and Thelen, M.H. (1984). Development and validation of a test for bulimia. *Journal of Consulting and Clinical Psychology*, **52**, 863–72.

Sperlinger, D.J. (1976). Aspects of stability in the repertory grid. *British Journal of Medical Psychology*, **49**, 341–7.

Strober, M. (1981). A comparative analysis of personality organization in juvenile anorexia nervosa. *Journal of Youth and Adolescence*, **10**, 285–95.

Szmukler, G.I. (1983). Weight and food preoccupation in a population of English schoolgirls. In J.G. Bergman (Ed.) *Understanding Anorexia Nervosa and Bulimia: Fourth Ross Conference on Medical Research* (pp. 21–8). Columbus, Ohio: Ross Laboratories.

Szmukler, G.I., Eisler, I., Gillis, C. and Hayward, M.E. (1985). The implications of anorexia nervosa in a ballet school. *Journal of Psychiatric Research*, **19**, 177–81.

Theander, S. (1985). Outcome and prognosis in anorexia nervosa and bulimia: some results of previous investigations, compared with those of a Swedish long-term study. *Journal of Psychiatric Research*, **19**, 493–508.

Touyz, S.W., Beumont, P.J.V. and Glaun, D. (1984). A comparison of lenient and strict operant conditioning in refeeding patients with anorexia nervosa. *British Journal of Psychiatry*, **144**, 517–20.

Tschudi, F. (1977). Loaded and honest questions: a construct view of symptoms and therapy. In D. Bannister (Ed.) *New Perspectives in Personal Construct Theory.* London: Academic Press.

Wadden, T.A. and Stunkard, A.J. (1985). Social and Psychological consequences of obesity. *Annals of Internal Medicine*, **103**, 1062–7.

Wakeling, A. (1985). Neurobiological aspects of feeding disorders. *Journal of Psychiatric Research*, **19**, 191–201.

Weinreich, P. (1980). *Manual for Identity Exploration using Personal Constructs.* London: Social Science Research Council.

Weinreich, P., Doherty, J. and Harris, P. (1985). Empirical assessment of identity in anorexia and bulimia nervosa. *Journal of Psychiatric Research*, **19**, 297–302.

Williams, P. and King, M. (1987). The 'epidemic' of anorexia nervosa: another medical myth? *Lancet* **i**, 205–7.

Winter, D.A. (1985). Personal styles, constructive alternativism and the provision of a therapeutic service. *British Journal of Medical Psychology*, **58**, 129–36.

Winter, D.A. (1992). *Personal Construct Psychology in Clinical Practice: Theory, Research and Applications.* London: Routledge & Kegan Paul.

Winter, D.A. and Gournay, K. (1987). Constriction and construction in agoraphobia. *British Journal of Medical Psychology*, **60**, 233–44.

Author index

Subject index